CONFESSION OF A RECOVERING MP

NICK DE BOIS

First published in Great Britain in 2018 by
Biteback Publishing Ltd
Westminster Tower
3 Albert Embankment
London SE1 7SP
Copyright © Nick de Bois 2018

ISBN 978-1-78590-335-9

10 9 8 7 6 5 4 3 2 1

A CIP catalogue record for this book is available from the British Library.

Printed and bound in Great Britain by
CPI Group (UK) Ltd, Croydon CR0 4YY

To Helen

*I am so very lucky, and very happy, to have you by my side. It really
is as simple as that.*

To Jessica, Laura, Madeleine, Alex

*Thank you for your patience, good humour, those wonderful
grandchildren and, above all, your unconditional love.
No father could ask for more.*

CONTENTS

INTRODUCTION

It's entirely possible that you may know what an MP actually does. After all, the work of an MP is by its very nature a very public job. Barely a day goes by when something they have done, said or been challenged over is not in the news. And that's not accounting for when a scandal erupts, usually over money, sex or both.

I do, however, want to add a note of caution.

When I became an MP in 2010, I thought I knew not only what I wanted to do but also how best to achieve those goals and what would be expected of me by constituents, party and Parliament. By 2015, when I left the House of Commons, I finally understood how bloody wrong and naive I had been.

So, who are these MPs and what do they do? Why do over 32 million people turn out to elect their representatives in the first place when, if opinion polls are to be believed, over two thirds of the country don't rate or trust them? What do we really expect from them, given that most of the time we barely give politics a second thought? Let's face it, most people have better things to do than think about MPs for more than a few seconds a day. We Brits tend to think about who is making the next cup of tea more than we think about who is making our laws.

You, however, are different.

While quite a lot of people think that MPs as a breed deserve abolition, and that the Houses of Parliament should be turned into a theme park, you on the other hand seem prepared to withhold judgement. After all, you have in your hands a book about Parliament and MPs. Don't worry, I've made the cover as harmless as possible to make sure you don't get disapproving stares from others as you read. With any luck, they may think you're reading a '60s spy novel or the latest offering from Jeffrey Archer.

Let me put my cards on the table, though.

I love the institution of Parliament and believe it serves our country well. Rest assured, I have not seen fit to write a dull defence of MPs, more a journey through both Westminster and the constituency that will help you reach your own conclusions on that score. I hope that you may also be left reflecting on the unique complexities of everyone involved in this extraordinary democratic process: the constituents, the ministers – Prime Ministers, even – and of course the humble backbencher, a mantle I happily and proudly wore for five years.

In writing this book, I have not set out to educate you on the processes of Parliament or to be included in the GCSE Politics syllabus. If it is deemed fit for academic reading lists, I will have failed. Instead, it will, I hope, cast some light onto a system that has outlived you and I some ten times over and seen the country through more challenges than any other institution or person could weather, except perhaps for the monarchy. All this despite the many foibles and weaknesses of both individual Members of Parliament and the very Palace of Westminster itself.

As you will discover, this isn't a political book; it's a book about political life. It's the inside story of a backbench MP, devoid of ministerial restriction but packed, I hope, with a little humour, a few anecdotes, plenty of irritation and some purpose. Oh, yes, and the odd kiss and tease.

Finally, let me assure you, no constituents or fellow parliamentarians were harmed during the making of this book. Although when you have read it, you may wonder how on earth that was the case.

I hope you enjoy reading it as much as I enjoyed writing it.

Nick de Bois
Hertfordshire
January 2018

1

WHAT DO YOU DO?

You are not an executive who can make and enforce decisions. You are a legislator who votes on making laws.

You are not qualified or trained on how to be a guidance counsellor, but you are often mistaken for an elected councillor and expected to do what a councillor should do.

You are not a housing officer, benefits clerk, bank manager or trading standards officer, but you are often expected to provide a new home, sort out benefits, provide a loan or settle a dispute about a computer game bought for little Jimmy that doesn't work.

You are, however, a bloody good listener. Well, most of the time, that is.

So, what are you? You are in fact a 21st-century Member of Parliament representing a population of about 100,000 good folk from your constituency by taking your seat in the oldest and most established of all the world's Parliaments and yes, quite frankly, probably the finest Parliament in the world, despite what you may read or hear in the media.

You are elected by a simple majority from roughly 50,000 people who turn out to vote and mark their X by your name at a general election. Some do it wholeheartedly and generously, some begrudgingly, and even a few by mistake, but most do it with a sense of hope that you will be able to make a difference somehow.

Unfortunately, when as a new Member of Parliament you walk through the Members' Lobby, dwarfed by the imposing statues of Lloyd George, Churchill, Attlee and, yes, the magnificent Margaret Thatcher, filled with a vision of how you will leave your mark on this place, this nation and this government, what you are almost certainly unaware of is that your constituents, your government, the press and the very institution of the Palace of Westminster have other plans for you. And that's before the odd fruitcake or two who persistently latch on to you.

So it was for me in May 2010 when, with an unimpressive and insecure majority of 1,692, I began the most marvellous journey of a lifetime as I met head-on the bizarre, the inexplicable, the touching, the shocking, the vitally important and, yes, thank God, lots of utter bollocks as well.

2

TRADITION – HELP OR HINDRANCE?

I confess, I went to a boarding school, more commonly known as a public school. Or, as the *Daily Mirror* would have you believe, a toffs' training ground.

To be fair, Culford School was no Eton, but it did a pretty good job of making this son of an RAF family fairly independent-minded, if not an academic achiever (one A-level grade E and five mediocre GCE O-levels). Although I had become quite fond of the place by the time I left in June 1977, I had thought that was the last I would see of an establishment built around patronage, prefects and privilege. A place where new 'bugs' and old 'bugs' (slang at the time for 'boys') were the inherent dividing line, where certain individuals were singled out, often inexplicably, for preferential treatment or rank and, where above all else, one man, the headmaster, carried absolute authority and the ability to dispense advantages on the favoured few. Fast forward to 2010 and thirty-three years later, as I began my first day in Westminster, it all came flooding back to me.

On any first day at school, the first thing you are shown is your coat hanger, and Parliament is no different.

During the introductory week, the doorkeepers of the Palace of Westminster, who are the most resplendent and amongst the most knowledgeable people in the place, are hosts for any MP who wants a guided tour. And that tour begins in the cloakroom.

'Here, sir, is your coat hanger, with your constituency name, Enfield North, above it.' (A gentle reminder that I was here on a temporary basis, hence the constituency name on the tag, rather than mine.)

Strange, I thought. Every coat hanger in the place, some 650 to be precise, had a pink ribbon attached to it with a small loop. I vaguely thought it might have something to do with the hugely successful Breast Cancer Awareness Day campaign.

'Tell me,' I ventured, 'what are these pink ribbons for?'

'For your sword, sir,' came the succinct answer – delivered, I might add, with a withering look. No further explanation looked forthcoming.

Bugger, I thought, I don't have a sword. It wasn't long before I realised I could really do with one.

That afternoon, the Commons met for the first time and, in keeping with tradition, immediately after the Speaker's Parade across the chamber floor, we commenced prayers. Halfway through those prayers, without any instruction, clue or secret signal, all the Members in the Commons about-turned and faced the wall, and prayers continued completely uninterrupted.

Not a murmur of surprise from anyone.

Bear in mind the country had just returned us all to Parliament, presumably to use our wise judgement and thoughtful counsel before making weighty decisions of state. Yet every single new Member in the House of Commons (by far the majority of those in the chamber that first day) without hesitation turned around and faced the wall. We followed without question, like lemmings throwing themselves off a cliff, those older

Members of the House who thought it perfectly natural to turn about-face in the middle of this solemn moment.

Eventually, as we sat down to begin the afternoon's session, I looked around the chamber to see if anyone else was remotely perplexed by this seemingly bizarre behaviour. Not a blank expression, except for mine, on any bench. I could contain myself no longer and turned to speak to a wiser and much older Member.

'Bill, why did we all just turn round and face the wall?'

Another withering look accompanied the answer: 'Your sword, dear boy, your sword.'

It transpires that the reason for this practice, as with so many things in the Palace of Westminster, lies in history. In the days when Members of Parliament attended the chamber wearing their swords, they found they could not kneel down for prayers facing forwards because their swords would get stuck on the benches or, more likely, poke the person behind them. They solved the problem by turning to face the wall and kneeling on the benches.

And, of course, the gap between the Prime Minister and the Leader of the Opposition at their respective despatch boxes is – you guessed it – two sword lengths apart.

How on earth do you get anything done in a place like this? Could history and tradition help my chances of actually delivering for my constituents? Or would the House of Commons model, used in public schools and elite universities in King Henry VIII's time, prove to be utterly outdated and ineffective?

Was I, in short, about to learn what so many of the public seemed to already believe: that Parliament was not fit for purpose, being completely divorced from the vast majority of modern-day British citizens?

3

IF IT AIN'T BROKE, DON'T FIX IT

To the inevitable polite enquiry by constituents as to how I was getting on during my first few months in Parliament, I always managed to demonstrate considerable enthusiasm for the place. Indeed, my sense of pride at having been elected never waned – but just getting there wasn't enough. I actually did want to 'do something'. Six months on from the general election, however, the single executive decision I had taken was which mobile phone to order. I was beginning to sulk. What had I done? Why was I here? Had I made a massive mistake? Was I set to be little more than cannon fodder for the government lobbies and not actually deliver anything specific for my constituents, all for a meagre dose of posterity?

Having spent twenty-five years starting and then running my own business, making decisions was a daily occurrence. Most were trivial but some had enormous consequences and were vital to the jobs and security of our employees and my own personal success and income. That's what being an executive in a small business means. Barely six months on as an MP, I was struggling to adjust to being a legislator voting on stuff, much of which was downright impossible to keep up with and, to boot, I was working my way around an antiquated and baffling system that was seemingly centuries out of date. On top of all this, I did not have a shred of executive power to do a damn thing, yet I was expected by all my constituents to have the power to 'do something' because 'you are my MP and that's your job!'

They had no idea, of course, of the mind-numbing dullness of life in those early days. The only real challenge was to see if you could reduce your intake of cups of tea, which threatened to drown you if you weren't careful. Wherever I went throughout the Palace of Westminster, a bloody cup of tea almost always appeared. Even the MPs' meeting room – moulded on a public school common room, of course – was called the Tea Room.

That was in fact the first place I visited in the morning, in my case around 8 a.m., and it was where I generally ended up around 10 p.m. every night with many colleagues, desperate for the vote to be called on whatever was being discussed so we could finally go home. Some days, I reflected somewhat rue-fully that I had spent eleven years trying to get in to the House of Commons, yet it seemed at times I couldn't wait to leave the place.

Before doing that, the second retreat of the day was my office.

Not quite the palatial grandeur that tabloids would have you believe MPs wallowed in. No ostentatious suite of outer offices to escort and impress visitors as they were ushered in to meet me. No spacious office, decked with sofas, elegant portraits and sweeping views of the River Thames.

Actually, that last claim is a bit of a fib. I did have a sweeping view of the Thames. Unfortunately, I shared it with anywhere between thirteen and seventeen other people, in an office not much bigger than your average living room. All right, maybe one and a half times the size of an average living room.

I also shared it with two high-flyers who appeared to launch their parliamentary careers by first competing with each other for who had the largest number of staff. This was then swiftly followed by who embarked on the most projects, followed by the first to publish a book. Their intensity could perhaps have knocked my self-confidence from day one. Happily, it reminded me I was not sent to Parliament to spend my time in an office, particularly one I could no longer barely fit in given the growing staff levels at the foot of my neighbours' desks.

I had, in fairness, managed to nick the best corner space, and plonked my parliamentary assistant by the door, probably far too close for her liking to both the door and a young and very enthusiastic intern who expressed that enthusiasm by talking incessantly. I then squeezed a small third table right up against the front of my desk, for use as a hotdesk by Tom Waterhouse, my former campaign manager turned chief of staff. That same table also housed the boxes of stationery we had nowhere else to store.

So glamorous.

By contrast, my nearest office neighbour, an assiduous, intellectual and bloody hard-working MP from East Anglia, occupied the middle ground of our office, again surrounded by three workspaces for his interns and staffers with his PA directly opposite my parliamentary assistant, who at the time was the delightful and incredibly patient Leslie Kiddoo. Clearly, owning your own personal space was not going to happen in our pad.

At the far end, though, was the outright winner: another East Anglian Member of Parliament, who arrived with connections that were second only to George Osborne or David Cameron himself from what I could tell. For his staff, he skilfully managed to squeeze a gallon into a pint pot when he at one point had some seven people in total. At times it felt like being in your living room tuning into *University Challenge* on the TV with some noisy students sitting on your lap, at your feet or even at your desk, as did happen on more than one occasion. That was our office. Nevertheless, his team must have produced some spectacular research papers and policy documents – at least, I imagine they did, since I don't think I read any of them. And, of course, he was first to publish a book.

I am perhaps being unfair to my colleagues, who both were and remain very generous to me. They arrived determined to map out a ministerial career, and they both succeeded. One, destined to fly high in the Cameron/Osborne era, is now an impressive survivor under the new leadership, still serving as a minister of state. Even his choice in sweaters and love of departmental cars did not harm his prospects. The other was inexplicably removed from a ministerial post in 2016 despite being competent, intelligent, hard-working and quite agreeable. More on ministerial qualifications later, though.

So, the huge change from actually running a business and making decisions in a decent working environment, to being a legislator struggling to get his voice heard at any level, particularly in his own office, which made even the Central line in rush hour look agreeable, didn't help me with my growing sense of frustration with Parliament. Frankly, I was beginning to sulk. As my huff threatened to engulf me completely, I realised that before descending into dark thoughts of a dramatic resignation born from the despair of not be able to 'do something', I needed to snap out of this funk and soldier on. After all, resignation wasn't that attractive since it would be followed by an unwelcome by-election and, of course, the inevitable lynching of Nick de Bois by the hugely alarming then Chief Whip Patrick McLoughlin, a former miner and, so far as I could tell, a trained killer. An unhappy prospect indeed.

The reality is that the only power you have as an MP is the power to influence, which comes about because of the apparent access you have to those who have real power – the ministers and, of course, ultimately the Prime Minister.

And so it has been for centuries. Why, I reasoned, was I so special in thinking the system was stacked against poor little old me? Thousands of MPs had gone before me, and many of them had made the system work for them and their constituents, so why did I think history and the whole Palace of Westminster had chosen this particular moment, and me especially, to single out for victimisation?

Silly arse.

Time to make the system work for me, not against me, and there was no better place to start than with the obscenity of knife crime. Before the general election, the Conservatives had promised that anyone convicted of carrying a knife would go to jail. If elected, they would introduce mandatory custodial sentences for the offence. With the number of young people stabbing each other reaching a high in 2008, particularly in north London, and including in my own constituency of Enfield North, this was, unsurprisingly, a popular policy even though judges and a pretty large chunk of the legal profession's practising criminal barristers did not like the idea. This attitude did not surprise me. After all, who likes being told what to do? But the fact is that multiple offenders, thugs who had been repeatedly convicted of carrying a knife, would get let off with cautions or community sentences time after time. They clearly saw this pathetic level of punishment as little more than an inconvenient interruption to business as usual. The judiciary was failing the public and needed a proverbial kick up the backside.

So, what's this got to do with trying to effect change as a backbencher?

Unfortunately, the 2010 parliament produced a coalition government, and the junior partners of the arrangement, the Liberal Democrats, did not like the idea of banging people up for carrying a knife. Instead, they said they would agree to the introduction of a new offence carrying a mandatory custodial sentence for 'using a knife in a threatening fashion'. In other words, if some offensive toerag threatened you with a knife, he would face a mandatory jail sentence. It was a start, but it wasn't good enough for two reasons.

First, it was not fulfilling the commitment in the Conservative manifesto at the general election. The government's half-baked measure dreamed up to appease the Liberal Democrats did not go far enough and they needed to develop a spine. Second, it applied to adults only. As my constituents knew only too well from some horrific stabbings in Enfield, more often than not the offenders (and the victims) were under eighteen. I, with support from my neighbouring MP David Burrowes in Enfield Southgate, wanted to ensure that the new offence and the sentencing rule would apply to young offenders of sixteen and over as well. I was hopeful we could eventually get the Conservatives to honour their pledge at the election to bring in automatic sentencing for carrying a knife, but in the meantime improving this proposed law was crucial and that became our main objective for now. Unfortunately, we didn't just have to overcome Liberal Democrat objections, but also those of the Justice Secretary, Ken Clarke, who was most definitely not a fan of the idea, and who was, of course, both a Conservative and a QC to boot.

We faced opposition from many quarters including the unwillingness of Ken Clarke and the Ministry of Justice to introduce the law in the first place, let alone adopt our proposal for mandatory sentencing to be extended to under-eighteens,

which Ken allegedly saw as 'bloody stupid'. We also faced further resistance from the high and mighty in the judiciary. That
was quite a powerful array of opposition, armed with the full
support of the civil service machinery to kill off our proposal.

And what did we have?

The backbenchers' arsenal includes the repeated use of parliamentary questions, even at Prime Minister's Questions, to
make the case. Then there is the press, who are often driven
by awkward parliamentary questions, and who love a potential troublemaker to brighten up their pages. In addition, there
is the voting lobby, where ministers can be cornered by an
MP without the civil service to fend them off and, of course,
parliamentary procedures such as tabling amendments and gathering shedloads of colleagues to back your proposal. We used
them all.

We planned, we plotted, we were supported by dozens of
colleagues, we tabled the amendments, we lobbied the ministers, we asked parliamentary questions. All this was good stuff
but it was frustratingly ineffective, as there was little sign of the
Ministry of Justice giving way. Even *The Sun* waded in and supported the law change.

'Ministers at War' raged their headline, after it seemed
that Theresa May (the then Home Secretary) and Ken Clarke
were busy arguing about the proposals during PMQs. No. 10,
we were told, was nervous but still backed Ken Clarke. David
Burrowes and I had a meeting scheduled with Ken that night
in his parliamentary office. His parliamentary private secretary (PPS), Ben Wallace, who had been lobbying hard to help
change Ken's mind, had set the meeting up in the hope that we
could convince him to support the proposal. We arrived a few
minutes early and proceeded down the corridor towards Ken's
office. Before getting to the door, we were engulfed in the strong

odour of cigars and the very recognisable tones of Ken Clarke
drifting down the corridor towards us.

'This is a bonkers plan, why on earth is someone sensible like
David Burrowes putting his name to it?' I didn't take offence,
but that, sadly, didn't sound encouraging.

'Well, mandatory custodial sentencing for carrying a knife
was in our manifesto,' Ben pointed out.

'Fag-packet populist stuff,' chimed in Ken. 'Hopeless, absolutely hopeless.'

We seized the moment and entered the smoke-filled room. I
spied what looked like a very good claret already being put to
good use.

'Gentlemen, hello! Something to drink?'

That, unfortunately, was as good as it got that evening.

David Burrowes is younger than me, better looking and far
smarter. He is a solicitor and undertakes criminal advocacy in
court, representing all sorts of villains, amongst whom he has
even inspired a loyal following. If they could, they would all
vote for him. David brought all that skill to bear in our meeting
with Ken, knocking back every single legal obfuscation that
Ken and his officials could throw at him to justify why our law
to automatically bang people up for threatening with a knife
shouldn't – or, as they argued, couldn't – go ahead.

Frankly, I was hopelessly out of my depth, burying my head
in my glass of wine and resisting the temptation to beg Ken for
a cigar, when he turned to me and said: 'I suppose that won't be
good enough for the backbenchers?'

I recall not having understood a single word they had been
talking about, given it was entirely on points of law. I did,
however, sense the moment was right for a robust and firm
argument from me.

'Absolutely not, Ken.'

And that ended my contribution to the debate. I think I had just threatened a backbench rebellion, without any basis for doing so, should he not support the changes we were seeking. It appeared not to have the desired effect.

A week later, our worst fears were confirmed when Ken's aide told us that we had fought the good fight but lost. The government would not back the proposed amendment.

So, in summary, we had a Conservative Party manifesto commitment, we had significant parliamentary support for the measure, and we had the public and *The Sun* with us. Clearly, though, this was not good enough, and I began to wonder if the Chief Whip would really lynch me if I quit. Still, I thought, *The Sun* would at least do a decent obituary.

The next day, the other ingredient required for a backbencher to get things done fell neatly into place. Opportunism.

I was tipped off that Ken Clarke was appearing before a public session of the Home Affairs Select Committee inquiry into gangs and crime. It was pretty clear that the Labour chairman of the committee was going to put Ken on the spot over mandatory jail sentences, so I rushed down to the committee room and slipped into the chairs reserved for the public, placed behind Ken, who was giving evidence and would not have seen me.

Having just listened to youth leaders and former gang members support our plan for mandatory jail sentences, Ken Clarke, who, until as late as the night before had resolutely refused to accept our amendment, indicated under some robust questioning that he 'still had an open mind' on the issue. Little did he know that I was less than six feet behind him, and the instant he rose to leave, I pounced.

'Ken, so pleased to hear you say that the door is not closed on our proposal, because last night your team indicated to me that you were definitely not going to accept the amendment!'

However dubious my tactics of barging in on him as he had barely risen from his seat at the Select Committee table might be; however inappropriate and unparliamentary my behaviour was to ask him publicly and within earshot of all the officials and Select Committee members to agree with me, Ken is above all else a pragmatist and a gentleman.

'Yes, very open-minded, not at all shut the door on the proposal, happy to see what we can do to help.' Ken's a decent man; he stuck to his word, and the new law was passed.

Two years later, we secured the further law to ensure that anyone convicted of carrying a knife for a second time would also go to jail. It seems you can, in fact, make a difference.

4

FEET ON THE GROUND

If ever there was any chance of basking in the rare glory of achievement for too long, every MP has the perfect antidote.

For me, it was sixteen miles from the rich and noble tapestry of the Commons and the so-called Westminster Bubble, and it is the best medicine any MP can have should they ever be in danger of believing their own PR and inflating their own importance. It's called the constituency office. In my case, it is exactly sixteen miles from the House of Commons, on Enfield's Hertford Road, an area sadly lacking in investment and trying to cope with significant cultural and local economic change at a fast pace. The very best of an outer London suburb is found here, but so too is the dark side of gangs, violent crime and social and economic deprivation.

I wanted my office to be here because it was in a part of the constituency that was far from Conservative leaning. I wanted people to be in no doubt that however they voted, I was here to represent everyone. We were nestled between a small news-agent run by a young Kurdish immigrant who always insisted I take my wine gums and Coke for free, an offer I routinely rejected, of course, and a flourishing hairdresser who never once offered a free cut and blow-dry. It was a great location, which became the scene for some memorable moments.

We got a taste of what to expect shortly after the 2010 election, when our constituency office door flew open and a very red-faced and angry middle-aged woman strode into the middle of the office, wheeling an old-fashioned shopping trolley behind her. Standing between my two caseworkers' desks, legs firmly planted astride, much like a parade sergeant major addressing a bunch of raw recruits, she demanded to see the MP immediately. Unfortunately, I was in.

'What', she thundered, 'are you going to do about this?'

Upon which, she produced from her well-used trolley an opened pack of Fray Bentos meat pie and pressed it right up against my nose.

'There's no meat in it!' she bellowed.

It was early days since the general election, so we all had a good prod in the congealed gravy and agreed that there was, in fact, no meat in the meat pie. After all, they say a new MP makes his mark in the first year, so every case mattered, surely?

With the pie lady duly despatched, along with a leaflet on how to complain to the Trading Standards Authority if the Co-op wouldn't refund her, I figured it was time for a team meeting in the constituency office about our priorities.

I was fortunate to have a constituency casework team consisting of Helen, a no-nonsense mother of two who had worked in the Enfield Conservative councillors' group office for years, and Leanne, who quite simply was a younger version of Helen in her no-nonsense 'just do it' approach to casework. Both had the good sense to understand that the work they did would reflect on my reputation as the local MP and, in turn, influence my chances of getting re-elected. As a result, they developed the art of making people feel valued and treated seriously, even when we were not able to secure the outcome they wanted. Caseworkers are often the stars of an MP's team.

They also have more common sense. 'Helen, why am I dealing with meat pies, for goodness sake?'

'For the same reason you'll be dealing with bin collections, trees that need cutting down, rats, dumped rubbish, immigration claims, social housing problems and more. That's what people expect their MP to sort out.'

'But I can't do anything about any of those issues. Almost all of those are matters for the council!'

'Tough, that's what you're going to get, and if you don't do it, they'll think you suck as an MP.'

'Why don't they go to their councillors?'

'They don't know who they are, and anyway, most people think you can sort it, and those that don't probably think you're a councillor anyway and no use.'

'But that's total bollocks.'

'Welcome to politics.'

In five years of casework, not all problems were frivolous by any means, but many were both memorable and indicative of the changing nature of society, as some looked to the state for problem-solving where the state had no business intervening. Worse, many more looked to their MP to 'do something' without making any attempts themselves. More of that later.

The consequence of handling so much casework that was not, strictly speaking, the job of an MP was that the most serious and demanding cases were at risk of not getting the attention they needed. Yet when I was elected in 2010, it was against a backdrop of broken politics, an utter lack of confidence and trust in MPs, and a general sense that they worked for their own benefit not their constituents'. Inevitably, only by delivering results on the ground could there be any chance of restoring some semblance of faith in our system. Those results were most evident in our approach to casework, so naturally we used the influence of the MP's office to persuade others to do their job, be it in housing, vermin control, the state of the roads, litter collection or elsewhere. It's commonly now known as 'pavement politics', and I can safely say it drives all MPs bonkers, whatever they might say publicly.

But some can be bloody funny, and some can be quite alarming.

Mrs Arnold – well, let's call her Mrs Arnold – was an early caller whose visit encouraged us to rethink the extent of our open-door policy.

At the time of her visit, we didn't even have desks for our office. We had the carpet, we had chairs and that was about it. Ever conscious of not splashing out too much taxpayer money, we had scrounged some desks from my old company, and Leanne had arranged for her grandparents' old dining table to be delivered for use when meeting constituents. As yet, however, nothing had arrived, which was why when Mrs Arnold walked into our office unannounced, she found all four of us sitting on the floor: Tom, my former campaign manager turned head of the parliamentary team, Helen, Leanne and me, all going through the casework left over from my predecessor.

'I need to speak to the MP.'

And of course, all pumped up with new-found enthusiasm, I volunteered to Mrs Arnold immediately that I was, indeed, the MP.

'Good, I'm glad you're here, I could do with some help because of some horrible anti-social behaviour I am having to put up with.'

Indeed, it didn't sound good. She shared with us all some frankly disturbing stories of bad behaviour. We listened intently,

FEET ON THE GROUND

our interest suitably piqued as we heard tales of unreasonable conduct and sensed the opportunity to solve a difficult constituency case only days into the job.

'And it all came to a head one Friday night,' she went on. 'I was just coming back from work when the door of their house opened and I was then covered in dog urine.'

'What?'

We all looked at each other, telegraphing the same question: 'Did she say dog urine?'

'That's awful,' I volunteered.

'No!' she blasted at me. 'Dog urine all over me, a huge bucket of dog urine.'

Tom tried.

'That's awful,' he said most sincerely.

Mrs Arnold then stood up, clearly feeling more explanation was needed, and proceeded to run from one side of the office to the other, throwing herself against the wall.

Now I was concerned for her safety. And our walls.

In all senses of the phrase, she provided a running commentary as she pivoted between either side of the office.

'They tipped dog urine over me, no matter how hard I tried to escape.'

They must have had a bloody good aim given the speed she was moving around our office, no doubt helped by the lack of furniture.

'They do it every day!'

Then the final word.

'Look at me, I am covered in it.'

Which, of course, she wasn't – as was helpfully confirmed when she shoved her sleeve under my nose.

What's difficult for MPs and their teams is that they have absolutely no training on how to deal with these all-too-frequent situations. The job does not come with training, but our task was to gently ease Mrs Arnold out of the door with some clear advice on how to seek help.

The only matter we did receive advice on was security. Back in 2010, threats to MPs were few and far between – aside, that is, from verbal abuse and threatening letters. It was not until later that year when Stephen Timms, the excellent Labour MP for East Ham, was stabbed in his constituency office that the police issued guidance on safety to MPs. The advice was basic, but did ensure we qualified for a door entry system at least. That was pretty much as good as it got.

The advice began with the recommendation that I sit during an advice surgery with a table between myself and the visitor. So far, so good.

Also, I should always sit closest to the back door so that I could remove myself quickly from any threat. The idea, it seemed, was that I should be prepared to abandon the team to the mercy of any assailant while I cut and run. I could not really justify that on moral grounds – or indeed electoral grounds.

'Trust me with your vote – after all, I abandoned my team to the mercies of a deranged assailant' hardly seemed a winning strategy.

As we saw with both the assault on Stephen Timms and the awful killing of Jo Cox MP in 2016, an open democracy carries huge risks. I doubt, however, that you will find an MP from any party who would want anything but an open democracy.

5

WHIP ME, AND WHIP ME AGAIN

I never intended to rebel against the government.

Sure, I said I would rebel if necessary, when asked by constituents both before the election in 2010 and after, but I was pretty confident that there would be no need to actually do it. After all, every new MP understands that the best way to bring about change is by being a good lad and getting a job on the ministerial ladder, don't they?

It was the same at school. Behave, don't grow your hair too long, be nice to the headmaster if invited round for tea and, of course, if you must smoke don't get caught. Simple enough, and almost always a ticket to being made a prefect of some level or another. Unfortunately, I broke all those rules except for being nice to the headmaster at tea, but that's simply because I was never invited.

So, less than ten weeks into the new parliament, some silly sod came up with a plan to agree to an increase in the budget for the grossly bloated EU Commission. The Commission would of course fritter it away in sun-bleached countries of the Mediterranean and a good chunk of Eastern Europe – after, that is, Commission officials had taken their extra slice for their own offices, cars, travel and entertainment budget. Unfortunately, at the same time as agreeing to this, we were busy warning the country that we would be cutting their child benefit allowance and other state giveaways that had become, by default, part of the household budget.

I didn't need to actually knock on the door of Mr and Mrs Enfield North to work out how the conversation might go.

'Morning, I am Nick de Bois, your local MP, calling round to introduce myself and see if there is anything you would like to raise with me?'

'How many kids have you got?'

'Eh? Four by my first marriage and two stepchildren.'

'How old are they?'

'My kids are grown up and my stepchildren...'

'So, all right for you then on your 65 grand a year, plus you had child benefit when you needed it, but now you seem to think it's OK to screw Middle England but give more money to the EU!'

'Well, yes, but I can assure you the Prime Minister has secured a cut in the EU budget for future years and...'

'Oh, it's all right for him, he can bloody well afford to lose the child benefit. I suppose that's what he means by "We're all in it together", then? Him, and the sodding Europeans!'

And the inevitable finish...

'I voted for you as well!'

The choice that faces every MP at some point or another is to cross your constituents or cross your party whips. All whips are MPs promoted by the Prime Minister to ensure that the programme of government gets through the House of Commons. They are there as managers of the government's business, not managers of people. It's not their job to care about people, but to care that the people they manage vote the way they want them to vote.

My general rule of thumb, established after my first rebellion, was simple. If a vote was on issues in the manifesto we were elected on, or in the Budget, then I had a duty to support it. Broadly speaking, that's what I was elected to do. As far as I was concerned, anything else was up for grabs.

First, though, came my initiation into rebelling, and my introduction to the whips.

First rule: to mitigate the wrath of the whips, give them warning that you intend to vote against the government. It's not fair on them to be taken by surprise and, much like duellists in the nineteenth century inviting opponents to choose the weapons, it is, after all, the decent thing to do.

Second rule: do not under any circumstances think this will lessen the assault on you. In fact, it just ensures that they have sufficient time to deal with you.

Third rule: remember that they are just doing their job.

Email is a wonderful invention when it comes to rebelling. The utterly cowardly thing to do is to send an email, often at peak time, forewarning of your impending rebellion in the hope that they don't read it until much later, and so narrow the window of opportunity to put the screws on you. You will have done your duty to notify them, but it's hardly in the spirit of fair play. Shamefully, in my first rebellion, this is exactly what I did. Even then it was strangely pathetic.

Email to: Whips' Office
Email from: Nick de Bois
Sent: 2.36 p.m.

Hi, somewhat concerned about government proposal on EU budget and will probably be voting against it.

Probably? Why not just invite them round to change your mind!

Email to: Nick de Bois
Email from: Your Whip
Sent: 2.39 p.m.

Thanks for your email. I would like to talk to you face-to-face.

Crap. That didn't work then.

Between 2.39 p.m. and 10 p.m. when the vote took place, there were three visits from the whips. The first was a simple chat on a one-to-one basis. 'I know you are new here, and you may not be aware that if you rebel, the Prime Minister will be told about this' (accompanied by a knowing look).

'Yes, I do, and to be fair, that's the point of my vote. I want him to know.'

'Well, wouldn't it be better if you just told him rather than rebel?'

Hmm, good point.

'That wouldn't be enough, because at the end of the day I have to explain to my constituents why we've increased the budget to Brussels yet we're cutting budgets at home.'

'Let's talk later.' First round: an honourable draw, I thought.

The fascinating thing about a rebellion is that they are rarely organised, yet those who plan to vote against the government tend to gravitate towards each other and effectively bolster each other's determination to see it through to the end. This unofficial network is very helpful, though in the early months of the parliament, no one was entirely sure if fellow rebels would see it through to actually going into the opposition voting lobby when it came to the vote at 10 p.m. Meanwhile, at least I knew where to find some mutual support: none other than the chamber in the House of Commons, where it was also not quite so easy for the whips to nobble you.

Sure enough, having found a measure of reassurance amongst colleagues, I watched my whip come into the chamber and start to pick us off one by one. We all expect this, but as we watch pressure being applied, and hear talk of banishment to the back benches and the abandonment of hope for a ministerial job for decades, all we are thinking is: 'Will they buckle?' There is no judgement by colleagues; it's always a personal decision to rebel or not.

The downside of being in the chamber hiding from the whips' wrath is that some ultra-loyal colleagues will take issue with you if it is known you are minded to rebel. The most prominent of these colleagues was Anna Soubry, MP for Broxtowe, who would gladly dish out a tongue-lashing to any potential rebel. Never shy of sharing her views with friend or foe, Anna found her telling-offs soon became a badge of honour. Most notable was her running commentary during PMQs if any fellow Conservative dared raise the question of the EU and in particular the then promise of a referendum.

'Utter nonsense, sit down and behave' or 'Oh, do stop going on and on, for pity's sake' were the sort of matronly comments we would hear as Anna's opinion carried across the chamber.

How deliciously ironic that after the Brexit referendum during which Anna campaigned vigorously to remain, her perspective on loyalty has changed. She is now the most vocal anti-Brexit rebel on the Conservative back benches. I saw her at the party conference in 2016 when I reminded her of this change of heart, and not least that I had been on the receiving end of an ear-bashing or two from her in my time.

'Well, there's no effective opposition so I have to do it,' she proclaimed. No double standards there, then.

But Anna was not my principal concern on this occasion.

Around 6 p.m., I received an email summoning me to meet with a senior whip.

Email to: Nick de Bois
Email from: Snr Whip
Sent: 6.02 p.m.

Please meet with whip in Whips' Office as soon as possible.

Email to: Snr Whip
Email from: Nick de Bois
Sent: 6.06 p.m.

Thanks, I'm having a cup of tea and will happily meet with whip in Members' Lobby in 10 mins.

There was no way on earth I was going to meet with the whip in the Whips' Office. There is no private office for meetings except the Chief Whip's. You would be grilled ostensibly by one whip, but in fact subject to about four other whips all keenly listening to every word and contributing as and when they wished. It would have been no contest. Manchester United against Altrincham, at Old Trafford, with eleven players against one. That was a non-starter.

Email to: Nick de Bois
Email from: Snr Whip
Sent: 6.07 p.m.

Fine.

The final showdown was something of a disappointment. Faced with two of us to persuade not to vote against the government, he easily turned my colleague on the grounds that the motion we were supporting, which was an amendment against the government, was in fact illegal. One down, just me to go.

'That's all very well, but my constituents won't see the subtle-
ties of the motion; they'll just see me voting for an increase in
the EU budget.'

'How about abstaining then?'

'I don't like abstaining. We weren't sent here to sit on our hands.'

'Don't be bloody stupid, your constituents won't even notice
how you vote.'

'They will if someone tells them, and I certainly intend to do
that.'

'You know this will be noticed in the Whips' Office, so think
carefully before you do this.'

'That's not a threat, is it?'

'No, but it does mean, well, we'll look at you differently in
the future.'

'How?'

'Well, it means…' Pause. '…We will look at you in a funny
way in future!'

And that's the moment it dawned on me. I was once told the
whips are all-powerful. Yet the reality is the whips are only as
powerful as you choose to make them.

If ministerial office and rank, both perfectly respectable aims for
MPs, are the most important things for an individual then, yes, the
whips have tremendous influence because they recommend you
for the position. If, however, you are not dependent on the patronage of the whips, if you value the role of backbench parliamentarian, then that's as close to becoming an independent-minded MP
as you can expect to be. The trick, of course, is to strike a balance
between that and maintaining a relationship with your ministerial
colleagues so that you can, if needs be, get something done. So,
don't piss your colleagues off too much or too often.

Meanwhile, on this occasion, the 'Noes' lobby welcomed me
with open arms, but needless to say, the government won.

6

DOES ANYONE NOTICE; DOES ANYONE CARE?

Returning victorious to the constituency office the following day (and happy to beat a retreat from grumpy whips the morning after the night before), I fully expected to bathe in some reflective glory of my virile demonstration of independence. I dished out some very decent pastries that I had picked up from Greggs to mark the momentous occasion of my rebellion. That's how good a mood I was in.

'Did you have a good week in the House?'

'Superb, I took a stand against the EU and protected my constituents' interests!'

'Good, can you sign these letters please, and we have a particularly tricky advice surgery this morning.'

'I take it you're not that interested in the vote yesterday?'

'What vote?'

'OK, pass the letters over for signing.'

Rarely do Westminster's events have any impact in the constituency office or go noticed by constituents, even those who attend the advice surgeries. The focus there was on casework, trying to solve problems, not debate weighty matters of policy.

Unlike the advice surgeries held before the days of 'pavement politics', it is now the exception for government policy to be raised by constituents during these weekly sessions. On one occasion, however, the two clashed, somewhat unfortunately.

At the end of a particularly challenging advice surgery, mainly filled with immigration cases that I could do little or nothing about despite the misplaced optimism of the constituents, a distraught young mother, toddler, baby and grandmother came into the office.

While Leanne was in the middle of trying to arrange an appointment for them to come in and discuss whatever their problem was, I heard the words 'knife', 'jail' and 'victim's my dad'.

Thinking the worst, I intervened and started to talk to them there and then, ignoring all the warning signals from my infinitely more experienced constituency team.

It transpired, in fact, that the young mother's dad had been victimised by some ghastly neighbours, in what amounted to persistent harassment, threatening behaviour and damage to property.

All too often in my constituency, I heard tales of families being terrorised by one or two individuals who made life hell for the targets of their abuse, often without any explanation. Many's the time, during my five years in Parliament, that I'd raise the question of so-called anti-social behaviour and, in fairness, the government did introduce measures giving more powers and rights to local people to try to contain this shocking conduct. Yet the bottom line is that unless councils use their powers to penalise those tenants who are either in social housing or in receipt of housing benefit, then many local communities will continue to suffer an intolerable disruption to the quality of their lives.

Not all anti-social behaviour emanates from those in social housing or in receipt of housing benefits, but an awfully high proportion does. Is it any surprise that, on occasion, victims of anti-social behaviour will take the matter into their own hands? They then, perversely, often end up on the wrong side of the law, while the perennial offender is not held to account for his or her actions.

And that's exactly what my constituents wanted to talk to me about.

'So, you see, Mr de Bois, my dad has had enough.'

'What happened, then?'

'Well, he had his window broken on his car, they chucked things through his letterbox and sat outside his house at night taunting him and keeping him awake. It's not right, is it, and the police did nothing.'

'Nothing. They just spoke to the thugs, which just made it worse for my dad.'

'Right, so what's happened now?'

'Well, they broke my dad's car window, as I said, and he'd had enough, right, so he took the kitchen knife and punctured the tyres on their car, and then these blokes saw him and gave him a kicking, so my mum called the police, right, and they arrested my dad, but he needed to go to hospital, right, but they just had him looked over at the police station. It's not right, and they didn't arrest the people who done this to him.'

'They arrested your dad for slashing the tyres, but not the louts who gave him a beating?'

'Yeah, and the police said he is definitely going to jail. My mum's heartbroken. It's so unfair.'

'It's not up to the police to decide if he goes to jail. That's for the courts.'

'No, it's not. The police told us that a new law has been

brought in, that if you use a knife in a threatening way you get an automatic jail sentence… Is that right?'

Oops. Time to beat a retreat to Greggs for a coffee break and sugar rush.

7

DUE PROCESS

Doughnut? What are they talking about?

No, I was not in Greggs again.

I was about to get to my feet in a very empty chamber of the House of Commons, and suddenly heard the irrepressible Colonel Bob Stewart DSO mutter to the two or three people near him, 'De Bois is on his feet. Let's doughnut him.'

I knew I was going to be called to speak, because there is an unofficial list of speakers made by the Speaker or Deputy Speaker and, assuming you don't hack them off too much, there's a good chance they'll share your place on that list with you. The good ones even give you a little nod to remind you that you're next.

Mind you, on this occasion, it was obvious I was next. There was hardly anyone in the chamber in the first place and, of the others, there was no one who looked remotely interested in speaking.

Television often shows the chamber of the House of Commons empty, with perhaps a dozen or so people in there. This is completely understandable because, after the opening speeches to any debate and perhaps one or two afterwards, there is frankly nothing new left to be said.

But that doesn't stop MPs from saying it anyway. Sometimes it just has to be said, simply to be on the official Hansard record that you said it, so you can enlighten constituents on your position on any given issue. Either that, or because it's not a good thing to have against your name 'Below-average number of speeches in the House of Commons' on that pesky 'They Work for You' website, which relentlessly measures how active you are in the chamber. Rarely is a contribution made to enlighten Members of the House.

Which is where the doughnut comes in.

Just before I got up to speak, Bob, along with two other Members he had marshalled to his cause, slid across the green benches and plonked himself behind me, leaned forward and adopted the listening mode. Phone away, iPad down, on best behaviour. Well, for a while, anyway.

The point of their doughnutting me was to provide practical support by ensuring that as the parliamentary camera is focused on me, any constituent who may be flicking through channels and notice that I am on my feet will see people behind or to the side of me, ostensibly listening to my every word. If only.

What they won't hear, because parliamentary TV microphones are brilliantly devised, is any heckling from the opposition benches, or any piss-taking from my somewhat unruly doughnutters on that particular day.

'Mr Deputy Speaker, I am grateful for the opportunity to highlight a couple of points…'

'A couple of points only? That's probably because de Bois knows sod all about the matter,' chortled one of the doughnutters behind me unhelpfully. I continued: '…to highlight a couple of points in favour of the government's measures.'

'Whips' nark!'

'You sold out, de Bois, sold out!'

The only people who can hear this are me and the perpetrators.

A pleading look to the Deputy Speaker, the affable and tolerant Lindsay Hoyle, who, incidentally, always called me to speak as 'Nick de Boy', and whom I never corrected because he was such a decent bloke and I knew he would be mortified. Regardless, he didn't look like he was going to come to my rescue on this occasion anyway.

I pressed on, defending in my speech the not quite indefensible, and continuing to subject myself to ribbing from my colleagues. In fact, Chuka Umunna, the lead opposition spokesman, was kinder to me than my doughnutter colleagues.

Eventually the mocking and teasing did come to an end when Bob, the ringleader, declared: 'De Bois, you are so tedious I am going to get some light relief by reading Select Committee reports on EU protocols.'

Fair enough – looking back over the speech, he did have a point.

So, what was I doing speaking out for something that I didn't wholeheartedly support, but was nevertheless making a pretty good fist of advocating in the House of Commons?

What was I, a man of supposed principle, doing on this occasion? Had I really sold out?

The answer lies in part with the very persuasive parliamentary private secretary to the then Chancellor George Osborne, Amber Rudd, who at the time of writing is the Home Secretary. The PPS is the lowest rung on the ministerial ladder and it can be a thankless job which includes (amongst other duties), trying to drum up speakers to support less-than-dazzling policy announcements from your minister.

When Amber called, I was, as it happens, sunning myself on

a beach in the Dominican Republic over the Easter recess. I was on a guilt-funded holiday from my wife who, unwittingly, had booked a skiing holiday for herself earlier that February with a friend, and at the time of booking had not realised it clashed with my birthday. Given that this came hot on the heels of her not being present for our last two anniversaries, my wife – in what I suspect was a panic move – very generously cashed in some timeshare points as a belated birthday present, and here we both were, by a sun-drenched pool, when the phone went off.

Amber is a very smart, no-nonsense, straight-talking person to whom it is very hard to say no. I have seen her close up in action as Home Secretary when dealing with both the police and the families of victims of knife crime, where she demonstrated a thorough grasp of her brief and the empathy and resolve required when meeting with the families. No wonder George Osborne wanted her on his team.

But at this precise time, she was effectively manipulating me into agreeing with her request. True, lying on a beach chair mid-morning in the Caribbean toying with the idea of your first cocktail means defences are low, so when the Chancellor's PPS rings you up to twist your arm into speaking, it was probably only ever going to have one outcome. I paraphrase:

'Nick, you know this is a policy George is personally very committed to?'

I bloody hope so – after all, it's his daft idea.

We were talking about the Chancellor's little-known 'Shares for Rights' employee scheme, the detail of which I will not bore you with just yet.

'I am really pleased to hear that, but...'

Clearly, I didn't have the willpower to put up much of a fight.

'And because you have started, run and grown a successful business, you would be the best advocate for this policy.'

'Indeed, though I am not sure I would have...'

Smooth interruption again by Amber, not letting one of my rebuttals be heard: 'And George knows that this parliament needs more people like you, with a background in business, people who have actually achieved.'

I can't believe I am falling for this.

'An entrepreneur speaking up for this scheme would be very significant.'

Ego was being seriously stroked here, with disarmingly bold claims. Both of us knew George hadn't got a clue what I did before I came into Parliament, yet damn it, it was working.

'When is the debate?' I conceded.

I could feel the smile as another weakling backbencher fell to the power of the Chancellor's office and, in particular, his PPS. God help them in the Home Office these days.

All over. Game set and match to the magnificent Amber Rudd. She had pushed all the right buttons and, for all I knew, had worked out that I would be eyeing up my first cocktail at this time of day and calculated I would be even more amenable.

Surprisingly, George and Amber missed a trick, as do many ministers. Having worked so effectively to stroke my ego and persuade me, on this occasion, to be the only Conservative who in fact gave a speech in the debate on this measure, therefore exposing myself to the questioning of Labour's front bench, it would have been impressive if a note of thanks had been sent after the debate.

OK, I agree this might seem like I'm a bit up myself, but it's always worth remembering that while George Osborne would forget about the entire thing less than a minute after he despatched the note, the impact of it on me, and no doubt others in similar circumstances, would be remembered the next time a PPS came trotting up trying to persuade you to speak up for some hopeless or even respectable cause.

In truth, I was more than happy to be a team player on many occasions, not only this time around. On this specific topic, I didn't feel particularly strongly about it, because ultimately nothing was being forced on companies or individuals, and no one had to accept a trade-off for shares in return for losing some employee rights, so there was nothing to get excited about there.

But most importantly, to be effective in Parliament, it would be crazy not to build relationships and allies when you could. I had absolutely no reason not to help on this and many other occasions, which ensured that when I did need to be awkward, or wanted to secure changes, I would not be dismissed as a serial troublemaker but someone who was generally quite reasonable.

That worked for me, and it worked for my constituents, albeit it was rather time-consuming. And in Parliament that matters, because the time available to pass legislation is short, not least as we are only there for about twenty-seven weeks in any one year.

So, given that time constraint, you would have thought we would have a very efficient modern process for scrutinising and then approving legislation, right?

Not quite.

In fact, it is a challenge to get things done in a timely manner, not least because we still use a parliamentary process that has evolved slowly over many centuries and is today essentially the same as it was way back in the early nineteenth century. Indeed, the building has little changed since the rebuild after the fire of 1834 that largely destroyed the palace.

The Commons is now a place of some 650 MPs, where about half will always complain that they don't have enough time to scrutinise and challenge the government proposals, and the government (the other half) will always complain that they can't give more time to allow bucketloads of scrutiny because they don't have enough room in the parliamentary calendar.

And that's in part because MPs only sit in Parliament for those twenty-seven weeks a year and there are only so many hours in any one day.

But even (generously) putting that to one side, MPs don't work to a system that makes it easy for themselves, and they eat up valuable debating time with some rather curious procedures.

They will, for example, have a debate to discuss how much time they will spend debating whatever it is that is up for discussion. Yes, seriously, we can spend one hour doing that, including voting. That's because the opposition wants more time to debate than the government will grant, so by having a motion to discuss how long they will be allowed to debate an issue, they eat up that time by a pointless debate on, you guessed it, how little time they have to debate.

And if that's not enough, the opposition (and awkward backbench MPs on the government side) will, of course, table amendments to Bills, which means there will be encyclopaedic quantities of amendments to discuss, of which a good few are simply not selected for debate by the Speaker. They can't even be mentioned under our breath unless in the third and final reading of a Bill someone wants to get up and say how much they regret they did not have a chance to discuss their amendment which was not selected for discussion. So we then talk about something that we were stopped from talking about despite the fact that we cannot even vote on the matter.

With me so far?

And that's before the grouping of amendments, which frankly I'm not even going to attempt to explain.

The point is that when the government wants to pass a law, they produce a Bill to put before Parliament, which becomes an Act of Parliament on signature by the Sovereign after it completes its scrutiny in both the House of Commons and the House of Lords.

As you can see, it's a lengthy process, which in theory allows just about any legislator who wants to comment on any Bill to do so. Particularly the formal opposition, which only exists to criticise whatever the government proposes. It figures that they are always keen to speak, and therefore the government whips and the relevant minister's PPS often have to drag members of their own party kicking and screaming to the chamber to speak in defence of the proposal, whatever it may be.

The only saving grace for the whips is that all MPs love to speak. But that's when we end up repeatedly hearing the same points, not least because the most reluctant of speakers (often less than knowledgeable about the subject in question) will be clutching the party briefing document, which unsurprisingly becomes the mainstay of any speeches.

Oh, and the measure of just how effective the whips are is when they have got so many committed to contributing to the debate that the Speaker imposes a time limit, maybe four to five minutes for each speaker, because there are simply too many of them.

And then we wonder why there is not enough parliamentary time to get things done.

The principle of having a long process to pass a Bill into law is based on the belief that we should vigorously scrutinise what any government proposes. Fair enough. But when I find myself spending hours just listening to the same old arguments time after time, albeit from different people, I can't help thinking we have not got this quite right after all.

In a place where it seemed we spent more time than necessary scrutinising Bills, adding up to an endless number of parliamentary hours, it's odd that we also have something called a Ten Minute Rule Bill. It's as if someone knows we take too damn long to pass legislation so, to compensate, we have a fast-track system, which does precisely what it says on the tin.

I can present a Bill to Parliament and have it scheduled for second reading within ten minutes. What's more, any opponent to the Bill has only ten minutes to oppose it.

And the great thing is you generally only need ten minutes to settle matters.

There is a huge catch, though: Ten Minute Rule Bills are not designed to actually make laws, even though they were meant to be. They are designed to make it look like you are doing something (which, as you might have noticed, is a growing theme of Parliament).

Confused? You have every right to be. I was too when I was trying to do something for the constituents who were sick to death of so many cases of 'neighbours from hell'.

More often than not, decent hard-working people would find that after a neighbour had sold their house and upped sticks, the new owners were remote landlords who made a mint out of renting the house next door to housing associations, councils and organisations providing halfway houses for those on rehabilitation of one sort or another.

And before I go on, no, of course not everyone who is housed under these circumstances is a troublemaker, but the ones my constituents came to see me about were generally these obnoxious sorts of people.

In short, troublesome tenants who lacked any sense of personal responsibility, making life hell for their neighbours. Fights, abuse, vandalism and aggressive behaviour were typical complaints. The victims of this behaviour would try to resolve issues themselves by speaking to the management organisation of the property, or the estate agents who had let it to the tenants. Neither usually responded positively and, if they did, they simply replaced one dodgy household tenant with another. And on it went.

Meanwhile, the new owner and landlord of the property just collected his rent and was quite possibly even unaware of the problems caused by his contract arrangements. Long-suffering neighbours nevertheless found it extremely hard even to track down the landlord, let alone to hold them to account. That's where my plan came in: to ensure the landlords did assume some responsibility, and the Housing Ombudsman could be the conduit for that.

So, what better than to introduce a law to that effect?

First stop, the government.

Could I raise a glimmer of interest? Not easily.

I lobbied ministers, who seemed sympathetic, but that frankly wasn't going to do it for my very grumpy constituents. They needed someone to 'do something'.

The state had fuelled this problem by lavishing housing allowances on people who seemed to have no sense of personal responsibility or respect for other people in their neighbourhood, not least because the benefit came with few strings attached requiring decent behaviour on pain of losing benefit. And if strings were attached, they were unlikely to be enforced. Ironically, more often than not the victims were supporting these troublemakers through their taxes. No wonder they felt the state should take action.

It seemed the state was not keen to intervene, however, so I calculated it was worth a try to force its hand. But how?

'This is one way a backbencher can introduce legislation, Nick.'

'How?' I asked eagerly. My mentor was, of course, a wiser,

longer-serving MP, the same one who had told me about swords being the reason we all faced the wall during prayers.

'A Ten Minute Rule Bill should do it.'

'OK, but how does that work?'

'Go to the Public Bill Office upstairs and work out what you want the Bill to say, as there is a special form of words needed, but they will sort that for you.'

'Good.'

'Mind you book your spot for the presentation of the Bill, first through the Whips' Office, then make sure you are No. 1 in line for the Public Bill Office on the Tuesday fifteen days before the presentation date. That means getting there for about 7 a.m. Some people sleep there the night before, even, to make sure they are first in the queue to grab the slot from you.'

Hmmm… I was going off this idea rapidly. Sleep in the corridor? It's all right if you have a nice taxpayer-funded flat around the corner, but I had a bloody awful journey in from Enfield most days, often taking up to ninety minutes to travel the twelve miles home thanks to a very unhelpful train timetable from Seven Sisters to Enfield Town out of rush hour.

'Then present it to the House on the date given, and that's it.'

'What? It becomes law?'

'Oh dear boy, no. Although I think in 1998 one Ten Minute Rule Bill did become law.'

Somehow, I had suspected this.

'Er, look, thanks for your help, but what is the point of this?'

'The point is: you have made your point.'

This, clearly, was meant to end the discussion. He even gave that same withering look he had given when he told me about the swords. And, once again, no further explanation was forthcoming.

I looked for comfort from a marginal-seat colleague to see if

I was, in fact, the only sane one here today or if others thought this Ten Minute Rule thing was a touch flawed.

'Have you done a Ten Minute Rule Bill before?'

'Brilliant stuff. Bit of a bear trap if you screw up the march down the aisle of the chamber to present the Bill, but the press coverage locally was amazing!'

Ahh… Being seen to do something, clearly.

'And I got a note from the minister saying he would look at the issue raised by my Bill, which he thought was jolly interesting.'

Bet that wasn't from George Osborne or Amber Rudd, then.

'Went down very well in the constituency!' he beamed.

'How long ago was that, and has the minister chatted it through with you yet?'

'About a year ago. No, nothing yet. We had a quick catch-up in the lobby a while back.'

Hmmm.

The way I saw it, Ten Minute Rule Bills exist so that back-bench MPs can introduce legislation in the full knowledge that it won't get onto the statute book and become law. Presumably that's why we don't waste more than ten minutes on it.

But, on the upside, you do look as if you are doing something.

I dug around and discovered that my mentor was right. One Ten Minute Rule Bill did become law about twenty years ago, something to do with divorce that the government backed. They therefore found time to debate it, and whipped it through the Commons and the Lords.

In fact, since 1945 some sixty Ten Minute Rule Bills have gone on to become law. That, however, is roughly one in every sixty presented to Parliament. Backbenchers really have the odds stacked against them.

Still, I reasoned, if that one Bill is, in fact, yours… so I gave it a go. Actually, I gave it two goes.

The Landlords Ten Minute Rule Bill was unfortunately con-
signed to the parliamentary dustbin, along with the thousands
of others that preceded it.

But, much to my surprise, another Ten Minute Rule Bill of
mine, while not coming into law in its own right, was adopted
into government legislation, namely: 'That leave be given to
bring in a Bill to amend the Adoption and Children Act 2002
to allow access to information for the descendants of deceased
adopted people.'

I won't even attempt to claim full credit for this because,
while the matter had been raised with me as deserving attention by my political assistant Jack Hart, there was in fact
a well-established campaign underway to address the matter.
My Ten Minute Rule Bill, and meeting with the very switched-
on then Minister for Adoption, Ed Timpson, coincided with
government legislation going through the Lords. The minister
wanted this issue dealt with by the Bill; I simply happened to
be doing the right Ten Minute Rule Bill at the right time and he
made sure it was included in the Bill going through the Lords.

But, once again, this bizarre, antiquated and sometimes utterly illogical place worked.

All right, we could clearly do it differently, but I am far from
convinced we could achieve a better outcome.

8

RIOTS

Sometimes in Parliament an event takes place that gets noticed by almost all of the constituency. These occurrences are rare, of course – indeed, almost unheard of – but when riots sweep through your patch, as they did in mine in August 2011, the ensuing debate consumes the attention of almost everyone. Just as unusual, it was a genuine opportunity for me to speak on behalf of all my constituents, and with no danger of either requiring supportive doughnutting from colleagues or being on the wrong end of their jokes. When it matters, the chamber is packed and the Members formidably attentive.

True, if you tune in to the Parliament channel any time, on any day, to any speech, you will hear MPs claim that they speak on behalf of their constituents, be it on great matters of state or the tortuous and incredibly dull minutiae of a very unimportant piece of legislation. They are making a legitimate claim, as they represent the constituency that elected them, but the implied unanimity with which he or she speaks is another matter. To be frank, the chances are not high, given there is at least a one in two chance that their constituents didn't vote for them anyway, and are therefore far less likely to be in agreement. Nevertheless, it is a long-established principle that the Member of Parliament speaks on behalf of his constituents, and is ultimately held to account by them for whatever words of wisdom he shares with the House. The difference is, following the events of August 2011 I was, for once, voicing the views of all my constituents on the shocking rioting we witnessed. True, not everyone would have agreed with my recommendations on measures to prevent future incidents, but there was no disputing the unanimity behind my decision to ensure that what happened in the constituency was understood by the House of Commons. How they voted didn't matter; how we responded as their representatives and their government did. The riots in question, and what I witnessed with fellow residents, presented that rare opportunity to speak in Parliament with one voice on behalf of all. Quite literally, my constituents demanded that I do so, so that they could be heard at the highest levels.

Helen (my wife, that is, not my constituency caseworker) and I were spending the afternoon of Sunday 7 August 2011 at Esher Park races, attending a birthday party for close friends, when it became increasingly clear that the riots that had devastated Tottenham the night before looked set to hit Enfield Town. At the time, I was hooked on Twitter, and could see that trouble was anticipated that evening. Two minor incidents had already been reported. The police were dealing with them, but social media was predicting more serious trouble later that night. It is perhaps difficult to recall now, but the atmosphere across cities was toxic, so it seemed perfectly clear to me at the time that Enfield was being targeted and I just had to be there.

Why?

There was absolutely nothing I could do to prevent trouble, and there was always the risk I could be seen as a nuisance by the police, and quite frankly a provocation to have a Tory MP wandering around the hotspots.

But I had to go.

It was inconceivable to me that if there was to be trouble I would not witness it first-hand and see the effect it had, both at the time and in the immediate aftermath. How could I seriously represent my constituents' interests if I did not understand the scale of the problem? Helen, understandably, thought I was bonkers, and left me in no doubt that the good folk of Enfield North would be right to question their judgement in electing an MP who would make such an insane decision.

Despite that risk, I ended up on the streets of Enfield Town for the next four to five hours in what was the most extraordinary event I have ever participated in. That sounds all wrong, but participate I did.

To my pleasant surprise, when I got to Enfield Town, all seemed very much under control. If you know the area, I was at the junction of Church Street with Silver Street, close to the town fountain and fifty yards from the main train station, essentially as close to a main meeting point as you could get. Although there were small groups gathering, it seemed peaceful: the police had dealt with the two earlier incidents and people were still on their way home after shopping, albeit many shops were closing early in anticipation of trouble. Because I was putting out on social media the odd report or two, it was no surprise that LBC phoned me up to ask if I could do an interview from Enfield. I happily agreed.

This was a time to be cautious, factual and definitely not flippant, and I nearly achieved it, but I did somewhat optimistically state that 'things were quite calm and I couldn't see any immediate threat of increasing disturbance'. After all, I was to rationalise later, I didn't want to unnecessarily alarm people.

I was so wrong.

Thirty minutes later it all kicked off and, notwithstanding the seriousness of the situation, Twitter understandably dubbed me the Michael Fish of the riots. Michael Fish, a much-loved BBC weather forecaster, became well-known for completely failing to warn of a devastating hurricane that swept the south of England on the day he dismissed predictions of a hurricane as somewhat exaggerated.

To be fair, I was pleasantly surprised that the subsequent ridicule was not far greater than it was. That, however, was where any frivolity ended.

Events soon became much more serious, as youths gathered on nearby St Andrews Road, where they reportedly broke down garden walls so they could collect bricks to throw at police and windows. Several shops were ransacked, including a frightening attack on the nearby pharmacy, and on Church Street a police car was smashed and set on fire. Riot police moved in to secure the area and close the train station.

Shortly after 8.30 p.m., a crowd of about 100 youngsters, some as young as eleven, broke into a long-established local jeweller's. When police arrived less than a minute later, I witnessed chaotic scenes, fuelled by young thugs' intention to loot not protest. For a moment, I took refuge in the porch of a restaurant, now closed, on the corner of Silver Street about thirty yards from the jewellery shop. The owner was next to me and was built like a front-row prop from the England squad. I felt perfectly safe next to him.

'What are you doing here?' I asked a kid of no more than thirteen who was clutching a metal rod and had his face covered by a scarf.

'Justice for Mark Duggan!' he yelled, Mark Duggan's death from police gunfire being the spark that had set off the riots in Tottenham the night before.

'Piss off back to your home you little prat,' came the response from the restaurant owner in whose porch I was standing.

Even though we were across the road from a line of police officers, who clearly had orders not to move, the looter stopped walking and came right up to us, removed his face scarf so we could see him, as could the police, and said, 'No one is going to stop us doing whatever we like, so it's you who can piss off.'

There was no fear of being held to account.

Around 9.30 p.m., the police began turning the whole of Enfield into a so-called sterile area. Hundreds of riot police arrived with vans and police dogs, charging at groups of teenagers, who swiftly disappeared into side streets and reappeared further along the high street. They smashed cars and shop windows as they ran. In Churchbury Lane, a pleasant residential street, I watched as a brute of a thug pushed a local out of his way as he charged up the pavement to his car, where the out-of-town louts drove off to park somewhere else and carry on with their carnage. It was a bizarre scene, as I stood there talking with residents in their front gardens with all this going on only yards away.

And it was only in Enfield that the marvellous character of my constituents presented itself.

'Nick, what do you say we go and slash the tyres of these little bastards' cars, then they have nowhere to run.'

'Are you sure you want to do that?' I replied. 'After all, don't we want the little sods to leave?'

'Turn around, Nick. An MP shouldn't see what we are about to do.'

The Prime Minister subsequently singled out for praise the efforts of Enfield residents to protect their own area.

But my lasting memory is from around 10 p.m. I was in Churchbury Lane again, speaking with ten or so residents. The trouble had now moved on.

'Nick, thank you for being here to witness what happened,

but now you have to make sure you tell the Prime Minister exactly what happened. They all need to know what really went on in our town. Make sure they bloody well know what we've been through.'

Parliament was recalled later that week, and that's precisely what I did. I couldn't have been prouder of my constituents, or the Parliament that meant their voice was heard, and heard by the Prime Minister and most of his Cabinet.

As I was beginning to learn, sometimes this antiquated old system works rather well.

9

MAD

Being on the frontline in the riots – and frankly not doing a bad job (even if I say so myself) representing the community during that time – didn't mean I would win any popularity contests with voters. Let's face it, even winning an election does not mean you are popular, and it certainly does not mean you are trusted or even liked. It just means you are less mistrusted than the other lot.

In fact, the only time I have ever been described as popular was after I lost my seat in the 2015 election.

'Nick de Bois, the popular former MP from Enfield North, will almost certainly be seeking a return to Parliament…' wrote my local newspaper, who up until that point I can't recall ever suggesting I enjoyed any support, let alone popularity, amongst residents.

Before defeat, it was more like 'Nick de Bois, the Tory backbencher, today defended the government's unpopular welfare reforms.'

Or, if I had been causing mischief within my own party and having a pop at the government, I was cast as 'Nick de Bois, the senior Tory, today demanded the government call a halt to their plans to increase funding to the EU' – 'senior' being a label given to errant MPs by the media.

But of course, being popular, while probably enjoyable, isn't what being an MP is all about, and is not what any MP should reasonably expect. More so since the expenses scandal of 2009 remains very much in the minds of the public.

One thing is for certain: the pollsters, whose reputation is currently pretty much in tatters themselves, do nevertheless get one poll consistently right, and that's the one that records just how many people don't like MPs. Ipsos MORI established in 2013 that 72 per cent of the population do not trust MPs whatsoever. Any doubts about the accuracy of the poll can easily be verified just by chatting to people about what they think of MPs. That's not something I try very often, as you can imagine.

I don't take it personally – well, not too much, that is.

Perhaps I am right not to do so, because that same poll concludes that the same members of the public trust their local MP more than MPs in general. In fact, just over half say they trust their local MP.

If you start to think about it, there is something quite illogical about that. The verdict seems to be that all MPs are lying, lazy toerags, except, that is, for everyone's local MP.

It's that sort of poll, nevertheless, that I clung to as evidence that I might be re-elected, and I can assure you that getting re-elected is an all-consuming obsession of even the sanest of MPs, and more so if, like me, you are defending a marginal seat. If not, and you have your backside firmly planted in a safe seat with a whopping 15,000-plus majority, you can both ignore opinion polls of any kind and be comfortable that no matter how inadequately your party may perform, or indeed how utterly useless you might be as a local MP, you are a shoo-in at the general election next time round. After that, and given the current political climate, who knows, you might just have to pull your finger out.

As a wet-behind-the-ears MP in 2010, I was distinctly unimpressed when my former campaign manager and then head of my parliamentary office announced on Monday 10 May, four days after the successful general election that saw me stagger into Parliament with my unhealthy majority of 1,692: 'The next general election starts now.'

Seriously? I had just got here, and he wants to think about the possibility of being fired? I was knackered. I wanted to enjoy it and savour the success.

'Tom, I have spent eleven bloody years and three general elections to get here, and now you want to start fighting the fourth, with five years to go. Sod that!'

Tom is one of those infuriatingly calm people. Young, talented and immensely efficient, he stands in complete contrast to my age, talent and efficiency. Nothing seems to ruffle him, least of all my odd rant. He can also be infuriatingly smug. Justifiably so, because he is far more often right than wrong. He is a great friend but, at that precise moment, rather annoying.

'You need to do a constituency newsletter.'

'But I haven't done anything yet.'

'You won the election.'

'But they know that – they voted for me.'

'Only just.'

That was so unnecessary.

'Anyway,' he went on, 'it doesn't matter if they voted for you or not, most people won't have a clue who you are, so your newsletter will introduce you, and you can thank them for voting for you.'

'I don't see why I should thank them for such a small majority.'

Childish, I know.

'Get over it, and do your newsletter. The 2015 election starts today.'

Everything I did in the constituency was, in truth, through the prism of it being a marginal seat. This had the effect of reducing me, at times, to a somewhat pathetically vulnerable and paranoid individual, despite the fact that for over two decades in business, I had demonstrated self-belief, confidence, some ability and lots of determination.

And, of course, your constituents know how to play that vulnerability to their full advantage. 'If you want my vote at the next election' became a mantra that fuelled the growing anxiety and paranoia that goes hand in hand with defending a marginal seat.

Almost every invitation came with a not-too-subtle reminder of how many 'voters' would be there. Every invitation became less of a pleasure and more of a threat. Your mind worked out torturous conclusions, with far-reaching consequences for your electoral prospects, with every single damned constituency function invitation that presented itself to you.

Don't go, and you would irritate the hosts.

Don't go, and you would annoy the members of the whole damned organisation.

They would tell their friends, their family, their bloody newsagent and, for all I knew, their second cousins, who undoubtedly would live in your patch, and that all of that would cost you over 100 votes! Turn down ten invitations and that's nearly two thirds of your majority gone, all because you didn't attend the event! Result? I tried to attend everything, seven days a week.

How is it that a normally sensible and rational person who has won the trust of his constituents (albeit just) can be so paranoid and unbalanced?

Part of the answer lies in my colleagues in the House of Commons, both those who have huge majorities and those who don't. The former irritate me and drive unreasonable levels of jealousy. The latter just worry me.

Take the Member for a leafy Midlands seat where, at his election count, they probably weigh his vote rather than bother counting it as his majority is so huge. Returning to the Tea Room for a break, having signed and read some eighty constituency letters prepared by my office, I was having a gentle whine about the time it consumes. The leafy Member proffered his unsolicited words of wisdom.

'Sign your letters? Don't be bloody silly, man [ex-military, incidentally]. No one signs their letters personally any more. And as for reading them...'

No one, that is, except a marginal-seat MP who happens to think that the extra personal touch really matters.

I foolishly challenged him and was wonderfully patronised for the next five minutes with a benevolent and collegiate, 'Dear boy, you will learn.' He continued chortling to himself, and slurped his soup just as nanny taught him, without spilling it over his regimental tie. Sometimes, I fear for the future of the Conservative Party if we go on electing people like that. Thankfully, they are a diminishing breed, often, as in this case, safely despatched to the Lords.

The whips don't help.

Being a Greater London MP, there is even more expectation that you can just pop back any time to the constituency to do whatever is expected of you. Fair enough, you must deal with that, but when there is a full-blown crisis, such as a public meeting to discuss the government's impending plan to close your local hospital's Accident & Emergency unit, the marginal-seat MP's normal symptoms of agitation can reach new heights. Not unreasonably, I felt that buggering around with my hospital was probably not in the best health interests of my constituents, and it was most certainly not in the interests of my health, more so as my blood pressure and heart rate escalated further when the so-called 'pairing whip' (who decides if you can be absent from Parliament) explained that I couldn't go to Enfield to a public meeting because I was needed for a vote in the Commons. At this point in time, it was the colourful blond bombshell Michael Fabricant who was the bearer of bad news.

'No, sorry, we could lose this vote, so no exceptions.'

'You always say that, and we never lose.'

I was acutely aware that on this occasion, unlike before, I was in the whips' open-plan office, which meant that every other whip was listening. Michael couldn't back down if he wanted to, as the brooding Deputy Chief Whip, John Randall, built much like his boss Patrick McLoughlin, and equally threatening, was listening intently at the other end of this office. The whip monitoring the whips, supervising my humiliation.

'Your job is to be in Parliament, that's why your voters sent you.'

'They expect me to be in the constituency, explaining why you want to close my A&E!'

'Your job is to fight your constituents' corner here, in Parliament.'

'You told me that nobody in the constituency pays any attention to what goes on in this place.'

'No, I didn't.'

'Well, OK, it wasn't you, but it was a whip.'

'It was me,' piped up his colleague nearby, and then somewhat unhelpfully added, 'When he rebelled on Europe, Michael.'

Oops.

I turned to pleading.

'I have a narrow majority. I can't afford to let this get out of hand.'

'I had a narrow majority too, when I first got elected. It was only 238 votes, and now look at it, 17,683.'

Smug sod.

'Yes, but you were increasing your majority when you were in opposition for a decade and no one could blame you for anything. I have to defend or explain some of these crackers decisions, for goodness sake!'

It was no use.

'Please...'

I was begging. I was definitely not too proud to do that when necessary.

Of course, well-intentioned colleagues sought to reassure me that all would be well as Parliament rolled on, along with my ever-increasing paranoia.

'Look, Nick, what was your majority?' said one of them, himself a former marginal-seat MP turned healthy majority in Buckinghamshire. An army man as well, but with his feet firmly in the real world.

'1,692.'

'Oh. Never mind, though, Nick, you will have double incumbency benefit.'

'What?'

In any institution, people have another language they often dip into, leaving newcomers like me flailing somewhat to understand what on earth they are on about. Still, at least we were not into acronyms or abbreviations yet.

'DIBS.'

My blank look said it all.

'Look,' he went on by way of explanation, 'you only won by 1,692, but that was against an incumbent who had been there since 1997. She had an incumbency benefit in her vote at the last election – a personal vote, if you like – of probably 1,000.'

'But nobody liked her, and she fiddled her expenses.'

'Lots of MPs aren't liked and had dodgy expenses, but they got back in with increased majorities. Anyway,' he went on, 'next time round you will have an incumbency factor of your own of around 1,000, and your opponent won't have any incumbency, which means you are really defending a majority of 3,692.'

Wow, I like that. DIBS worked for me, acronym be buggered. This would keep a smile on my face for a while.

Unfortunately, come the 2015 election, that turned out to be utter tosh as well, and I am still waiting for his explanation.

We marginal MPs naturally gravitate towards each other. We form an unofficial self-help group.

Experts in this club included successful campaigners like Robert Halfon, serial rebel Andrew Percy, former marketing and campaign guru Justin Tomlinson, and the vocal and gritty Tracey Crouch amongst their number. They, like me at the time, didn't realise we were members of this club, but membership was demonstrated by how often our conversations would turn to maintaining our profile in the constituency, capturing the contact data of our constituents so we could communicate and hope-fully earn their support and, more generally, how we could use our incumbency to best effect. And for a long time it drove me bloody crazy.

Not because I didn't think the topic was important – it was very, very important. I used to dread talking to fellow marginal MPs though, because it always fed the paranoia. And I used to dread talking to these four in particular, because of their competence.

Just when I thought I was getting a grip on my challenging seat and believed I was making headway with the voters, I would hear from Robert, Andrew, Justin or Tracey about their latest campaign project in their constituency, which was always so bloody good. They were campaign geniuses who had a natural ear for their constituents and knew exactly the right buttons to press. I was in awe of them and their campaign work. Consequently, after one of these chats I would more often than not find myself beating a retreat to my office, tearing up whatever scheme I was working on and trying to adopt theirs.

Rational?

Of course not.

But, much like alcoholism cannot be dealt with until you admit you have a problem, I too had to finally admit I had a serious condition. I was a victim of MAD, otherwise known as Marginal Agitation and Despair syndrome. In fact, I discovered this condition.

I knew I was in deep trouble when a plan was launched to help those in critical marginal constituencies like mine retain their seats at the next election and yet I just saw it as an attempt to fuel my growing insecurity. The proposal by the Conservative Party planners was to formalise our status as critical marginals and create a club boldly called the 40/40. Hold forty seats (including mine), and target forty new ones to win an outright majority.

It is the only club, within a House of Commons that thrives on clubs and groups, that no one, absolutely no one, wanted to be a member of. For me, being a member of this 40/40 club only confirmed the legitimacy of my increasing sense of vulnerability, and the torment of defending my narrow majority. As far as I was concerned, the party were rubbing salt into the wound rather than helping me.

Absolute rubbish, of course. But that was how MAD presented itself in the most severe cases.

I would have been the first to complain had the party not planned anything to help marginal seats.

For too long, MAD drove my behaviour and, like any recognised condition, I had to get it under control. More balance was required, more objectivity, and I needed to stop letting the pursuit of votes drive my work as an MP. To some extent I succeeded, but it never really went away completely, not least, as you will read, because of what one Prime Minister famously called 'events, dear boy, events'.

A constituency can be the main beneficiary of a marginal seat. Marginal status all but guarantees that constituents will be served by an assiduous, hard-working Member of Parliament. The MP may also, of course, be driven by a genuine desire to serve and succeed. Be in no doubt, however, that always lurking at the back (or front, in my case) of their minds will be the knowledge that their future in Parliament hangs by a numerical thread, and therefore they will be chasing votes.

That is not to say all safe-seat MPs are lazy bastards. Of course not.

But you know that, right? Because, as the poll shows, we all think our local MP is the exception to the rule that all MPs are lying, lazy toerags.

10

HOSPITAL TREATMENT

Despite the presence of MAD, I must confess that I was in danger of patting myself on the back for doing what I thought was a pretty good job in the constituency so far. I believed I had proved I was prepared to stand up for my constituents by how I voted on the EU budget increase, and I had made sure Enfield's voice was heard after the chaos of the riots and, so far, no one had thrown noxious materials at me when I was out and about. All in all, I was beginning to enjoy the role of local MP focusing on local issues. Who knows, maybe I could increase my majority.

I would not say this was a moment of hubris – I could never feel confident enough for that – but, whatever it was, it was sadly short-lived.

I burst into the constituency office, clutching my latest packet of wine gums from Mehmet next door. This time he had refused to take any money, so I felt obliged to share them out, such was my generous mood.

'You are getting a lot of correspondence on the hospital, Nick.'

Ah, back to reality, and the direct assault on my sense of well-being, this time by Leanne.

Leanne, when she joined the team, was a mild-mannered, somewhat diffident and quiet individual. I had some doubt whether to hire her, simply because I thought she would not cope well with the more obnoxious type of constituent, of which, fortunately, there were not many, but enough to make case officers' lives a nightmare at times. The few obnoxious constituents we did have ranged from the mildly threatening to the downright offensive.

Helen, my senior caseworker, was adamant that Leanne would be more than a match for them, and insisted on hiring her. Once again, my judgement was found wanting, as Leanne moved seamlessly from polite young interviewee to a cloned version of Helen, who balanced charm and the highest standards of service with the demeanour of an untamed Rottweiler on speed should anyone misbehave. Myself included.

'I don't know how to answer these ones, so I need your guidance,' announced Leanne.

The reality of a constituency office is that a large chunk of the correspondence is on issues that can be skilfully dealt with by the casework team, and policy responses were generally drafted by Jack or Tom in the Westminster office. Those that fell between the two, or were more complex and needed input from me, were flagged by Leanne for my wisdom, such as it is.

'Nothing that can't be dealt with, I'm sure!' My good mood and optimism persist.

'Well, they are all blaming you for the closure of A&E at Chase Farm Hospital.'

'But it hasn't been closed yet. The decision isn't final. It's another review!'

'Well, it will be, won't it? That's what they all think, anyway, judging by these letters, and you are getting the blame.'

Helen joined in.

'You are the MP, and you are getting the blame because it's your government doing it.'

'You said most people thought I was a councillor, so how come suddenly everyone knows I am the MP?'

'That's when they want something, but now they want to blame someone, so it's you, the MP.'

'That doesn't seem fair. Anyway, Labour started this mess.'

'Deal with it.'

'You always say that.'

'I mean, deal with the hospital. What are you going to do?'

Chase Farm Hospital has so far been mentioned over 294 times in the chamber of the House of Commons or through parliamentary questions. I think that's more than any other hospital, ever. It has been visited by one Prime Minister and, since 2003 alone, five Secretaries of State for Health. That in itself may be unsurprising, but it is one of the few hospitals that has also attracted visits of a less welcome nature, from demonstrators, academics, TV crews, radio stations, councillors, newspapers, property developers and even the Enfield Preservation Society. Not forgetting, of course, endless government review bodies about its future – and now, in 2010, there was to be one more.

Sadly, none of these visits was to celebrate the huge number of successful operations and outpatient clinic visits, but rather to witness the slow and painful downgrade of what was once a thriving district hospital with an Accident & Emergency unit to a smaller, centralised hospital without an A&E.

It is also the hospital that successfully delivered my wife Helen into the world, and now even the maternity unit was under threat. And this time it was for real.

On the eve of the momentous 1997 general election, which saw Labour swept to power in a huge landslide, a spurious front page of the local newspaper, the *Enfield Advertiser*, carried a headline claiming the then doomed Tory government of John Major had a secret document planning to close the hospital's A&E unit. Total bollocks at the time, but nevertheless, so effective was the perceived threat that a few more Tory votes drained away under the Labour landslide, overturning even Michael Portillo's Enfield Southgate seat, where he had been defending a 15,563 majority. Portillo lost to a young Stephen Twigg by some 1,400 votes. Enfield North, my seat, where the hospital was actually located, was swept aside, leaving Labour with a 6,812 majority.

The hospital had claimed its first political scalp, and so was born a local cause for just about anyone of any political persuasion to champion, regardless of facts, and most definitely with more fiction than you would find in a Jeffrey Archer novel.

In 1997, there was no threat to the A&E unit, but nevertheless that election had launched the cry of 'Save Chase Farm', which was echoed repeatedly wherever there was an audience ready to listen. It was several years later, in 2005, shortly after an election in which Labour had promised to invest hugely in expanding the hospital, that the first of many con tricks was pulled when, weeks after the election, the money disappeared and the Labour government announced plans to 'consult' on closing the A&E.

That was the first time a claim that the A&E would be down-graded could legitimately be made, and campaigners seized the moment, not to let go for the next decade.

After a carefully constructed sham of a consultation worthy of any self-respecting dictatorship, the then Secretary of State for Health, Labour's Alan Johnson, promptly signed the death warrant approving the A&E closure in 2008. Unfortunately for him, he wasn't paying too much attention when he signed the letters letting local MPs know of his decision, because he got the hospital name wrong – not that this made any difference.

Meanwhile, in Enfield, we had the bonkers prospect of a

Save Chase Farm group of councillors fighting local elections on a ticket to, you guessed it, save Chase Farm, even though the council could do bugger all about it as the matter was in the hands of the Labour government. What's even more mystifying is that the Save Chase Farm candidates all stood in Conservative-held council seats, proving that you don't need logic or a political strategy targeted against the right people to win elections. Which is precisely what they did by gaining two seats on the council and achieving absolutely nothing in the fight to save the hospital A&E.

So, where does the then wannabe MP for Enfield North fit into all this?

I certainly did my bit in making sure the public knew who to blame for this mess, and felt things were ticking along quite nicely. Obviously, no one in their right mind thought for five minutes I could do anything to prevent the hospital A&E downgrade but, as opinion polls show, people do like a local campaigner. And that was fine by me, until I had to go and overreach myself and actually try to save the hospital from downgrade, which would lead to the biggest bite on a local MP's arse you may ever have witnessed.

Some may recall that in the autumn of 2007, Gordon Brown was enjoying a superb honeymoon as the newly enthroned Prime Minister, having forced his one-time political soulmate and now lifetime political enemy Tony Blair out of office earlier that summer.

Speculation was rife that he would call an election, and everyone on the political scene was keenly anticipating the contest. I was, for sure, and thought there was a very real prospect of winning, more so if I could persuade our lot to commit to not closing the Chase Farm A&E unit.

Brown eventually bottled it, but the threat of the election created a perfect window of opportunity for me to angle for a commitment from the Conservatives not to close the A&E, and I was definitely up for trying.

As luck would have it, in September 2007 we were gathered for the Conservative Party conference in Blackpool, where all candidates were summoned for the traditional one-on-one photo opportunity with David Cameron, Leader of the Opposition at the time. The idea being that we could then plaster the photo over all our election literature and hope that some of his shine would rub off on us as local candidates. With what was to become trademark political opportunism, I collared David while standing for the photo and managed to register the opportunity to 'Save Chase Farm'. By the end of the day, I had also nobbled his parliamentary private secretary, Andrew MacKay, who was hugely supportive.

'We could use Chase Farm as an iconic example of precisely the A&E units David has pledged to save from the threat of closure by the Labour government! I will see if we can get a statement from the boss.'

'Specifically on Chase Farm?'

'Absolutely.'

Sounded good to me.

With Andrew Lansley, the shadow Secretary of State for Health, making positive noises as well, I felt that things were going quite well, and that if elected we were clearly not going to go ahead with these planned countrywide closures, including Chase Farm. My local press release was waiting: 'De Bois secures pledge to Save Chase Farm Hospital.'

I could picture the headlines. I could taste the victory. Four days later, it got even better.

'Nick, just to let you know that David Cameron is coming up to Chase Farm Hospital tomorrow morning with Andrew Lansley.'

'Coming up? I thought he was just going to make a statement for use in a press release?'

'He is going to make a statement at the hospital, so please arrange for some people to meet him, and maybe a banner or two about saving the hospital's A&E and maternity units.'

'Really? You're sure about this?'

'Er, yes, isn't that what you wanted…?'

'I mean, this is a policy announcement, right? We don't want banners saying Save Chase Farm and then we just get warm words, right? No disrespect meant, obviously.'

'See you tomorrow, Nick.'

The next day, around 10 a.m., about forty of us gathered with the appropriate banner, along with neighbouring MPs Charles Walker from Broxbourne (bounding around with his unending energy and enthusiasm), Theresa Villiers from Chipping Barnet (who stood at the back looking, not unreasonably, like she did not want to be there at all, possibly because her constituency would benefit from the downgrade of Chase Farm with investment in her local A&E), and David Burrowes, my neighbour from Enfield Southgate (who was eagerly awaiting the announcement like me). The TV and press were gathered in force and were herded into position by the advance CCHQ press officers. David Cameron and Andrew Lansley were on their way; their car was due here in fifteen minutes.

The phone rang. It was Andrew Lansley.

'Nick, slight problem: the hospital is trying to ban us from coming to the hospital. Where are you exactly?'

'Just inside the grounds by the main road entrance, with forty people and banners.'

'Right, don't trespass on the hospital grounds. Get off the grounds and move to the pavement. You must not go onto the grounds of the hospital.'

'What, even if some of the protesters get run over, which is what will probably happen if we all try to squash onto the pavement?'

'That's not helpful, Nick.'

The chief executive of the hospital, Averil Dongworth, was a ruthless operator who, before coming to Chase Farm, had been in Bedfordshire, where she was caught up in a scandal over the bugging of hospital staff. Her chairman, Baroness Wall, was appointed by the Labour government, and the hospital certainly did not welcome the attention of senior opposition politicians as Chase Farm tried to push through its reorganisation plans. In a conversation with Andrew Lansley, who was in the car on the way to the hospital, Averil tried to ban the opposition politicians from coming:

'Andrew, I can't allow you onto the hospital site.'

'Averil, that's absurd. I am with the Leader of the Opposition, who wants to visit the hospital.'

'Well, we should have had more notice.'

'We will make an announcement outside the entrance then.'

'Fine.'

'Averil, this is a public service. It's utterly illogical for you to want to stop us visiting.'

And so David Cameron turned up and I met him for the cameras about fifty yards away from the entrance so that we could be seen walking and talking as we made our way to greet the campaigners. Posterity, in the digital age, would capture this moment for ever, but fortunately not the conversation.

'How are you, Nick?'

As ever, David was a commanding presence: tall, in control and very personable. But, for the first time in a long time, he was wearing a tie on a public visit, rejecting his trademark smart-casual look.

'Fine, thanks. I thought you didn't wear a tie?'

You silly arse, Nick, I said to myself. What sort of question is that to a future Prime Minister?

Having mulled over the dress code, I had made the sartorial error of a striped shirt with no tie, thinking this firmly aligned me as a sincere, modern Conservative MP in waiting, rather than the underdressed and out-of-place wally I looked in all the ensuing photographs. This marked the first and last attempt I made to dress like a Cameroon. After that, I reverted to a more comfortable and traditional suit and tie.

Rightly, David looked at me curiously, then remembered the camera, smiled and ignored my question.

'Glad we can help you with the hospital.'

'Are you going to save the A&E and maternity?'

'No reason to close it,' he said carefully.

But there it was. Publicly, David Cameron had made the case for keeping the A&E open and the maternity ward in place. No ifs or buts as far as the public was concerned.

Andrew Lansley was photographed happily brandishing a signed pledge card to 'Save Chase Farm', as if it was the most significant document since Prime Minister Neville Chamberlain came back from Munich with the 'Peace for our time' document from Hitler in 1938.

Worse, people never seem to tire of telling me that I look very like Andrew Lansley, and how it looked like me holding the signed pledge. This came back to haunt me with a vengeance, much like the pledge cards on student fees that came back to haunt Liberal Democrat MPs in the 2015 general election.

Nick Clegg and the Lib Dems brandished signed cards pledging to abolish tuition fees if they ever got into government, and then, on breaking that pledge, were subsequently annihilated at the next election. They lost forty-nine of their fifty-seven MPs.

Andrew Lansley, on the other hand, managed to produce only one card, for one hospital, and broke one pledge that helped defeat only one MP, me, in that same election. He subsequently chose to stand down from Parliament, and is now sitting comfortably in the Lords. I am sitting on my sofa, writing this book.

I am appalled, and a touch ashamed, to admit that I spoke with my good friend and neighbour David Burrowes, the MP for Enfield Southgate, shortly after the 'announcement', and said I had doubts whether David Cameron or Andrew Lansley would actually deliver on the pledge. Yet I still ran with the general impression across the constituency that it was in fact 'job done'. As local champion and campaigner, I, Nick de Bois, had delivered the pledge from the man most likely to be the next Prime Minister, the message everyone wanted to hear. Chase Farm was saved if a Conservative government was returned at the next election.

And the leadership of my party did nothing to dispel that idea.

Andrew Lansley even printed a letter in the local paper two weeks before the 2010 general election promising to deliver his pledge, although with some weasel wording that 'guaranteed' the A&E would not be closed 'without the consent of General Practitioners, patients and residents'. He ultimately won the support of the vast majority of local GPs, shame on them, but not the residents. It was shamefully misleading of him to make such a pledge, not least because both David Burrowes and I questioned the content of the letter, seeking his assurances that he meant it.

Roll forward to 2011, and Andrew Lansley, now the ill-fated Secretary of State, signed off an independent review that defied not just his assurances but all logical arguments, and as such condemned Chase Farm A&E to a downgrade to an urgent care centre, along with closing the maternity unit and despatching patients to neighbouring hospitals that, to this day, cannot cope with the extra demand.

For the two years preceding the downgrade, and the three years after, I began to almost enjoy my ritual bashing of the Secretary of State and, when possible, the Prime Minister for their about-turn. I made representations both privately and publicly. Yet I knew it was futile, my constituents knew it was futile, the Labour opposition who had started the whole bloody mess in the first place knew it was futile, but perversely, and supporting the findings of the Ipsos MORI poll on local MPs, constituents constantly thanked me for trying.

And then despatched me to oblivion at the next general election.

Perhaps another reason to think that our system of democracy is not so bad after all. Two people who aspired to high office broke a promise, and the electorate made their views clear in the only way they could.

11

THE POWER BEHIND THE DESK

Even prior to my defeat in the 2015 general election, my electoral track record was not that impressive (played four, lost three, won one). It beggars belief that, having finally got into Parliament, I then subjected myself to more elections. This time, however, the electorate was tiny, the campaign would only take up a week at most and I had a magnificent secret weapon in the shape of my new parliamentary assistant, Madeleine Smart.

The electorate were the Conservative MPs and the elections were for Select Committees and, later, secretary of the 1922 Committee, which is to all intents and purposes the trade union of Conservative backbench MPs. Often described as 'the men in grey suits', the officers of the 1922 would be responsible for telling the Prime Minister when he or she had lost the confidence of the party and should exit No. 10 as swiftly as possible. Such influence was partially diminished when the Conservative Party started electing their leaders in 1965. Until then, leaders and Prime Ministers were chosen from amongst an elite group of members, including the influential 1922 Committee officers. Nowadays while the chairman meets weekly with the Prime Minister, and the officers meet him or her on a quarterly basis, their role is subtly changed. New rules mean that if the chairman receives letters expressing no confidence in the leader of the party from 15 per cent of Conservative MPs, the 1922 launch a process that leads to a leadership challenge. After the poor general election outcome of 2017, there were 318 Conservative MPs, meaning that today, if only forty-eight MPs chose to write a letter of no confidence, Theresa May would almost certainly be toast. Given her predecessor David Cameron had a regular cohort of some thirty MPs who would have happily plunged the political knife into his back by writing letters denouncing him as leader of the party, she should not be obsessively worried about this. No leader is loved by all.

In fact, though, the complete reverse happened in the summer of 2017, when, with some members of the Cabinet squabbling post-election and jockeying for position as a new leader on the assumption that May would go quickly, the 1922 chairman, with the full support of his executive, made it perfectly clear that backbenchers supported Theresa May and the squabblers should get back in their box.

At the time, most understood that a new leader would probably mean another general election, and with it the distinct possibility of losing their seat, which may have strengthened some backbenchers' resolve to rally around Theresa May. Let's face it, after the 2017 election there are now quite a few more Conservative MPs suffering from MAD.

Yet perhaps the most notable case of Marginal Agitation and Despair syndrome was suffered by David Cameron, who within days of becoming Prime Minister in 2010 was struck down by the condition. Or at least he behaved as if he had been.

True, he had a safe constituency seat, so that was not the issue, but despite having struck a robust coalition deal with Nick Clegg and the Lib Dems which looked set to keep him in office as Prime Minister for the next five years, he seemingly became obsessed with the risk that the Conservative 1922 Committee would do for him as it had done with some of his illustrious predecessors. So, having just moved his furniture into No. 10, he was getting a touch paranoid about being kicked out of his new home, and he seemed to think the 1922 would be the ones to do it. His symptoms were not kept very private.

I was being educated on the issue by an east of England MP who had been in Parliament since 2005, had a demographic seat similar to mine and, despite his scepticism of our leader, was keen to develop a ministerial career now that we were finally in government. He almost towered above my six-foot-three frame, but not quite. A robust Conservative, he thought along similar lines to me on many policy issues and the broad direction that the government should be taking.

'Cameron is launching a takeover bid to limit the power and influence of the 1922 executive. He wants to put his people in to make sure he is not given any problems by the committee.'

'Why?'

'Don't forget, Cameron worked for Norman Lamont and watched the 1922 give John Major hell. He wants to kill off the 1922.'

And finally: 'Look how he tried to change the rules on membership of the 1922 in the first week of the parliament!'

Which is true, and he partially succeeded. The 1922 Committee is open to all backbenchers, but not ministers. It was conceived as a voice for backbenchers and founded, somewhat surprisingly you might think, in 1923. The first meeting to set up the committee took place in April 1923, whereas the 1922 refers to the year the members who founded it were elected. Nothing is simple in the Palace of Westminster.

Its purpose at first was essentially as a self-help group for

new Conservative Members. It was then expanded in the subsequent parliament to incorporate the next new intake of MPs
before being opened to all Conservative MPs other than the
leader of the party when in opposition, and all Conservative
MPs other than ministers when in government. And that's what
David Cameron wanted to change.

As he put it to us in 2010, days after his victory, 'We all work
together in opposition, so I want to us to do that in government.' Which of course was code for: 'I know I messed up the
election and have forced a coalition with the Liberal Democrats
on you all, but I am Prime Minister and leader of your party
and I don't expect any crap from you. That's why I want ministers to have a vote and say in the 1922, because they will toe the
line and squash any independent thinking or outright rebellion
if I annoy you all too much.'

I don't blame him for trying, but his coup failed to win ministers the right to vote (although they were admitted to meetings), which is why I ended up on the ballot paper for election
to the executive of the committee.

'So, Nick, that's why you need to stand as co-secretary of the
1922 Committee,' said my colleague.

'Why?'

'Because he is having another go at neutering the 1922 executive by getting his people into place.'

'Why me, I meant?'

'You are not a Cameroon, and you are too old for him to give
you a ministerial job of any worth.'

'Thanks for the positive vote of confidence.'

So obsessed was David Cameron with trying to control the
1922 that, following his failure to win ministers the vote, his team
developed a Plan B: to put forward 'Cameroons' as candidates
for the elections to the 1922 executive. By parachuting in these

ultra-loyalists (all of whom were seeking ministerial office, and few of whom wore ties), they hoped to bind the hands of the executive and the chairman, who was most likely to be the popular, principled and somewhat urbane Graham Brady. Aside from my colleague's dim view of both my prospects and my age, I was approached to stand because I was seen as neither anti-David Cameron nor ultra-pro-David Cameron. To be fair, I was utterly indifferent to him as an individual so long as he did a good job.

My opponent was to be Charlie Elphick, the new MP for Dover and Deal, and by any definition ultra-loyal to whomsoever was in No. 10. Nothing wrong with that, and he was on the face of it always gracious and eloquent, so I knew we would have a civilised campaign. The question was: how to win an election amongst your peer group?

The answer lay with my very well-connected and well-informed parliamentary assistant, Maddie Smart.

I ended up with Maddie on my team almost by accident. She came to me by recommendation; indeed, I don't recall even interviewing her, feeling that since the recommendation was so good, and she had plenty of experience around Parliament, she would do. I can't think of a more unprofessional approach to staff recruitment. My poor practice continued, as, when this somewhat petite, almost shy-looking new parliamentary assistant began work, I made mistake No. 2, which was to judge her by appearances. I foolishly thought she would be lucky to last a month in the rough and tumble of my office. I was of course magnificently wrong.

She took charge of my campaign, or rather, she made the best of my poor campaigning tactics.

What I had completely failed to understand was that Maddie was remarkably well connected and, as far as I could tell, knew more MPs than I did. She was irritatingly popular, to the point that one MP expressed complete amazement that she had chosen to work for me. I was not offended – far from it, as I enlisted her charm to campaign for me, which probably explains the ultimate victory for Team de Bois. But not before I had put her through some unique campaign experiences.

In every election campaign there is always literature, and this election was no different. Maddie produced letters from me for every backbench MP, which I had to personally sign and, where appropriate, write an additional note proclaiming my warm admiration for the recipient. At this point, most candidates would bung the letters in the internal mail and hope for the best.

'You need to hand these out personally to the MPs, or at the very least pop into their office and be nice to their staffers to make sure they pass the letter on to their MP.'

'Why can't I just post them?'

'It's the personal touch and also it makes you less intimidating.'

'I am not intimidating.'

'No, your saving grace is you are, most of the time, quite nice, but you are very tall and don't look very friendly or approachable, particularly to other staff members. You can also be very grumpy.'

'Rubbish! Anyway, staff members can't vote for me.'

'No, but they can make sure your letter gets through when others may not.'

'Hmmm.'

'Give them out and make an extra effort.'

And off we went.

I soon got into the swing of this and started to develop a technique that probably fooled no one but was designed to make it look like I was casually dropping in on people rather than undertaking a sophisticated rapid swing-by of all the backbencher offices. Maddie trotted along behind me as I strode on ahead looking for willing victims to knobble as part of my charm offensive. All, I felt, was going well until I popped my head around the corner of the next corridor and spied Liz Truss, the newly elected MP for South West Norfolk.

I retreated behind the corner, out of sight of Liz.

'Maddie, hide.'

'What?!'

'Hide, I don't want you trotting along clutching a box-load of letters, this is meant to be a personal campaign!'

'Don't be ridiculous.'

There was no time to argue but, as is the case across all the parliamentary estate, no matter where you stop, there is always a door to somewhere else nearby. With Maddie still protesting about my absurd request, I pulled open the nearest door and gently but firmly pushed her in, shutting the door behind her.

'Liz, glad I caught you on the off-chance...' And off I went with my pitch as to why she should vote for me as secretary of the 1922. Maddie had at least the grace not to continue complaining from behind the nearby door. Anyway, I was quite considerate because I ended the conversation with Liz as soon as possible and went to retrieve Maddie from her fate.

Or from what looked like the janitor's cupboard.

She was remarkably sanguine about her solitary confinement. 'That's never happened to me before,' she noted, 'and I would rather you never did it again, but did you secure her vote?'

I have no idea if Maddie had suffered in a good cause or not, as I never discovered whether or not Liz voted for me. In the meantime, Liz continued on her way to her office, and eventually on to become a Cabinet minister, while I went on grubbing for votes.

We didn't do badly at all. I was at least capable of winning some elections, it seemed, but what role my charm offensive played in that victory I have no idea. Even on voting day, while Maddie was despatched to sit outside the committee room where votes are cast in a last-ditch effort to capitalise on her connections, I morphed into the lounge lizard of the Portcullis House lobby and seating area on the ground floor of this magnificent building. My job was to use what remaining influence I had to remind people to vote, preferably for me, which I did by maintaining my 'casual' approach to lobbying individuals, loitering in this well-populated area so I could manufacture a chance to stop and chat with them. I cringe with embarrassment at these clumsy efforts, but despite them I still managed to win.

And how did I show my thanks to my loyal parliamentary assistant, who had suffered the indignity of being shoved into a janitor's cupboard and compelled to sit outside a committee room for a day smiling at a seemingly endless trail of Conservative MPs?

I forgot her.

Graham Brady notified me of my win by email (although, annoyingly, he was as ever being insufferably discreet and not revealing the actual number of votes cast for each candidate), whereupon I promptly left the building to join some other MPs on a boat to listen to MP4, the remarkably good rock band made up of MPs and one former MP.

Maddie was nowhere to be seen and I had not rung her either to thank her or to let her know the result.

Finally, she called.

'Have you heard anything about the result yet?'

Bugger. I felt such a heel.

'Charming,' was her one-word reply, but I deserved much worse than that – and, to be fair, Maddie extracted suitable penance over the next two years that she worked with me. I won't attempt to offer any defence; there is none that any jury would pay any attention to.

Once again, sorry, Maddie.

Parliamentary assistants, much like constituency staff, are the unsung, often low-paid heroes of an MP's office. They can of course ensure efficiency, but the really good ones also prevent you from making some bloody stupid errors. They share your disappointments, they support your ambitions and they feel your failures, but they also look out for you.

'What did you think of that interview, then?'

I had just concluded a three-way interview for *Sunday Politics*, appearing alongside a token Liberal Democrat and the feisty Emily Thornberry on behalf of Labour. Emily's interview technique is very much like Gordon Brown's: just talk. Ask them one question and they could fill the rest of a half-hour programme droning on. It's a good technique to avoid difficult supplementary questions from inquisitive journalists, but on a panel discussion it can be quite frustrating for other guests trying to get a word in. My apparently intimidating appearance clearly didn't bother Emily, who hogged the air time with a ruthless determination.

I don't like it when politicians talk over each other in interviews, as I think it turns the viewer off, but with Emily I had no choice but to do so. I thought I had done quite well despite the challenge of getting a word in, so I was optimistic that I would have earned perhaps a glimmer of acknowledgement for a job well done from my team, or maybe even some praise. However, Maddie dashed that prospect quite swiftly as she met me outside the studio door.

'You must stop touching Emily!'

'What?!'

That just sounded wrong on every level.

'Every time she was speaking and you tried to interrupt, your right hand went out to touch her arm.'

'Did it?'

'Yes, and if she had called you out on it you would have died a slow death on TV – stop doing it!'

She was right, of course, but I was utterly oblivious to this habit, and to this day I have no idea if Emily noticed and chose not to humiliate me or if she was equally oblivious to it, but Maddie had put the fear of God into me and for a time I thought I should keep my hands in my pockets. Well, not really, but she most definitely made me aware of what must be an irritating habit for anyone on the receiving end. Better to know than give the tabloids a good laugh at my expense.

'Patronising Tory shamed by female Labour MP on TV' or worse '"Keep your grubby hands off me, you pervert," says tormented Labour MP'.

Being candid, open and frank with your boss is not an easy task for some members of staff, but my team never hesitated to set me straight, not least when it was in my interests. That candour and loyalty was priceless to me, and it was only the limit on salaries set by IPSA that meant I could not pay them what they deserved. The good news is that all of my parliamentary office team who stayed with me for the longest period of time, Maddie, Jack and later Leanne, have gone on to greater things, and rightly so. I, in the meantime, have been practicing my 'approachable friendly look' and keeping my hands under control.

I think.

12

MEDIA TART OR
MEDIA MANAGER?

First, let me declare an interest. While an MP, I found out that I love the media – or rather, I love doing media.

If I had to choose, I would always do radio, followed by press, and then, finally, television. I always prefer to do interviews live, so that some awkward leftie in the production office can't edit me so that I sound worse than I actually do.

Sometimes, of course, malicious editing wasn't necessary, as a few of my efforts were, quite frankly, a car crash. The most notable being when Tim Donovan, the very polished and smooth political commentator for London's *Sunday Politics* programme, sprang a surprise on me at the very end of the recording of one edition, when I was up against Sadiq Khan in 2012. At that point, honours were even between Sadiq and myself – until, that is, Tim raised the thorny and, for me, utterly unexpected issue of housing.

I got smashed all over the studio simply because I was ill-prepared. Worse, I had brought it upon myself because, when Tim's producer had called earlier that week to discuss the content of the show, I had foolishly joked, 'Anything but housing, please.'

I was so bad, I only have a vague recollection of the interview.

'Nick,' Tim began, 'the Tories have claimed their reforms will fix the housing crisis in London. Will they? Will these reforms do what they say on the tin?'

Bloody hell! Reforms, what reforms? Have we published any?

I felt the first hint of a cold sweat on my forehead. Actually, it wasn't cold: it was raging hot.

'Tim, I think we should be wary of over-simplifying this issue ... which is very complex indeed.'

Which, as he well knew, was code for: 'All right, I haven't got a clue, you got me, but I am now going to waffle on because I hope we will run out of time.'

Sod.

'Tim, as you know, it's the supply side of housing that matters, which means simply getting more homes, and affordable homes as the priority, just built, and built soon. That's precisely what our reforms will do.'

Please don't ask me how...

'How will they work, then?'

Complete sod.

'By allowing us to build more homes, and build them quicker.'

Sadiq, of course, the master of spin, knew a waffle when he heard one, and in this case was probably helped by the sheer look of terror in my eyes when housing was raised. He opened with something like: 'Labour is committed to building more affordable homes to own and rent, so that we can protect "Generation Rent". I don't know if Nick actually knows what the average rent in his constituency is.'

'Do you?' chipped in Tim, rather unhelpfully.

Definitely off this year's Christmas card list.

Not wishing to let go of the initiative, Sadiq jumped in, completely uninvited: 'I will help, Nick. It's more than £1,100 a month for a two-bedroomed house, and how he thinks that's affordable...'

And then, showing my complete inexperience, I tried to cut off Sadiq in mid-flow to assure him that I was well aware what rents were in my patch, which is precisely what he hoped I would do. He pressed on ruthlessly: 'What Nick also knows is that it's Labour's policies that will help his constituents.'

To which I blundered in again, now feeling hopelessly out of my depth, with words to the effect of: 'Sadiq and his Labour colleagues don't have the answers for my constituents, or any Londoners, on housing policies which are inconsistent and contradictory, and even he can't explain them, as is all too evident.'

Sadiq tried to come back, and all I was doing was looking at the clock thinking, why have they not run out of time... then, somewhat late, it dawned on me that this was a bloody pre-record, which means they can go on, and on, and on.

Bugger.

'No, forgive me, Sadiq, you have had your say. Let me finish this point...'

'But Nick, you have just asked me to explain what our policies are, so that's what I want to do, to answer your question.'

Tim added, somewhat unhelpfully, 'He does have a point.'

My face reddened. I could feel it. I so wanted out of there.

And then Sadiq had a one-minute free hit, outlining Labour Party policy. De Bois had been firmly knocked out of the court.

Outside the studio, having watched it on the monitor, my research assistant Jack Hart was busy trying to look anywhere but at me. He then confirmed how poorly I had performed: 'Most of the show you did really well.'

Notwithstanding this particular disaster, which I am pleased to see is nowhere on the internet these days (hence my vague recollection of how it went down), my love affair with the media began soon after appearing on LBC, shortly before it became as well-known as it is today. Then, it was still essentially the only London talk radio station, rather than the national broadcaster it is today. Iain Dale hosted the evening programme, which included the LBC Parliament, where he gathered at least three representatives from the major parties and ensured as much lively debate as possible.

Iain generously encouraged me to do lots of radio, both to help my profile in my marginal constituency and because he thought I had a good voice for the format. Personally, I think he had seen my interview with Sadiq and realised radio was my best remaining shot for good media coverage. On three occasions, Iain engineered it so that I stood in for David Mellor on his Saturday morning programme on LBC, with comrade Ken Livingstone.

Yet it was not a radio interview that made me a target for media comment and speculation, or gave me my most unwelcome fifteen minutes of fame. The BBC launched that entirely single-handedly, thanks to the efforts of James Landale, their current diplomatic correspondent, who is often on our screens with the news headlines.

In short, I gifted a hugely topical and controversial statement to him without any concept whatsoever of what I was letting myself in for, on a subject I was least qualified to talk to my own family about, let alone debate at a national level across TV, press and radio.

That subject was the NHS, and in particular the hugely controversial reform the government was proposing for this great British institution.

For someone who has never worked in the health sector, who has had the good fortune so far not to have to worry about their own health, or indeed worry too much about the health of their family, it was odd that so much of my time in Parliament was consumed by health policy.

Perhaps the closest I got to a personal stake in health was with my first wife, who was a nurse with the NHS for over thirty years, and my eldest daughter, who trained first as a physio, then as a doctor. Jessica, incidentally, thinks it's her patriotic duty to lambast me every now and then about the NHS and the government; a self-imposed duty she fulfils with rather too much enthusiasm.

In May 2011, the coalition government had announced a 'pause' in the progress of a Bill through Parliament that was becoming hugely controversial: namely, the Health and Social Care Act, which would mean the biggest reforms to the National Health Service since its inception. The pause had been announced because the Liberal Democrat junior partners in the coalition had started to lose their nerve as opposition to the reforms mounted from the health unions, and the British Medical Association in particular. (Most people overlook the fact that the BMA is little more than a posh title for a union that has a history of pretty much opposing any change, including, ironically, the foundation of the NHS itself.)

The NHS was crying out for reform, but the Prime Minister 'wobbled' after intensive lobbying from his Deputy Prime Minister and leader of the Liberal Democrats, Nick Clegg, and he therefore promptly implemented a pause in the Bill 'as a listening exercise'. It did, however, seem as though he was only listening to Nick Clegg and not his own Conservative Party.

Enter the rather naive Member for Enfield North.

'Nick, can you pop round to my office? I need to speak with you urgently.'

And off I trotted.

Now, this mystery caller, who is a good friend of mine, is also still a serving member of the government at the time of writing, and will be, I hope, for some time. So, it's only fair for me to show some uncharacteristic discretion at this point and keep their name out of it, and resist the temptation to drop some not-so-very-subtle clues.

But she is effective, and clearly good at persuading reluctant people to play their part in what she described to me as a 'team effort'.

'Andrew Lansley', said my own Deep Throat, 'has been sat upon by the PM, and must stay silent about the whole bloody "pause" bollocks on the Health Bill. He is hoping that someone might step up to the mark to rally Conservative MPs.'

'Good for you, go for it, and how can I help?'

'Well, obviously, I can't do it.'

'Why not? You would be amazing, and colleagues like you.'

'I know nothing about the Health Bill.'

'Nor do I, really.'

'De Bois, you just spent six weeks in Bill Committee going through it line by line!'

Hmmm... fair point. Bill Committee is precisely that. It is when about twenty-four MPs from both the government and opposition parties meet in a committee room on the upper corridor of the House of Commons for two days a week, sometimes three. They are there, under orders from the Chief Whip, to listen to endless debating points on the finer detail of the Bill. Theoretically, we are all there to scrutinise it for possible improvements; however, if you are a government MP, then it is made clear that you are there for votes only and not to intervene, as this is regarded as a waste of time. Of course, asking a group of MPs not to speak is like asking performers on a stage not to take a second curtain call, but you get my drift.

What's more, this means that one doesn't, with the best will in the world, pay as much attention as we should. To be more accurate, and fairer to my colleagues, *I* hadn't paid as much attention as I was now beginning to think I should have…

'So,' I ventured, 'what are you thinking? An email to Conservative MPs saying it's important we are listened to, and not just the Lib Dems who clearly want to water the whole thing down?'

'Oh, that's nice, I shall add that into this note.'

'What note?'

'Think of it as a suggestion that would look so much better coming from you.'

'Seriously, you don't think I can write my own note about the Health Bill?'

'Oh come on, de Bois, you just said you didn't know much about the Health Bill, so what's wrong with a bit of help?'

'Fine, let me look at what you have.'

Unsurprisingly, it was a very well-constructed note, setting out why Conservative MPs should not let Nick Clegg derail the Bill and, more importantly, giving some backbench muscle to the Prime Minister in his dealings with Clegg. I didn't think for one minute my 'Deep Throat' source had written it.

This note clearly came from Andrew Lansley's office; he may even have written it himself, though it's more likely to have been drafted by a special advisor. Either way, I am absolutely convinced Andrew knew all about it. That's why, truthfully, it was a very good note, and I was quite happy to send it to Conservative MPs in my name, in an attempt to make sure our voices were also listened to in this 'pause'.

As anticipated by others, I couldn't resist the challenge and was oblivious to how this would play out.

On reflection, I am horrified at my naivety at the time. I really did think this was a note for MPs, when in fact the authors knew damn well it would leak and the corresponding ruckus would play well to their cause, regardless of what might happen to the messenger, i.e. me!

I arranged for the email to be sent to colleagues at around 5.30 p.m. on 26 May 2011. At 5.40 p.m., James Landale from the BBC tracked me down on my mobile. We had never spoken before. There was, in his view, clearly no time for introductions, as he had a looming deadline that I was happily oblivious to.

'Have you just issued a series of red lines that Tories won't accept being deleted from the Bill?'

'Er, yes, you could say that.'

'Well, have you or have you not done that?'

'Yes, put like that, I suppose I have.'

'Can I have the memo you sent to colleagues.'

'No, I can't leak my own email!'

I was pleased with myself. See, even I had principles.

'Well, I need it. Now. I am about to go on air for the 6 p.m. news with this breaking story.'

Breaking story? It's not that big, surely…

'Er, OK. Try this person. I know they have a copy.'

Well, perhaps I don't have principles. On this occasion, at least.

What on earth had I done? I was soon to find out, as the BBC six o'clock news led with: 'Conservative MPs are preparing to oppose changes that Nick Clegg wants to make to the government's NHS overhaul in England, the BBC has learned.'

I didn't say that!

'One MP, Nick de Bois, who sits on the parliamentary committee looking at the NHS Bill, has set out a series of "red lines" from which he says his fellow Tories should not retreat.'

Technically that's true…

'Some of them appear to clash directly with proposals from

the Deputy Prime Minister and challenge the stability of the coalition.'

Really? It was just a note to colleagues. Oh crap.

This could be interesting.

I was, at the time, nowhere near the Houses of Parliament. In fact, I was on my way to visit my children, who were all in Huntingdon, where their mother lived. The phone rang. It was my co-conspirator, who led with: 'Wow, what have we done? You are all over the news! Amazing!'

'We?' Suddenly I felt very much like a team of one.

Whether I liked it or not, I was about to have my fifteen minutes of fame. All the national dailies contacted me over the next two hours as I sat with my kids, who were somewhat bemused by all the press calls I was getting. Each time I said the same thing: that all I was doing was ensuring the Conservative voice was not lost in this debate. Then, to my horror, the BBC Radio 4 *Today* programme contacted me and invited me on the show for the 7.50 a.m. slot the next day. Seriously, the *Today* programme? People get lynched on the *Today* programme. Very experienced people included.

Help.

And help was much needed. I turned to the two very talented policy research people working for me, in the shape of Jack Hart, a former Communist (well, not quite) turned Labour turned libertarian Conservative, who had even made a pilgrimage to North Korea as part of his political journey, and Adam Hawksbee, who will, I am sure, be a major policy thinker for the next generation. Two very bright people.

Though they were clearly somewhat bemused by what I had got myself into, I could see they were secretly pleased with my venture onto the national stage. This could spice things up for them, but that meant they had to make sure I did not cock up *Today*. They worked their socks off to anticipate the line of questioning and prep me. We found out that I was also up against former Lib Dem MP Evan Harris, something of a health campaigner, who had described me only that evening as a 'health zealot'. This was going to be lively.

The three of us were so edgy and keyed up for the *Today* programme that we met at 6 a.m. in a coffee shop close to the BBC's Millbank studio.

Final rehearsals took place and I was rubbish. My fifteen minutes of fame may have stretched into about twelve hours, but it was still going to end in tears. Thank goodness, however, for rehearsals, because that is the best time to screw up and get the demons under control before the live event.

It was Justin Webb, I believe, who kicked off the interview and, with a moment of realisation, I recalled the fabulous *Yes, Prime Minister* television series, written by Antony Jay and Jonathan Lynn, where James Hacker, the PM, gives advice to his Cabinet Secretary on how to avoid bad interviews: by simply preparing what you wish to say before the interview and sticking to it, regardless of what the question might be.

That's precisely what I did, and God bless *Yes, Prime Minister*, because it all went fine after that.

So, while I was basking in self-declared glory for avoiding a car crash and making a mark on a big national issue at the time, I had completely overlooked the underlying reason for the successful media coverage.

I was off-message.

The media do not like to give a troublemaker a hard time. I am sure Justin Webb could have happily skewered me had he so wished, but why would he? I was making news, and ostensibly being a pain in the arse to the coalition government. The real story here was not my red lines but tensions within the coalition. The media loved it.

And, given there were very real tensions in the coalition, on the back benches and in some government departments, by sheer luck I emerged unscathed by colleagues, who were generally delighted that the first substantive skirmish with the Lib Dems to play out in the media was seen as a Conservative win.

Unfortunately, the Prime Minister was not happy, and slapped me down in a private meeting with backbenchers when, in answer to a question on the progress of the health reforms, he said it was very unhelpful to go rushing to the press to make colleagues' voices heard.

Cheeky sod. I never rushed to the press. They trampled over themselves to get to me.

What's more, I had walked into the whole thing clueless but, I believe, emerged much wiser about the media as well as about the Lib Dems. In fact, I would say that this episode defined my working relationship with the media throughout the parliament. Most significantly, it taught me that they, the media, need us as much as we, the politicians, need them.

For a new backbencher, this was an important lesson, and a useful weapon in 'getting things done' in the future.

Even on a much smaller, but no less significant scale, understanding how your local press works can help increase (hopefully) favourable coverage.

Journalists, believe it or not, are much like the rest of us: overworked and under pressure. They are always hunting out the next story. Particularly at a local level, where you can only report on so many flower shows before tearing your hair out.

Using social media to pump out a useful line, or piece of information, can drop a story into their laps even without a press release. I learned that the local press probably had the word 'Enfield' in their Google alert system, which meant that any time Enfield was mentioned on the web, they would get a notification. So, if you were ever browsing my questions and speeches in Hansard (perhaps as a cure for insomnia), you would see that I mentioned Enfield repeatedly in the Commons, which all but guaranteed a free hit in that week's paper.

Now, it's unfortunate that one of my local papers thought itself the local equivalent of the *Daily Mirror* and were therefore quite resistant to my efforts, but a few hits got through.

Meanwhile, not a word from Andrew Lansley. Not even a note of thanks for my efforts on the 'red lines' media drama.

It was some time later that I went to see him to once again plead the case for Chase Farm Hospital, which coincided with a settlement of differences between the Conservatives and the Liberal Democrats. The red lines, however, had in part been crossed and the compromises weakened the objectives of the Bill.

'Nick, I think you have every reason to be content that none of your red lines have been crossed.'

That struck me as a touch optimistic.

But that was it. No hint of his office's involvement. He simply carried on with the Bill, which was inevitably compromised, leading to some startling errors and problems within the Health Service.

And the sod still downgraded my hospital's A&E.

13

AIR MILES – WITH BENEFITS

Far too much of my constituency office time was taken up by immigration, particularly when I could have been spending time on the hospital. Difficult, because day after day, people would troop into my office trying to make sense of their immigration claim. Some claims were lost, some were rejected, some were taking years to sort out, and each and every one of them ended up in my office.

The system in 2010 was in meltdown. Applications were phenomenally high and the Home Office was struggling to keep up. Actually, it wasn't keeping up, but more on that later. For now, let's concentrate on those immigrants who had successfully settled here in the UK, and in Enfield in particular, because they presented me with a huge upside.

For me, a large immigrant population also meant the opportunity, should I choose to take it, for shedloads of foreign trips. After all, most immigrant communities welcome their local MP traipsing off to their country of origin to touch base with the motherland for whatever reason.

That reason could be the hope that I would beat up the current despot running the country, be they elected or otherwise, or it could be to build links with their hometowns and use the growing diaspora in the UK as a reason to strengthen economic ties between our two countries. Unfortunately, there weren't many immigrants in my constituency from the French Riviera, the Canary Islands or Italy's Amalfi coast to justify a few sun-soaked days on a beach in their country of origin.

True, I had a large Cypriot community, but as will become clear later, that only led to sweeping up old churches rather than sweeping up the odd cocktail on a beach in Limassol.

My immigrant community originated from far-flung places such as northern Bangladesh, Kurdistan, Turkey, Nigeria, Somalia, Poland and Azerbaijan. Not all top holiday destinations, as you can see, but, as most national leaders show, when the going gets tough at home, packing your bags and going abroad can be just the right antidote.

For a backbencher like me, it primarily relieved the routine of the day job, especially in the winter months, and offered a measure of understanding about countries with whom the UK either had or sought a close political and economic relationship. And getting away from local politics, not least the hospital, was always a good idea. Sometimes we even did some good on a trip.

Sceptical?

Of course. Who wouldn't be, at the thought of me taking off for different parts of the world in the lap of luxury, enjoying five-star cuisine, top-class hotels and the courtesy and respect offered to foreign political dignitaries?

If only.

In fact, of the nine international trips I made in five years, only one fitted that description. The rest were more 'I'm a Politician, Get Me Out of Here' than 'A Place in the Sun'.

So, let's deal with the sun first: the one that greeted me in

Kuwait when I joined a trip with the Conservative Middle East Council (CMEC) for a brief visit early in the parliament.

The trip was led by Baroness (Trish) Morris, accompanied by Lord (Norman) Fowler and three MPs in total. The reason? Under New Labour, relationships with the Gulf states, many of which had a colonial background with the UK and valued links with Britain since independence, had to all intents and purposes been ignored by Blair and Brown. The 'Cool Britannia' mantra of New Labour had no room for 'Old Colonial'. Given that Kuwait was the largest foreign sovereign fund investor in Britain, this seemed somewhat short-sighted, and our trip was designed to mark a reversal in policy. Trish Morris had carefully and diligently maintained relationships with Kuwait for years, and commanded huge respect from the Kuwaiti royal family and institutions of the state. She also had the distinct advantage of not having to worry about elections every few years so, regardless of who was in power, she could maintain her work as a peer of the realm.

As I noted, this was early in the parliament so, naturally, I was puffed up somewhat at my new-found status as the elected Member of Parliament for Enfield North and now, having travelled business class to Kuwait, I was looking forward to a bit more pomp and circumstance on our arrival.

On touching down in the early hours following our night flight, our small delegation was ushered through the VIP lounge with no hint of passport control. This was how to travel. We finished our refreshment, completed the hand-shaking with the official welcome party and were escorted to two highly polished waiting limousines, complete with flags and escort. There was even a red carpet.

With a little prayer of thanks to the voters of Enfield, I joined Trish Morris, who was escorted first from the VIP lounge to the cars. I was alongside her, chatting as we walked towards the lead vehicle, then, with a not-too-subtle sleight of hand, Trish was shown to the nearside passenger door of the car and invited to take a seat. As I made my way to go around the back of the car, to the other side, I was firmly but politely sent packing to the second car in line and encouraged to take the passenger seat along with my fellow MPs. Meanwhile Lord Fowler, who had been modestly loitering at the back of our line, was escorted to the front car to sit alongside Trish. And off we went.

In the UK, members of the House of Lords sit in what is known as the second chamber. They are a revising chamber, which ultimately accepts the will of the democratically elected MPs who sit in the House of Commons, the primary chamber of Parliament. We had fought a civil war to establish this primacy of the commoner over the aristocracy but, clearly, this historic change had not yet reached the old colonial states and modern-day Kuwait. Here, in the sun-drenched splendour of the Gulf, lords and ladies were hierarchically in a class of their own, and MPs, it seemed, trailed a very distant second.

Or was it a simple oversight that my bruised ego could easily recover from?

The luxurious hotel we were driven to certainly helped. It would most definitely not have been found in a Thomson holiday brochure; it was more Mayfair than Magaluf, and that suited me fine. After all, this was not at taxpayers' expense, but that of the Conservative Middle East Council.

A delegation from the hotel was there to meet us as we poured out of the cars and, after some considerable fawning to Baroness Morris and Lord Fowler, we followed on behind after brief handshakes and gallant attempts by Trish to introduce us as part of the delegation.

We MPs, meanwhile, carried our own bags, as the others'

were whisked away on gold-plated trolleys, no doubt to be unpacked by some poor sod before the rooms were occupied.

Doing away with the necessary check-in procedure, we were handed our keys along with a welcome drink and then escorted through the plush foyer to the lifts, where I was firmly put in my place. As the door to the first lift opened, a burly individual leading our party stepped aside to hold the doors open for us. Trish stepped into this spacious lift with Norman, and I tried to follow them but, in a very blunt gesture, the escort held his hand out, palm facing upwards, much as a police officer stopping traffic. I obeyed and meekly retreated into the foyer.

Ever the pragmatist, I began to adopt the 'When in Rome' philosophy, suspecting that without Trish leading this delegation we would probably have been in the nearest Kuwaiti Travelodge.

Having finally joined the others upstairs, we were welcomed into a beautifully spacious room with lounge chairs, a bathroom to freshen up in, fruits and more drinks laid out. Not unreasonably, we all, including Norman and Trish, assumed this was a reception room for us until our rooms were ready, given our very early morning flight arrival.

Wrong.

As I plonked my case down on the thick carpet and then flopped into a settee when all the pleasantries were concluded, someone picked up my case and offered to escort me to my room. Somewhat confused, I looked around and saw that my fellow MPs and Lord Fowler were being summarily escorted from the room for the same purpose.

It was then that I twigged what was happening.

Trish had been given the royal suite, and we had been in the antechamber of the suite. So large was it that we had not even seen the bedrooms, separate lounge and study. It was that big.

Clearly, the riffraff had to be swept from the room as quickly as possible so as not to ruin the carpet, hence our prompt despatch to our very nice, but now somewhat disappointing, rooms after a brief taste of how the other half lived.

So what? Serves me right for getting up myself? (Again.)

Indeed so.

Trish Morris has helped forge considerably profitable relationships with the Kuwaitis over the past two decades. The respect accorded her is to the UK's benefit, and we were all quick to recognise that, not least because she commanded the attention of the Emir of Kuwait himself, as we saw during our meeting with him. The head of the Kuwait Investment Authority, the man who decided which countries to spend his vast sums of money with, sought her counsel, as did the Speaker of the Kuwait Parliament. The political culture within Kuwait, and indeed the wider Gulf states, relegates Parliaments to little more than talking shops; real political power rests with the royal families. Lords and ladies are therefore held in far higher regard than mere MPs.

This is what drove me, subsequently, to make the case to David Cameron to appoint trade envoys from across Parliament, either as peers, for countries where that status and position carries greater influence, or as ambassadors where that title confers seniority and influence, such as in South America. Politicians come and go, but trade envoys could exceed the life of any one parliament and help build sustainable long-term relationships.

While the Prime Minister did not see fit to offer me a trade envoy role, following my insistence on asking an awkward question during PMQs, I was delighted that his first appointment was Baroness Morris as trade envoy to Kuwait. She paved the way admirably for those who followed by giving a first-class example of how to do it, and is still doing so, I am pleased to say.

Traditionally, when visiting other countries in delegations, there is always an exchange of gifts for the pre-arranged meetings. The quality of the gift matters, and depends on the level of the meeting. You would not expect to hand to the Emir of Kuwait a plate with a picture of a London bus on it and an invitation to 'Kiss me quick'. Yet I have, at the last minute, been rushing around a London airport terminal looking for anything remotely acceptable to give as a gift to a foreign host. We often fork out for these ourselves rather than the taxpayer, which in part explains the limited expenditure.

Presents have included, somewhat embarrassingly, a Harrods plate (thank God for Harrods in airport terminals), tea cups, a set of spoons and a teddy bear with a Union flag emblazoned across his chest, which we tried to pass off as a lucky charm to put on the recipient's desk. I imagine that went straight into the file marked B, for Bin.

In return, I have received a huge chest of tea from hosts in Bangladesh, engraved decanters from Turkey, plates engraved with the date of our visit from Azerbaijan, a gorgeous tea set from the Prime Minister of Bangladesh, and many traditional host country costumes. The difference is, their governments pay for the gifts, whereas we often end up forking out ourselves. Fortunately, over the years, I don't think I truly offended anyone with the tat that I dished out, as it seems the concept of 'It's the thought that counts' crosses all borders.

While we narrowly avoided offending anyone, or embarrassing them with the gifts we offered up, the reverse was not always true. I was faced with the difficulty of either offending a senior parliamentary figure and member of the royal Kuwait family by refusing a gift he had generously bestowed on me, or facing difficulties when I got back to England. And it was all James Bond's fault.

I had returned to my hotel towards the end of our trip and saw a large shopping bag perched on my pillow, where these days you normally find that the cleaning staff have made a swan or something out of the bathroom towels in anticipation of a healthy tip. Curious, as anyone would be, I unpacked a traditional national dress outfit (which I still have), a very nice leather belt, aftershave, a wonderful pictorial book on Kuwait, a pen and a watch. Not just any watch, but the Omega James Bond watch, as I was subsequently told, which was considered quite fashionable at the time and was worth over £5,000.

Hmmm. Dilemma.

First, where was my moral compass at this point? Let me be clear, I did bloody well consider keeping it.

The chances were, however, that whatever I did would backfire. My constituents would not take too kindly to the idea that I profited from my role as their MP, yet, if I didn't accept it, more than likely our hosts would be offended.

Would my constituents, for example, understand if I published in my official register of Members' interests that I had received a gift of a £5,000 watch? Would they violently object, or just, with typical Enfield character, take the piss out of me?

'Good evening. Apologies for knocking on your door out of the blue, but I just wanted to introduce myself and see if there is anything you would like to raise with me, as your local MP?'

'Jean, love, it's our wannabe James Bond, the wealthy local MP.'

'Oh, that's nice dear, ask him if he can AFFORD the TIME to come in for a moment?'

Or, more likely, 'Typical scumbag Tory, on the make for himself as always.'

Keeping it, therefore, was not looking too clever.

Then I cracked it! Give it to an Enfield charity for an auction. That really did seem like a good idea.

My wife, however, a trained accountant, spiked that plan rather swiftly in a phone call home.

'Tax.'

'Tax? But I'm not keeping it, I'm giving it to a charity!'

'Import duties.'

'Well, I suppose there might be...'

'Tax on a gift like that will be about £1,000.'

'What about if I auction it, on condition they give me the money to pay the import tax?'

'Really? So, "Tory MP keeps £1,000 of money raised from a charity auction."'

'That would be unfair!'

'It would make a great story, and scupper any chance you had of winning again.'

Bugger.

So, getting a gift I did not ask for and could not keep would cost me a thousand quid to bring back and give to a charity auction. Added to which, I would almost certainly irritate the Speaker of the Parliament in Kuwait for not accepting his gift.

Time for a consultation with colleagues and the team from CMEC.

'Leave it for the chambermaid as a sensational tip?' suggested one.

We thought about that as we stared vacantly into our evening glasses of wine.

'Nope. She would hand it in as lost property, and then the Speaker would really be fed up with you.'

'Smuggle it into the UK?'

A moment's silence.

'Not a good idea really.'

'I was joking!'

'Sure.'

Another slug of wine.

'Give it back?'

No chance, a sure way never to be invited back.

'Got it!'

We all looked up expectantly.

'Leave it with me to sort out, so there are no red faces here or in London.'

Hmmm.

'So, let me get this right. I don't accept the watch, and that's the last I see of it?'

'Absolutely, and no offence will have been taken by anyone. You will have behaved honourably.'

Hmmm.

Oh well, what you never had you can never miss, I thought, as I handed over £5,000 of watch for the last time.

I truly wonder whether my considered thought process would have won the day had I not been planning to stand again in the 2015 election. I would like to think so, and I will continue to do so, regardless of what you may think. And if you're wondering what happened to the watch, I haven't got a clue, but I do know some people who would be aghast at the frivolous treatment of such wealth. I came across them some years after the Kuwait visit, when in south-east Asia.

This later visit certainly dispelled any lingering doubts I may have had about the value of sending backbench MPs abroad, and what's more it did make me wish I had kept the watch, paid the tax and given it to a charity in their name.

'When you get out of the car, please be prepared for a strong distasteful smell,' warned our host.

We were on a trip to Bangladesh with the Conservative Friends of Bangladesh, and our next stop was a school on the edge of a slum. Our host was right: the noxious smell was sewage, and it made you retch instinctively. The ground we were standing on was a combination of mud and other things I could only begin to imagine, and which I had much rather not imagine at all.

Located in Dhaka, the capital of Bangladesh, this slum was home to thousands of people living in the most squalid conditions. Yet most of the people who lived here had parents who went out to work for a pittance to help feed and clothe their families. Worse, rampant child labour was exploiting the young and keeping many out of school while they went to work for pennies to help supplement the family income, such as it was.

'Dhaka is a fast-growing city, which is densely populated, sir, with over 2 million people living in slums.'

'*How* many?'

'There are 14 million people in the city of Dhaka, sir. That's nearly as big as Greater London, because everyone comes here to find work.'

'Nearly 15 per cent of all the people in this city live in slums?'

'Yes, sir.'

I was both sickened and humbled to see the conditions in which these people lived. The fact that in the UK, almost all of us go to sleep with full stomachs, or even waste meals, while people in this slum work for a pittance and can be forced to scrounge for their meals on a daily basis, couldn't escape me. I resolved that the next time someone came into my office talking about poverty, I would tell them to buy a one-way ticket to Dhaka so they could get some perspective. There's poverty and there's relative poverty, and the failure to distinguish between the two irritates the hell out of me.

And here I was, in hell.

'Come here, sir. Come to the school.'

In this cesspit called home to so many people, a small, shoddy

building was used as a school for the local kids. It was a remarkable school to be found in the centre of this slum. The children
were so pleased to see us, and were all lined up so politely, so
respectfully and so cheerfully to greet us, it brought a tear to my
eye. I know I'm a wicked old Tory and should not even have a
heart, according to my political opponents, but these beautifully
turned-out children, so optimistic and so welcoming amid such
squalor, would cause the hardest heart to melt.

The youngsters put on a wonderful singing and dancing performance for us, which led to the remarkable sight of me, Anne
Main MP (our chairman and devoted advocate for the dispos-
sessed in Bangladesh), Bob Blackman MP and others dancing
along with the kids. There is a photo, I am told, but I won't share
it with you.

Children always tell their parents not to dance, but we
middle-aged politicians, who defied the wishes of our own
kids, were rewarded with delightful howls of laughter from our
audience as they coped with the sight of us waving our arms
and legs in all directions, hopelessly out of time with the music.

Education is the way out of poverty and, as we all do with
children we meet, I asked one little girl what she wanted to be
when she grew up. She didn't hesitate: 'I want to be a doctor.'
The ambition of these children will only be stifled by a lack of
opportunity, and if our international aid money gets to schools
like this, and helps lift children and their families out of the
slums, then I reckon that's money well spent.

And that's precisely the point we made to the British High
Commissioner that evening in his residence when we were all
quaffing gin and tonics in comfort. So it was with a genuine
sense of disdain that we learned where some of our international aid money was going at the time. And it wasn't going to help
youngsters like those we had just seen.

It was funding projects to support 'democracy', which in this case meant funding a bunch of TV producers to come up with a Bangladeshi version of *Question Time*. Lawyers were also being paid to further the cause of women's rights, and consultants were ticking boxes to ensure they had their fair share of our international aid money.

'Well, these projects are part of the Millennium Development Goals, such as gender equality and empowering women.'

'Don't you think you would empower women by getting them out of slums?'

'We do think that would be a good idea.'

'That's encouraging.'

Is it me? Or am I being patronised? Surely not.

'How about funding the school? That will give these kids a chance.'

'We do send aid to the government in Bangladesh, who distribute the funding to schools.'

'Well, they obviously missed this one, but maybe they were busy preparing for bloody *Question Time!*'

I know the UK can't solve Bangladesh's problems and, in addition to the aid, there are many British companies investing in the country, providing jobs and work for thousands of people. But if we are going to have an international aid programme, it must hit the spot where it can be most effective. At the time of our visit, this was not happening, and it was with a huge sense of purpose that we helped shine the light of transparency on some of the more questionable uses of British aid, which, in turn, has led to much more scrutiny in how we spend taxpayers' money today.

This hell I visited is something I will never forget. These people have been either forgotten or overlooked by their own neighbours. Knowing the reality of the hardship people face in

the slums, and knowing that we in the West can make a difference, renews my belief that international aid matters, so long as
it is getting to those who need it.

And, yes, be sceptical about foreign trips, but some trips like
this matter. They matter to the taxpayer in the UK to make sure
they are getting value for how we spend aid money, and above
all, they matter to those kids in the school.

In truth, every time I see wasted food, I still think about them.

14

DON'T YOU KNOW WHO I AM?

Who really, in their right mind, would say 'no' to some serious VIP treatment?

Just occasionally, I suspect all of us would like to be treated like a very important person. I know I would. I also know it's not politically correct to say that, but it's true, and what's more, be in no doubt, it is also very, very nice when it happens.

Visiting Kuwait, despite being relegated to temporary bag carrier to Baroness Morris and Lord Fowler, was quite splendid, and thoroughly enjoyable as well as indulgent. If that happened to MPs every day, we would well and truly be out of touch with the real world inhabited by our constituents. That it is so enjoyable when it does happen simply underlines the fact that we do not live in the lap of luxury, and that our parliamentary system is pretty good at keeping most MPs' feet firmly planted in reality. At the very least, I can promise I have never resorted to that painful last refuge of the deluded: 'Don't you know who I am?'

This phrase is generally delivered by the un-self-aware individual seeking unearned respect, often during a confrontation or, more likely, when stopped for speeding. It is to be avoided at all costs. Not simply because it is plain wrong, but because it will ensure copious amounts of derision are rightly heaped on the pompous arse who delivered the question in the first place.

This is not to say that I don't have a healthy respect for – and enjoyment of – the VIP treatment. I have always lapped it up whenever it was on offer, not least because it happened so rarely. The best place for it, curiously, is either abroad on a foreign delegation, as you have already witnessed, or when visiting one of the many groups run by our growing diaspora communities across the UK. The one very much goes hand in hand with the other.

In Enfield, we have a very diverse community, but the most prominent are the Cypriots, both Greek and Turkish, and it's fair to say that while they have always demonstrated the utmost courtesy, respect and immense hospitality (at least a stone's worth in weight!) the politics of Cyprus meant that, at times, our relationship was truly tested, both at home and abroad.

First, a little bit of history.

Cyprus is one of the most beautiful islands on the planet, with an extraordinary history. It is the mythical birthplace of Aphrodite, the goddess of love, and the burial site for the aunt of the prophet Muhammad. It has been under the rule of Romans, Greeks, Egyptians, Ottomans and, of course, the British, most recently until 1960. And that's only a small sample. But it is the legacy of British rule on this gorgeous island that left me, at times, overwhelmed and bewildered, and always over-fed.

For the Greek Cypriots in my constituency (approximately 3,500 households, or 8,000 voters), the issue was all about the tragic consequences of the 1974 invasion of the island by the Turkish armed forces. For the Turkish Cypriots in my constituency (approximately 5,000 households, or 12,000 voters), and, also with some justification, it was about the protection of the Turkish Cypriots' interest from a discriminatory Greek Cypriot leadership going back to independence in 1960, when Archbishop Makarios III became President. His subsequent overthrow in a coup in 1974 was led by a particularly nasty chap called Nicos Sampson, a former newspaper photographer turned gunman with EOKA, the paramilitary organisation seeking independence from the British. Sampson, along with his cronies, also took a few potshots at my father, but more of that later. As the self-appointed post-coup President, who believed in the unification of Cyprus with Greece, Sampson went down like a lead balloon with both the Turkish Cypriot community and, more worryingly, the Turkish military government in Ankara, which promptly launched an attack on the island and occupied the north of Cyprus up to the so-called UN Green Line. This buffer zone, which had been established a decade earlier to keep the peace, obviously didn't really do the trick in the face of this perceived provocation.

The Green Line 'border' is still in place to this day, and Nicosia, the capital, remains the only divided city in the world, where you must pass through a checkpoint to get from one side to the other.

Thankfully, in Enfield, we don't have a Green Line, but we do have Green Lanes, where Greek Cypriots and Turkish Cypriots live, work and play together. They even serve in the same political parties on Enfield Council, and devote considerable energy to trying to make Enfield a better place to live. When it comes to Cyprus, however, there is little accord amongst the local politicians here in England, or the national politicians back in Cyprus. Yet wander down Green Lanes and most people – though not all, I accept – shrug their shoulders and hope the politicians will finally catch up with the wishes of the people and sort the matter out. Unsurprisingly, when I met with people, rather than politicians, in both the north and the south of Cyprus, there was a similar response.

Were the politicians out of kilter with the public, and were they making it harder, not easier, to reach an agreement to reunify? If so, what could or should British politicians do to reflect that view, and would this help or hinder the settlement process?

I would have been content with making this point during meetings of Cypriot representatives from both the north and the south on the many occasions we met. Our job, as MPs with a stake in the Cyprus question, was to inform, debate and listen to the prevailing views, and feed that into the British government. But David Burrowes, the then MP for Enfield Southgate, which had an even larger contingent of Cypriots than my constituency, came up with a bonkers plan to intervene at a grassroots level that was at best controversial, at worst highly inflammatory.

It involved volunteers from London and Cyprus embarking on a pilgrimage across the island to restore sites of 'religious and historical' interest. In a nutshell, after the division of Cyprus in 1974, some wonderful and historical churches had been desecrated, and others left to ruin in the north (Turkish Cypriot territory). Some, it was alleged, had been obliterated and turned into car parks. In the interests of balance, we also had to identify similar sites in the south (Greek Cypriot territory), where mosques and burial sites had been treated without respect. Although many of the acts of destruction had taken place in the immediate aftermath of the conflict, many other sites had, shamefully, been left to rot. It's no exaggeration to say that on our inspection trips we walked across graveyards with bones exposed. To this day, I don't know whether they were animal bones or human bones, but the state of the graveyards did leave me wondering. And it was into this hugely sensitive yet intolerable situation that David Burrowes chose to tread, bringing along me and two other MPs, Jim Sheridan and Matthew Offord.

It is difficult not to be swept along with David's enthusiasm. He has the advantage of a naturally generous and exuberant disposition, which sometimes hides the steely determination to do what he thinks is right. On this particular issue, he has the added motivation of his deeply held faith, always present but never intrusive to those of less conviction. Helen and I became very close friends with David, his wife Janet and their large family, for whom I shamefully but regularly forget the precise number of children they have. I think they could field a full subs bench at David's beloved Arsenal. What I do know, however, is that his solid foundation at home, and his faith, made David, regardless of one's views on his politics, one of the most effective and principled MPs I ever had the pleasure to work with. But on this trip, he was never really in my good books.

On a normal parliamentary delegation to Cyprus, the official welcome is marvellous. Yes, my colleagues and I were made to feel extraordinarily important and significant. If I had a share price, it would be at an all-time high following one of these trips if value were based on ego, vanity and self-importance.

It begins at the airport, where you are escorted through all the formalities with absolutely no wait. Your passport is taken from you, and the details of immigration and your baggage retrieval all officially sorted out while you relax in a comfortable VIP lounge. From there, a smart, air-conditioned limousine escorts you to the finest hotel, and the hospitality only continues to exceed expectations. Wonderful meals (and, to be frank, endless pastries throughout the day) ensure your energy levels remain at their best for the round of meetings and continuing receptions, all requiring substantive toasts with an endless supply of thirst-quenching local wine. This is how to travel, and stands in stark contrast to the return journey back to London, when you are ejected from the plane and join the end of a very long and unwelcoming queue for passport control. The upside is that at least the long wait gives you a chance to find your Oyster card for the Tube back into London.

Sadly, like share prices all over the world, what goes up can come rocketing down, which, thanks to the well-advertised purpose of our trip, happened on this occasion. David had managed to annoy both the Greek Cypriots and the Turkish Cypriots. The Greek Cypriots thought we should not even be in the north, and the Turkish Cypriots felt that this was a provocative and anti-north propaganda trip. On the plus side, David had uniquely united these two opposing sides in common cause: sadly, not on the question of reunification, but against this mission to highlight the state of religious and historical sites.

So, on this occasion of our arrival at the airport, no cars, no VIP lounge, no pastries.

Our pilgrimage across the island began in the north, where, at the first stop, we encountered a beautiful but decaying church in Assia. We turned up like a bunch of scouts, armed with brooms and shovels, and set about sweeping, collecting, restoring and sweating an awful lot. This was not part of the de Bois MP action plan, and indeed the last time I had picked up a broom to sweep a church was when I was on detention at school, but David's enthusiasm was infectious, if not mildly irritating.

Not only were we clearing up what was evidently an unused church, without much of a ceiling or a congregation from what I could tell, this symbolic act was not going unnoticed.

As we toiled away, sweeping up copious amounts of bird crap, we had the ominous presence of Turkish Cypriot police following us around from village to village on instructions from the Turkish Cypriot administration. Not unreasonably, the police officers appeared utterly baffled at what on earth we were doing. I suspect they struggled to understand why we might be a threat to Northern Cyprus, as we swept and shovelled away, and that they were more likely to be taking us away for questioning of our sanity rather than our political intent.

Burrowes was, of course, oblivious to all of this, as indeed were the fifteen or so volunteers who joined us on this curious day trip. Eventually, after playing the 'I'm older than you lot' card, I negotiated a break at the village café, which was reluctantly agreed to by our task master Sgt Major Burrowes but, as it turned out, he was pleasantly surprised at the outcome, which gave us a chance to chat to some of the locals.

Remarkably, one of our group, who had joined us from the south, recognised a Turkish Cypriot villager. It seemed they had been childhood friends, subsequently separated during the invasion. At the time, many Greek Cypriots simply grabbed what they could and fled to the south when the Turkish army started marching across the island. There was no time for taking more than the possessions you could carry, and many people left not only property but community and friendships behind during that distressing time. If you want modern-day evidence of this, visit the sealed town of Varosha, left precisely as it was following the invasion of 1974. There are poignant reminders of garden tables left with now-broken bottles on them as people ran from meals, taking with them only what they could carry.

Some forty years on, it was a huge delight to be sipping coffee and making pidgin conversation in the way so many do when language divides us, notwithstanding our translators. We were seated around small tables outside a tiny café that had probably never seen so many guests this early in the morning. The atmosphere was relaxed; villagers expressed their sorrow at the state of the church and committed to doing their best to maintain and restore it and, for a moment, we were reminded of our purpose. We had the feeling that if it wasn't for politicians, the people could and would have reached an accommodation far sooner, had they been allowed to get on with it. I don't wish to overstate the significance, but watching two people, one Greek Cypriot, one Turkish Cypriot, recognise each other after so much time, and share the warmest embrace, was one of the most satisfying moments of all my dealings on Cyprus.

On we pressed, from village to village, welcome at some, slightly less welcome at others, but in all cases we witnessed derelict and neglected sites of both historic and religious significance. There is hope, however, as the beautifully appointed church of Apostolos Andreas Monastery, situated just south of Cape Apostolos Andreas, the north-easternmost point of the island of Cyprus, in the Karpass Peninsula, has finally had much-needed renovation work authorised. I am not sure if our visit had any influence on the restoration and care of religious sites, but the fact that this work is taking place and, more importantly, with local people wishing to exercise due care and attention, is most encouraging.

We also travelled to several mosques, and one in particular: the Ibrahim Aga in Limassol, where Greek Cypriots took pride in showing off its condition and the tolerance of freedom of worship. Unfortunately, this was tinged somewhat since our visit coincided with an arson attack on the very same mosque, which, in the heat of political tensions at the time, was swiftly condemned by the Turkish Cypriot leaders as a sign of Greek Cypriot intolerance and lack of respect for Turkish Cypriots and their religious buildings.

More relevant to us was that our group leader, David Burrowes, was held personally responsible for the attack by the Turkish Cypriot newspapers. Across a front-page spread was the

DON'T YOU KNOW WHO I AM?

picture of the burning mosque, with David's superimposed face (along with his customary boyish smile) peering down at the flames. The caption simply read: 'Is he going to clean this up?'

Never have brooms and shovels had so much to answer for.

When we were not annoying Cypriots of any origin, we were always treated with considerable respect and made to feel very welcome. On all but the one occasion, we enjoyed the trappings of public office and the benefit of very well-organised trips to meet Cypriot politicians, diplomats and representatives from civic society. While I genuinely enjoyed these types of trips wherever they took place in the world, Cyprus had a very special meaning for me.

My father served in Cyprus with the RAF during the independence campaign, which saw him being shot at on many occasions by EOKA terrorists. It was a dark time for British servicemen, who would be brutally gunned down, often shot in the back by terrorists as they walked down Ledra Street, the main shopping area in central Nicosia. Outside the main entrance to the UN HQ at the Ledra Palace Hotel, there is a statue in tribute to EOKA terrorists. Until a few years ago, the subject of the statue held a sculptured grenade in his hand, but it was finally removed on the grounds of sensitivity. My mother would have agreed; after all, EOKA chucked a grenade into her house, where my elder brother, then aged one, was sleeping. Fortunately, everyone survived. None of that has displaced my huge affection for the island, and for all Cypriots, but history did throw up a rather curious meeting in 2013.

At a lunch with the UK Conservative Party's sister party in Cyprus, called the DISY, I found I was seated opposite the son of Nicos Sampson, the former newspaper photographer, gunman and eight-day President of Cyprus. His name was Sotiris Sampson, and he was an MP in the Cypriot Parliament.

It felt distinctly odd to be sitting at the same table as the son of a man who had murdered British servicemen and would have happily killed my father. Equally, I was in little doubt that my father would have held a similar view of Nicos Sampson. I thought this deserved mention.

'If my father, an RAF Intelligence Officer in Cyprus between 1956 and 1958, had done his job, you realise you would not be here, and if your father had done his job, I would not be here.'

Lunchtime chit-chat was rather stilted after that.

• • •

We may, quite literally, have broken ground when trying to clear up the churches across the island, but David and I also broke new political ground by actively engaging with politicians in the north. This was hugely frowned upon by many in the Greek Cypriot community, both at home and abroad. David risked considerable political capital in his constituency, which was predominantly Greek Cypriot, by doing this at a time when a solution to reunifying the island looked very unlikely. Nevertheless, with the prospect of a new administration in the north, we both felt that, as parliamentarians with a significant interest in Cyprus, we should be building relationships. This had not been done before, and we were determined to do it.

Now, if the idea of these talks conjures up images of fleets of official cars sweeping us across the Green Line control points in Nicosia, with outriders and blue flashing lights, think again. We were left entirely to our own devices. In fact, we were all but disowned by the UK and Greek Cypriot establishments. In practice, this meant tracking down the email addresses of the different party leaders and representatives, explaining who we were, overcoming the understandable scepticism (not least because David was not exactly seen as neutral on the question of Cyprus by many Turkish Cypriot politicians), and agreeing meetings. No official help from the Greek Cypriots, Church or civil service. Go north? Go on your own.

Instead of official cars, we ended up walking across the Green Line through the Ledra Palace checkpoint at night. Now, I don't want you to think that this is anything like Checkpoint Charlie, the famous Cold War crossing point in Berlin, where endless stories have been told of illicit crossings and spy swaps from the then Communist East Germany into West Germany, but certainly the Ledra Palace crossing is a time warp, thanks to the bizarre and tragic circumstances of Cyprus's history.

Although many buildings have been maintained for UN use and cross-community civic society groups, you walk past buildings and structures that have remained untouched since 1974. There is little activity at night apart from bright lights and a definite sense – mostly imagined, I grant you – that you are being watched.

Within fifty yards, we found ourselves in the north, and very close to the first of our meetings. We met with many political parties, of which currently only four are represented in the assembly. I won't attempt to relay the content of the meetings, but all followed a similar theme. Warm welcome, bountiful eating and hope.

I know I am guilty of being both naive and an optimist, which are not always the best qualities for a politician, as this book has already demonstrated, but I left all these sessions convinced that there was a real thirst for an agreement on the ground in the north. However, the reality that Ankara and the Turkish government were still pulling the strings meant that this hope was tempered with frustration that politicians in Northern Cyprus were not in control of their own and the island's future.

Hope, however, was best illustrated by our meeting with Özdil Nami, a senior member of the then opposition party. We met in his home, a modest detached house, where we chatted in his living room eating the most delicious apple crumble I have ever tasted.

Nami was born in London in 1967. He completed his Master's degree at the University of California, Berkeley, in 1991, spoke perfect English, and was very much a man of the future. Our talks revealed that he was a young man who was clearly looking ahead and deeply engaged in the prospect of the reunification of Cyprus. Many of the older politicians we had met were understandably heavily influenced by their own experiences during the conflict and before. This often meant that it was difficult for some to see a way ahead for the island. A younger generation did not have that emotional history and personal experience, yet had the good sense to be fully cognisant of the big outstanding issues of missing persons, property displacement, security and so on. I couldn't help but feel these younger politicians held the key to future success. Nami subsequently went on to be the foreign representative for the new President after the elections, and at the time of writing is the Turkish Cypriot Special Representative in the present negotiations to solve the Cyprus dispute. I am guessing he will produce his wife's apple crumble when things inevitably get tough.

In contrast, the very next night, we had one of the most intimidating meetings I have ever experienced, and I shamelessly admit leaving it all to David Burrowes to manage. After all, he had arranged it.

We had been invited to a dinner with a group of former

leading 'influencers' who were apparently no longer active in Turkish Cypriot politics or the administration. We were told that we would be meeting with former negotiators on the settlement talks, as well as industrialists, academics, commentators and former ministers of the Autonomous Turkish Cypriot Admin-istration. What we were not told was that these individuals were clearly the power brokers representing an ultra-conservative level of thinking that I am quite sure had an audience amongst a number of influential Cypriots, but most probably not the majority of the north Cypriot public.

Our driver, a very vivacious and engaging young lady called Fevzi, who worked for Özdil Nami, dropped us off at a remote but somewhat grand building on the edge of Kyrenia. She quickly drove off, leaving us at the entrance, where we faced two rather large and imposing doors. It was dark, isolated and very unwelcoming. I fully expected a resurrected Boris Karloff or Christopher Lee to open the door. They didn't, but the at-mosphere that greeted us as we were escorted to an imposing hall was certainly chilly enough for a 1950s horror film that Karloff or Lee would have been very much at home in.

After brief introductions, we were invited to take our seats at the conference table, which felt very much like being invited to take your place in the dock at the Old Bailey. All eyes were on us from the sixteen men who now took their own seats. They bore no resemblance to a jury, however, because a jury would have been prepared to weigh the evidence before reaching a verdict. It was clear that we were guilty; it only remained to determine the precise charge. I mumbled to David that we should try to speak at the end of the dinner, so we could have a chance to break the ice and warm the guests up. He nodded enthusiasti-cally. 'I will leave that to you to organise then?' he added.

The first course was served alongside a very subdued level

of conversation. To my right was David. To my left was one of the more right-wing members and chairman of the group, who leaned across and startled me by quietly murmuring, 'It is a pleasure to meet you, Mr de Bois. You have been very fair in your comments about Cyprus, and we appreciate that very much.'

'Thank you, Mr Chairman,' I said. Somewhat relieved at this unexpected turn of events, and with growing confidence, I noted, 'I do believe that at this important stage in Cyprus's future, balance and perspective is sometimes required. A word out of place here, a nuance there, can cause unnecessary problems.'

'Indeed, Mr de Bois, which is why it is so unfortunate that your colleague, Mr Burrowes, does not heed your advice. It troubles some of us here greatly.'

It would have been entirely in character had a furry white cat then jumped up onto the chairman's lap, allowing him to slowly stroke the beast just before consigning David to a murky end by pressing a button. Perhaps sharks were swimming hungrily beneath us at that very moment. After all, not one British official knew we were there, and I reckon I would have happily maintained a silence at the disappearance of my colleague, had it guaranteed my safety.

I returned to reality and uttered something loyal about David.

'I am sure he will surprise you with his open mind on the subject. After all, he has Cyprus's interests at heart.'

'Well, let us hope so, Mr de Bois. Maybe we should invite Mr Burrowes to address us now, rather than later as planned.'

Oops. A touch earlier than we wanted. Well, considerably earlier than we wanted. I should try to help David out here, shouldn't I?'

'Perhaps we should let him eat something first?'

'No, I don't think so, I am sure his Greek Cypriot friends have fed him well enough.' He beamed a warm insincere smile at me.

'Come, come, Mr de Bois. I am only joking. Let me introduce David now. We're all keen to hear what he has to say.'

'OK, fine by me.'

Shame on me, shame on me. So quick to sell him out.

David's self-defence antenna was up and running, as he clearly sensed something was afoot and he caught my eye. I shrugged and offered a helpless look. Good luck, I thought.

And off he went. He did his best, setting out the UK government's position, underlining the importance of our visit, describing his hopes for the future for the reunification of the island and the resolution of the key critical issues.

He was met with stony silence.

Not even the odd nod of acknowledgement at any single statement he made. He ended with a brief acknowledgement to me, asking if I would like to add anything.

I began: 'I know I speak for both of us when I say how pleased we are to be here. David has set out *his* views, gained over his many years as an MP.'

Nicely distancing myself there, I think, without being too obvious.

'For me [note the 'me'], tonight is about making sure I have the knowledge and understanding to ensure that a balanced view on Cyprus is presented, resisting the temptation that many other politicians have to capitalise on any single partisan event during what is, as we all know, a long journey to a settlement.'

Lots of nodding.

Then, the clincher to maintaining my chances of getting back to the hotel safely and keeping the chairman's finger away from the eject button.

'*My* job is to listen. Listen, and continue to learn, because I am proud of the fact that you have two MPs – the first two, I might add – who have come here to engage with you and your current political leaders.'

My good friend David was smiling and clapping (as were the audience), but his eyes said it all.

Treachery.

I could not disagree with that analysis.

The evening had two phases. The first was a cathartic opportunity for the hosts to lambast David and the Greek Cypriots (frankly, they didn't distinguish between the two) and the European Union's hostile attitude to Turkish Cypriots.

The second was simply to leave us in no doubt that, in their opinion, a two-state solution by dividing the island on a permanent basis was a realistic possibility. But given they had all been close colleagues of former hardline leader Rauf Denktaş, this was not altogether surprising.

David, tiring of fielding questions and, truthfully, not getting to eat very much, would occasionally invite me to comment. It struck me that this was entirely unnecessary as they had David firmly in their sights. I could see no advantage in disappointing them. I simply slipped lower in my seat and engaged in deep discussions with my host to my left.

My affection for Cyprus remains undiminished, and my hope for a final settlement for reunification never wavers. I find it shocking that those who endured the misery of 1974 are still waiting to see Cyprus reunited in their lifetime. As we learned on our trips, the people of the island retain a huge thirst for unification, yet it is the politicians who have failed to present a solution for approval by a second referendum. What role does the UK Parliament have in this?

Under the 1960 Treaty of Guarantee, the British government has a responsibility to guarantee Cyprus's independence as a nation state. However, nothing I have experienced or heard in my dealings with Cypriots has persuaded me that British politicians should adopt a partisan ʼapproach to the divided communities, either for domestic political advantage in their constituencies, or in the belief that doing so will assist in finding a solution. I accept I am probably in a minority of one on this.

What we can all do is build trust through visits with both communities, and ensure that the British government undertakes its full responsibilities as a guarantor of Cyprus's independence by helping bring the two leaders from the north and south to a successful conclusion to their talks.

Opinions change as time passes.

One of the most outspoken people at the rather strange dinner we attended spoke to me in 2016 on a subsequent delegation I led to Shakespeare House, the UK government's office in the north zone of Nicosia.

He spoke of the opportunity for successful settlement talks leading to reunification in much more optimistic tones than he had at our dinner. 'What's changed', I asked, 'that has made you think this?'

'Time and opportunity,' he said. 'The former we have plenty of in Cyprus, as the past forty years show, but opportunity has, until now, been in short supply.'

Sadly, his optimism was misplaced as once again, at the time of writing, the Cyprus settlement talks sponsored by the UN have collapsed.

15

NET IMMIGRATION INGENUITY?

Even after the least successful of trips, returning to London's airports can be very depressing. No VIP lounge awaiting, no collection of my bags, and certainly no car to whisk me off to my next destination. Out with the Oyster card, to join the great British public as they too suffer the frustration of arriving home to airports that still, inexplicably, allow themselves to be ranked so badly in the world, according to the latest AirHelp rankings of 2017.

Only Heathrow scrapes a passable 20th place. That's not good enough for a country that is 'open for business'. Four of our airports are ranked the worst in the world, for goodness sake.

But the great thing about this?

By the time I arrive at the constituency office, clutching a bulging suitcase and yet another packet of wine gums forced on me by Mehmet next door, I am ready for the realities of constituency life again. Fresh from the sunny island of Cyprus and the wonderful people there, I was then brutally brought down to earth by a meeting with a lady of Turkish origin, now a British citizen, along with her child and her friend.

'Sir, I am the translator, accompanying my friend here who needs your help.'

'I see, welcome. And what can I do for your friend today?'

We were in Kingfisher Primary School in the east of the constituency, where the head teacher had invited us to host a constituency advice surgery for local residents.

'My friend has been here eight years, and she has trouble getting a job, and now her house is in an awful condition, with damp, and windows that don't shut properly, and the council isn't doing anything about it.'

'Is it a house provided by the council?'

'No, it is a private rented but we get housing allowance to pay for it from the council.'

Wise nodding of heads around the table.

'I am sorry to hear you have problems. What can I do for you?

Moment for translation.

'Sir, my friend says she has spent much time with the council, but they say because she has been moved once before, there is little chance of her having another move for some time. My friend would like you to get her a council house.'

'Has your friend applied for a council house?'

'Yes, but they said she will not get one as the wait is too long which is why she wants you to help her get one please.'

'This is entirely a matter for the council and your councillors, and I will happily refer you to them with a letter summarising your wishes.'

With that explained, I started to draw the meeting to a close.

'My friend says she is also short of money now that your government has introduced a limit on benefits. She has lost almost £200 a month, and finds it difficult to feed her children regularly, so she goes without food to feed them.'

Ah.

'Your friend may not know this, but if she gets a part-time job, then the benefits cap will be removed and she will have money for more food and maybe to move to a better house.'

A pause for translation.

'My friend has not been able to get a job. She can only work part-time because of the ages of the children.'

Which, in this case, meant she could work.

Perhaps I was tired from the journey, and a bit jaded. It was, after all, ambitious to host a constituency surgery the same day we came back from Cyprus.

'Did your friend come to this country to get a better life?' I asked.

Translation.

'Yes, sir, but so far she has not had a better life, but thank you for asking.'

'Do you think your friend, who has been here eight years, might be able to get a better life if she learned to speak English?'

Translation.

I did not need to wait for a translation from her friend, as the rising volume of her voice, the agitated waving of arms, and her body language spoke volumes.

'My friend says she did not come here to get criticised. She came to you for help.'

'I am helping. This is an advice surgery and my advice is that if after eight years she has not yet learned English then it undoubtedly makes it harder to get a job and provide for her family. I can recommend some language classes.'

The offer was not accepted.

Although my constituent, let's call her Asha, had not come to see me about her immigration status, she had come to this country from Turkey as an economic migrant. Good for her.

But there was little chance of her improving her circumstances unless she won the lottery or learned the English language to get a job.

True, the wider established local immigrant community provided some jobs that required only the native language, but these jobs were few and far between. I knew there would be exceptions, but generally, if you come to this country to work and improve your economic circumstances, it's unlikely to happen if you don't learn the language. The alternative, of living on taxpayer handouts, defeats the object of becoming an economic migrant, surely?

Having the time to actually learn a language was not an issue, not least because bureaucracy and mismanagement of asylum and immigration claims made damn sure there would be time to learn a language, and a lot more besides.

The average length of an immigration application cycle that came into my office was four to five years. The administrative chaos of the Home Office meant that some unfortunate people had waited ten years for applications to be processed. The last government had opened the doors to immigration without considering whether they could manage the migration process, which left many people in a vacuum, unclear about their future, for years.

The upside, if you were looking for one, was that there was plenty of time to learn English, so if they did get the formal 'leave to remain' status, getting a job would be much easier.

After all, learning five words a day over eight years would have enabled a vocabulary of 14,600 perfect English words. An average eight-year-old child has command of that, for goodness sake.

But what really surprised me was that people would come to see their MP about immigration in the first place. I, for one, can list three reasons why, on the face of it, no one should have been coming to see me about immigration:

1. I can't do anything about an application except check it is in the system. No MP can, because MPs don't make the Yes or No decision.
2. Your immigration lawyer, who has probably fleeced you to represent your claim for immigration status and leave to remain, was lying when he said I must help you and would give you a reference.
3. Of course I won't endorse your application, because until the moment you set foot in my office, I had never heard of you.

Oh yes, and one more:

4. I was elected on a pledge to reduce net migration to the tens of thousands.

This last point didn't seem to cross the mind of anyone who ventured into the constituency office asking me to 'do something' about their immigration request and, to be fair, it never was a factor in dealing with constituents, but it always struck me as odd that this policy seemed divorced from most people's minds.

Probably because no one believed it, including the immigrants.

During five years in my constituency office, we had about 5,000 cases. If that was repeated across the 650 constituencies in the UK, then that would be 3,250,000 applications – and that's only counting the ones that MPs would have been involved in. It didn't need Her Majesty's Loyal Opposition to tell me our manifesto pledge was unattainable. It was bleeding obvious within the first few months of being elected.

In the end, the constituency office team devised a system to simply check that constituents' applications were underway. Frankly, for the vast majority of cases there was little else we could do. True, if there had been an absurd amount of time with no response from the Home Office, we would have tried to prod them into action.

But let me be clear. There were some cases we really went to town on, not because we could do very much about the individual case, as I have explained, but because I felt the law was profoundly unfair in some circumstances and should be modified.

A very cheerful, chatty and engaging lady, originally from the West Indies, came to see me. She was a retired nurse who had worked in the NHS all her adult life and seemed only to see the positive in people, even when she had been dealt a blow by our own Immigration and Border Protection department.

Annie had been sent to the UK by her parents back in the late '60s to live with her uncle and aunt, because her parents wanted her to have a good education, as was her entitlement at the time. Subsequently, her native British Caribbean island colony assumed independence, a welcome but unremarkable day for Annie, who pressed on with her studies.

As she told me, she had had a wonderful adult life after leaving school, becoming a nurse, marrying, and being blessed with children. Sadly, Annie divorced, and soon after that was advised to apply for pension credit. Her whole life she had done the right thing, and made a wonderful contribution to her adopted country and the NHS. When asked to provide proof of status, she was unable to do so and, mainly because of her divorce from a British citizen, she no longer had status in her own right. She was therefore denied pension credit.

Although there was little doubt she would get British

citizenship, she had to pay £1,200 for the process, which was both a rip-off and an insult. And what did she say to me when I broke the news?

'Sweetie, you tried and you failed. You win some, you lose some, but I reckon you put in at least £1,200 worth of effort for me, so I will just look at this payment as an investment to get me the pension credit I am due.'

The irony is that because her children had a British citizen for a father, they got British citizenship.

I was angrier than Annie, but she was by far the better person. The UK continues to discriminate against families who came to this country from former British colonies, often to help rebuild the nation after the Second World War. Decades later we thank them by imposing onerous immigration rules, often resulting in nonsensical decisions to divide families or, as in Annie's case, fleece them for thousands of pounds. In contrast, because of our membership of the European Union, our borders remain open to anyone from member states where there is little or no historical or family legacy associated with the UK.

As I said, Annie was by far the better person, and her case stood in stark contrast to some of the scams we discovered.

'Mr de Bois, I have come to talk to you about my brother, who wants to come to this country.'

'And he wishes to come and stay here permanently with you, or is it just to visit?'

'My brother coming here is a problem, which I need help with, please.'

This didn't sound like an immigration problem; more like a family dispute.

'What can I do for you?'

'As far as the immigration people are concerned, my brother is here already, you see.'

'I'm afraid I don't.'

'I am my brother, you see. This is hard for me to explain.'

It's bloody hard for me to understand.

Leanne got it. This chap had come to the UK pretending to be his brother, with his brother's country of origin passport. He had therefore entered the country illegally, and now his brother wanted to come over, and that was his problem. Being found out and what to do about it.

'I see. So, let me get this right. You came here seven years ago in your brother's name, you now have a partner, and you have two children.'

'Yes, sir. And I have legal status to stay in this country with my children.'

'Well, to be strictly accurate, your brother has legal status to remain in the UK.'

He had the good grace to look slightly ashamed.

'Yes, sir. So, sir, I want your help please. Can my brother stay in this country, and can I claim to stay in this country because I have a family?'

I didn't have a clue, but I was impressed with his cheek.

To be fair, while I did not have any sympathy for his dilemma, I was always sensitive to the children's plight in all this, as the innocent victims of their parents' decisions.

Perhaps the most awkward and, to some extent, disturbing case I dealt with was the student who came to see me to ask if I could help get her UK passport sorted out as her parents had mysteriously misplaced it.

'I need the passport for my university, to prove my nationality, but according to my parents it's lost in an embassy in Cyprus, which is where they were from originally. I was born here and I am a British citizen, yet we are struggling to get hold of it. Can you help?'

NET IMMIGRATION INGENUITY?   139

Odd. But it seemed straightforward enough. Even I could manage that, I thought.

'So, your British passport is at the embassy in Cyprus. Do you know why?'

'Yes. It was sent there for renewal by my parents.'

'But you all live here and are British citizens?' asked Leanne, who was babysitting me through the advice surgery. Clearly, she scented something was wrong and, having been trained by Helen over the past year, she had undergone a Doctor Who regeneration from a sweet, innocent and trusting soul to a somewhat more worldly wise, sceptical and questioning case-worker. So young to be so cynical.

'We are Turkish Cypriots by origin, but yes, British citizens.'

It was time to look into this, and time to wrap up the meeting. We promised to get back to her as soon as possible, given the urgent need of her passport to get her to her university of choice.

Renewing a passport in Cyprus was done online and by post. You wouldn't take your passport to an embassy in Northern Cyprus, not least because there was no embassy, just a small High Commission working office.

If you lived in Enfield and were a resident of the UK, I could not think why you would want to try to renew your passport through an overseas embassy.

This young lady seemed as baffled as we did, but fear not, the feisty Leanne was on the case.

The first port of call was the High Commission in Nicosia, which had no record of any contact with the parents or the daughter. With the persistence of a private investigator, Leanne next spoke to the Home Office, who had absolutely no record of the family. That was a little odd, as the parents had, according to their daughter, immigrated to the UK fifteen years ago. It could be a clerical error, of course. And on went the search for an explanation of where this passport may have ended up.

Much like a good detective thriller, Leanne followed the evidence, or rather, the lack of evidence, determined to find this passport though clearly smelling a rat. We checked the immigration status of the parents and set the Home Office off on a search for information, which they duly turned up.

To cut a long story short, this poor girl's parents were not British citizens. They had never sought UK citizenship, but arrived in the UK with fake documents. They had remained illegally in the country for over two decades. Their children were educated here, they used full public services, and at no point had the family's status ever been questioned. The consequence was that their daughter was not eligible for a passport and they had broken the law.

Worse, the parents had not told their children that they had in fact been born in Northern Cyprus, not the UK.

I arranged for the parents to come in to the office to discuss the passport situation.

'My daughter was born here, eighteen years ago, at Chase Farm Hospital.'

'Are you sure?'

How stupid did that sound?

'Of course I'm sure. You don't forget having a baby. Only a man would say that!'

Polite laughter all round.

'Well, I agree. You wouldn't forget having a baby, but it seems you have forgotten where you had the baby.'

Silence.

'Please…?'

'You arrived in this country about fifteen years ago on false papers. There is no record of you, and you are not British citizens.'

Silence.

'I'm sorry, I realise this is difficult, but I have your daughter's interests to think about. Where was she born?'

'Cyprus ... But in Greek Cyprus, so she is an EU baby.'

'That's not true, though, is it.'

Silence.

'No.'

Throughout all this, her husband offered no comment, apparently speaking no English. The chickens had come home to roost, but more for his daughter than himself. She was completely blameless in all this, but looked set to pay a heavy price for her parents' actions. We could help her, by encouraging her to make a claim for leave to remain in her own right, which she did, and she has now completed her university course.

But who is to blame for this mess? The parents are ultimately accountable for their actions and for breaking the law, yet a flawed immigration system, which one Home Secretary made clear was unfit for purpose, gave room for people to use their ingenuity to either get around it, or, as in this case, just ignore it, with unfortunate consequences many years down the track.

In one day, I met with eight different people and families to listen to their concerns over their immigration applications. Of eight applications, only one was straightforward. All the other cases confessed that they had played the system and/or broken the law to further their ambitions of achieving British citizenship.

A foreign national explained, 'I have been asked to leave the country three times, and did so, but within days I returned and started a new application.'

'How?' I would ask.

'I got on a train or a van and hid, sir.'

Determination is quite an admirable quality.

'I overstayed my visa and now my girlfriend is pregnant, and I am applying to stay under the right to a family life,' adding, 'Is this OK, and the way I can stay here, Mr de Bois?'

Cheeky sod.

'Look,' I said to one person, 'you were told that you would be removed by the authorities from the country, so how are you still here?'

'I know, but the border force was very polite as they wrote to me to let me know when they were coming round to question me and arrange for me to leave.'

'Really? So, you moved before they came to see you?'

'No, sir. I am still living there, but I'm sorry, I lied. I told them that the person they were looking for had moved.'

I didn't make that up, I promise you.

And on it went. I truly admire the determination of people to come to the UK, and some of these people were clearly setting out to make a new life, work and settle down. But a constituency surgery is a strange place to be when so many people feel able to come and sit in front of a national law maker and freely admit to breaking the law as a demonstrable sign of their eagerness and suitability to become a British citizen.

Yet there is no question that the Home Office (which at the time had the responsibility for managing immigration cases) was considerably out of its depth. Unable to meet the enormous workload of processing and verifying immigration claims, it caused appalling delays that drove some people to take these extraordinary measures. Many were, of course, just chancing their luck.

Obviously, there is another side to immigration, and I am not just trotting that out for political correctness. In particular, I am referring to the skilled and conversant people who come to work and live here. As a rule, those were not the people who came to my attention, but it is a point worth making to provide context to this narrative, which focuses on the less positive side to immigration that I saw far too much of in Enfield.

That less positive side led to a shameful targeting of Turkish people during the Brexit campaign, when much political capital was made out of the prospect of Turkey joining the EU. Amid threats from the Leave campaign that millions of Turkish migrants would pour into the UK, even arch-remainer David Cameron – who up until then had been an ardent supporter of Turkey and its bid for EU membership – jumped on board the anti-Turkish bandwagon. In answer to a question about Turkey joining the EU, Cameron said: 'I'm not going to be Prime Minister in three decades' time. If this was going to happen in the next couple of years, *I would not support it*. But it is not going to.' (Emphasis mine.)

It was a sign of desperation, perhaps, that David Cameron was targeting a crucial ally of NATO and the UK. But that's for him to explain.

He could have asked me about Turkish migration. Yes, there are scammers, abusers and crooks from Turkey, and I have just introduced you to some of them. That's not surprising, and there are others from Germany, France, Spain, America, Greece and more.

I can, nevertheless, also testify to the extraordinary contribution from the medical profession, small business entrepreneurs, lawyers, accountants, shopkeepers who work twelve to fifteen hours a day, academics and musicians. I have worked in the UK with institutions dedicated to sharing best practice in healthcare, such as ITSEB, the Association of Turkish Speaking Health Professionals, and I have worked with Turkish business investors looking to invest in the UK.

They are choosing to put their ingenuity and effort into

legitimately living and working in this country. That's a win–win for them and for the UK.

As most Brits know, not all migration is bad, but that should not stop our understandable indignation about those who play the system, and about the fact that the system can be played so easily.

16

VIRGIN DELIGHTS

There is no doubt in my mind that I entered Parliament at the worst possible time. That has nothing to do with the fact that immigration seemed to dominate the parliament, and my constituency office for that matter. Or that we were in a coalition with the flaky Liberal Democrats, or even that I had to deal with the fallout of a broken promise by the Prime Minister on my hospital. They were all challenges that certainly made life interesting, but had nothing to do with the view that this was the worst possible time to be an MP.

No, it was the worst possible time if I had wanted to max out on the perks of a job that for decades had lavished a wealthy lifestyle, endless free travel, bucketloads of expenses and the right to a second home in your own name, funded entirely by the hard-pressed taxpayer.

Those perks were available right up until 2009, when the *Daily Telegraph* tipped a large dose of transparency onto the whole rotten system, with inevitable consequences. By the time I entered Parliament in 2010, you could barely claim for office stationery without undergoing the most vigorous scrutiny from the newly formed IPSA, which showed all the characteristics of a zealous police force, working on the assumption that all MPs were guilty the minute they submitted a claim. Its full name was the Independent Parliamentary Standards Authority.

The pendulum had swung from a system that favoured abuse to one that favoured those with a private income. The stench of dodgy expense claims still permeates the political atmosphere even now, but in 2010 our much-loved tabloids were desperate to keep the toxic issue alive, and therefore sought to ridicule and shame MPs wherever possible in the new 2010 parliament, when expenses were published every three months by IPSA.

So when some innocent parliamentary assistant ordered some loo roll for the constituency office and put in a claim for it, the tabloids would publish their outrage that an MP on £65,000 a year was getting the poor old taxpayer to pay for 'his' loo paper. I am struggling to think of any business that asks its employees to pay for the company loo roll, but then again, I may be wrong.

Unsurprisingly, those who, like me, had the benefit of a private income from their previous business life wouldn't risk claiming for such luxuries. Likewise with air freshener, coffee, tea, paper clips and goodness knows what else. The rules would allow it, but the court of public opinion would not, according to the tabloids.

I was bloody furious about this. Not because of the cost, but because I knew I was making a bad call and should have toughed it out. The post-expenses scandal climate was now creating two classes of MPs: those who could afford not to claim and those who could not and therefore had to run the continued risk of widely inflated headlines. For me, though, with early Marginal Agitation and Despair syndrome in full flow, I chose the easy option.

Nevertheless, it was with a certain sense of well-being, and a hint of smugness, that I came into Parliament in 2010, quite content that, having not been caught up in the expenses fiasco of the previous parliament, I would have no problems whatsoever. I would not be claiming any meal or food allowances, and had no second home to worry about, since I lived well within reach of my home from Westminster. Expenses were, for me, not an issue.

Unfortunately, not everyone thought so.

I was leaving the House of Commons at 2 a.m., after the most irritating but effective member of the then Labour opposition, Ed Balls, forced a late-night sitting on the first Budget debate in June 2010. Under the expenses rules, I could claim for a hotel as the sitting overran past 11 p.m. However, given I only needed to get back to Enfield, some sixteen miles away, it would be cheaper to get a taxi, and even better value as I shared it with my neighbouring MP, David Burrowes. So, about an hour later, at 3 a.m., I was duly dumped outside my house, some £64 lighter for the whole journey. The taxpayer had done well, I thought.

The *London Evening Standard* did not agree.

With a wonderful tabloid sense of disproportion, the paper ran a headline on page 3 on the day the first batch of all MPs' expenses was published.

'London's Most Expensive Travel Claim', it screamed in outrage, citing my lavish trip home.

It was a slow news day, I suspect.

Regardless, having met with the wrath of Fleet Street's finest, that was the last taxi I ever took at the taxpayer's expense, and then I retreated to cowardice by taking the easy option of not claiming at all for most incidental expenses.

But not all was doom and gloom.

Far from it. Along with the huge privilege of being a Member of Parliament, there came a handful of extraordinary events that my wife and I would never otherwise have had the chance to experience.

But first a word about my wife, Helen.

The year before entering Parliament in 2010, I married Helen Seaman, a professional accountant who had been working in my company since 1995, having become financial director in 2000 and then managing director in 2010.

Helen is five foot three to my six foot three. She is elegant, whereas I am clumsy. She is considered, as opposed to my impulsiveness. And she has patience, where I hurry. In short, we are a perfect match.

Perhaps her only flaw, and one that I am at a loss to understand, is why, having married me, she won't take my name. Seriously, keep Seaman and not adopt de Bois?

Notwithstanding that one weakness, the company she has run since 2010 has gone from strength to strength under her leadership, and she has now established Rapiergroup as a major player in the international events and exhibitions arena. I am very proud of her, and of the company's efforts. But let's be clear, she can be formidably opinionated and is rarely shy of voicing an opinion, whether asked for or not. This is simply an expression of the genuine passion she feels for the work she does, more so about matters that truly excite her. I never doubt, when she commits to do something, that she will in fact do it.

Which brings me to the first of the memorable events that we were invited to shortly after my election: a reception with HRH Prince Charles at his royal palace, Clarence House, on the Mall.

For those of us who grew up with the Charles and Diana romance, marriage, family and subsequent divorce, and then her tragic early death, the subject often divides opinion. On this, Helen and I disagree profoundly. But, for the purpose of this story, let's just note that I was very firmly in the Charles and Camilla camp, while Helen had both feet entrenched – no, more like cemented – in the Diana fan club tent. With the arrival of the formal invitation to take tea with the Prince as part of a group of MPs invited to Clarence House, Helen's preferences became once again very evident.

'I don't think I'll be going to this, but don't let me stop you.'

'Oh, come on, it will be an amazing experience and you will get to see a beautiful building, which is his formal residence and palace in London! Not everyone gets to take tea with the Prince of Wales.'

'I don't want to "take tea" with him. You know what I think, so just toddle off and cosy up to royalty if you wish.'

'I didn't take you for a republican.'

'I'm not. I just don't like what he did to Diana.'

'I really would like you to come. I won't ask ever again, but on this one occasion, it would be wonderful to have you with me. Think of it as supporting me at work, where you can meet some of my fellow MPs?'

'No.'

'Please, just this once. You probably won't even have to meet him, as the place will be packed, I'm sure.'

'Fine. Then I won't be missed.'

'I will miss you,' I said simply, accompanied by my best lost-puppy expression.

'Fine.'

Oh, that didn't sound good. More clarification needed.

'Is that fine, you will come, or fine, you won't come… darling?'

'I will bloody come, but don't think for five minutes I won't let him know what I think of him and that woman if he speaks to me.'

'Just check out the treason laws before you do that,' I said, as I fled the room before she could change her mind.

Two weeks later, we were strolling down the Mall, approaching Clarence House. Me, with a little trepidation, but with no chance to think about it as Helen was in full flow.

'I'm not staying long, just long enough for form's sake. And don't expect me to curtsey. I'm certainly not doing that. He shouldn't be king anyway, it should skip to William. He's looovely.'

I spied the Chief Whip, Patrick McLoughlin, up ahead, heading in the same direction. I wonder if he could help? Perhaps not; he might like the idea of me having to deal with a rebel for a change.

Helen and I entered the rather sparsely furnished but ornate reception room in Clarence House and joined the liveliest of groups already well into their first drink (no sign of tea anywhere). Holding court was the magnificent Colonel Bob Stewart DSO, the newly elected MP for Beckenham, along with his charming wife Claire. It wasn't long before we all relaxed, and in fact we barely noticed the Prince of Wales enter the room and start doing the rounds. Helen was nursing her second glass of wine, and I risked a joke.

'Darling,' I whispered. 'He may well be with us soon. Don't forget to curtsey, will you?'

'Oh, bollocks to you.'

She rightly ignored me and carried on chatting to Claire on the subject of whether they should curtsey or not. I did indeed sense a rebellion, and thought the Prince, should he come over and chat to us, would be getting a marginally frosty reception. Or was I being over-sensitive?

And then, there he was, trademark hand in left pocket and thumb curled over the top. Elegantly dressed, perhaps a little shorter than you might expect from being brought up on television news pictures. But definitely there, in person.

Bob led the way and introduced himself as only a military man can. I got the impression they had met before. He was followed by a delightfully respectful handshake (no curtsey) from Claire.

I put out my hand to introduce myself, then turned to Helen. With a new-found sense of dignity and purpose, she promptly capitulated. Not even a flicker of disapproval swept across her face as her hand swept out to greet the heir to the throne and she flashed her most sycophantic smile. So warm was her greeting, I was anticipating a grovelling curtsey to a degree not seen in the Royal Household since Sir Walter Raleigh laid down his cloak for Queen Elizabeth I.

OK, that was never going to happen, but you get the point.

They then shared a little joke about the curtains, or some such nonsense. The wine had done its trick and mellowed the great lady, and the Prince moved safely on.

'Well, darling. That really told him, eh?'

'Oh, bollocks to you.'

My inability to refrain from gloating is often a matrimonial downfall of mine, and having been quite irritating for the rest of the day it was a pleasant surprise not to be banished to the sofa that night. Having said that, one of the less notable pleasures of being an MP is waking up in bed with your wife.

Well, to clarify, waking up with your wife when, on most mornings, you discover she has an opinion on some latest policy announcement, be it the Budget, free school meals, tax, prisoner votes, maternity leave, or whatever may take the fancy of that morning's news programme. We watch Sky News, and I frankly began to think there was no room in our marriage for a third person, namely Eamonn Holmes, who at the time led the Sky News *Sunrise* show.

He would sit on our bedside table, less than two feet from

my face, all wide awake and chirpy, delivering some crushing verdict on one government policy or another, often leading to a poke in my ribs and a now all-too-familiar demand for me 'to do something' about whatever he was spouting on about.

Bless him. I sent a fiver to Sky News as a contribution to his leaving gift when he retired in 2016. Nothing personal, as I am sure he will appreciate.

As I nursed my bruised ribs, I knew I was simply the conduit. The opportunity that presents itself, when you have your MP in bed with you, must be irresistible. Irresistible, that is, to give him a good kicking on a policy issue, confident that the message might get through to a member of the Cabinet, or maybe even the Prime Minister.

So, with good fortune, an invitation arrived from No. 10 at a time when Helen was somewhat less than happy with the general direction of the government, who seemed to be making it quite tough for 'strivers', with whom she readily identified. By this point, Helen had added other weapons of persuasion to her arsenal, including 'If you want my vote at the next election…', and was quickly progressing to drafting questions for me to ask ministers in the House of Commons. To be fair, they were not bad questions, and by agreeing to ask them it marginally reduced the amount of bruising on my ribs.

Thus, when salvation appeared in the form of the invitation to No. 10, I am not sure who was more pleased: me, my ribs or Helen.

'Perfect,' she announced, as I set it before her along with her morning cup of tea. 'Just what I have been waiting for. I have some thoughts I would like to share with Mr Cameron. I will get to speak to him too, won't I?'

Too bloody right you will, I thought. Even if I have to crawl over broken glass to get him to you. See how his ribs cope.

10 Downing Street is much like the good Doctor Who's Tardis. Hidden away behind security gates just off Whitehall sits a very plain and rather small-looking terraced house. Once inside, however, the full scale and size of the building becomes clear as you walk down the long, elegantly furnished corridor complete with Henry Moore sculpture. At the end is the entrance into the Cabinet Room, which we are firmly shunted past. Receptions are held two flights up the stairs, where visitors pass the now-famous parade of former Prime Ministers whose photographs adorn the walls of the staircase. The present-day incumbent is not displayed, not until he or she leaves Downing Street for the last time.

Four splendid rooms await you, of which one is a beautiful state dining room that, truthfully, visitors for receptions are not encouraged to enter. Mainly I think to stop us trying to damage or, for the more opportunist, perhaps, swipe the priceless silver gifts and memorabilia that decorate the tables and open display cabinets.

Oddly, there is a rose pink-coloured fluorescent sign above the door to the entrance of the Terracotta Room. It greets you as you approach the room, much like a red light does above an Amsterdam brothel. The sign reads 'More Passion'; it was created by Tracey Emin and, I presume, spurred David Cameron on to great things.

'It certainly would have been well-suited to the streets of Amsterdam,' Helen noted. She sounded uncharacteristically prudish, but I put that down to her growing focus on how to skewer David Cameron.

In the Terracotta Room, we joined about 100 other guests, all hoping to have their moment with the Prime Minister.

Given the lessons of Clarence House, you might have thought I would be confident that Helen was never for a moment going to raise any complaint with David Cameron. Far from it. I thought she had every right to do so, and I knew she would handle the matter well. I was curiously looking forward to it but nevertheless, somewhat patronisingly, thought it prudent to instruct Helen on how best to take advantage of the PM's time so she could make her views known.

'Keep it brief, but make your point. You won't get anything more than a non-committal response but, who knows, he may take note. And, you know what, I think he will enjoy a bit of a challenge as, let's face it, most people here will just be nice and on their best behaviour. You go for it, darling!'

And then, much as with Prince Charles, suddenly David was with us, making introductions as he worked around our little group. As predicted, the conversation was limited, trite and utterly unmemorable, as MPs' other halves all gushed their unanimous praise for the PM.

He turned to Helen.

'You must be Nick's wife, Helen.' An impressive start, I thought. The man is a pro. Good luck, Helen. You go, girl! Huge respect to you.

'Oh, Prime Minister, how lovely to see you. I can't tell you how wonderful it is to be here and to meet you.'

That's my girl. And then, the coup de grâce, the killer statement.

'I run my own company, and know how tough a job you face, but think you are absolutely right to focus on spending and the economy. It doesn't make our life easy, but we all know it's just got to be done.'

'Thank you, Helen. That's good to hear, that we can count on you and the support of business.'

'Can we have a photo?'

'Of course.'

Next…

I didn't say anything.

'Oh, bollocks to you.'

Speaking truth to power is no easy thing when you actually have the chance to do it. Many a brave armchair critic has seen their planned proclamations disappear on being introduced to the PM, but that didn't stop me enjoying the moment my wife lurched from bedroom critic to slavish admirer in less time than it takes for Eamonn Holmes to say, 'There you go…' – his usual sign-off having just demolished another government minister on TV.

However, when a critic does leave their armchair it can be a politician's nightmare, especially if they're confronted in the street by an angry and distressed member of the public, and with television cameras within inches of their face.

It does take a certain courage to speak up, and that deserves respect. More so when that person has the genuine conviction and determination to be heard. It is perhaps worth reflecting that Tracey Emin's message, if not the design, was apt. 'More Passion' is no bad thing. Unless, of course, you are simply a political agitator looking for five minutes of fame, in which case no one gives a damn.

Helen and I were enormously privileged to enjoy these treasured visits and more. Her Majesty the Queen hosted a reception for MPs at Buckingham Palace, and Westminster Hall was the stage for addresses to Parliament by the Pope, President Obama and other famous world leaders invited during my time as MP.

These are moments that money – and, let's face it, expenses – cannot buy. I would not have had it any other way. The institution of Parliament was right to clean up its act and set about restoring trust in politics, but I am immensely relieved that, as yet, no one has tried to stop MPs attending these amazing events.

17

IT'S NOT WHAT YOU KNOW BUT WHO YOU KNOW

I t's all very well enjoying the privilege of access to the great and the good but, truthfully, a visit to Buckingham Palace for a few minutes with royalty, or a glass of warm white wine with the Prime Minister in a packed and stuffy No. 10, is unlikely to be in the interests of your constituents or the country. What is being served up on these occasions is simply vanity and ego, albeit this is quite enjoyable at the time and I shamelessly indulged whenever possible.

Access to the great and the good, however, is arguably the most important tool at the disposal of an MP when trying to act on a constituent's behalf. To be fair, though, that does not mean I ever brought up Mrs Jennings's missing meat from her Fray Bentos pie with HRH the Prince of Wales.

The point is that it's very unlikely that many people in positions of authority will ignore a call from their local MP. So, when a constituent is understandably enraged at the lack of response from the police to a burglary, or a council taxpayer is tearing his or her hair out because some faceless bureaucrat is passing them from department to department in a mind-numbing exercise in stonewalling, an MP can circumvent the whole system by effectively picking up the phone and kicking arse. The outcome may or may not eventually satisfy the constituent, but at least there is an outcome, and the constituent is somewhat mollified by the fact that someone has tried on his or her behalf. Giving voice to the little things often matters to people as much as giving voice to the bigger issues of the day. This is the day-to-day fare of the job and, frankly, it was quite enjoyable listening to very well-paid executives squirm on the phone as they were presented with a catalogue of system failure.

My constituency office team were masters at this, and quite often I did not even have to get involved unless they too found themselves being stonewalled or, as Helen and Leanne would describe it, they 'sniffed the noxious odour of bullshit'.

Access to the powerful, on the other hand, is another thing altogether.

It is assumed by most constituents that, as their MP, I am on regular speaking terms with all the Cabinet and, of course, the Prime Minister. It is accepted that if I work some magic, these close colleagues of mine will crack the whip and sort out whatever it is that is troubling them.

This, in the main, is utter claptrap.

I barely exchanged more than a dozen impromptu conversations with the Prime Minister in five years apart from, of course, always trying to ask him questions in the formal setting of the House of Commons. The longest casual conversation I ever had with him was at a No. 10 reception (without Mrs dB), and it lasted six minutes. I know because he uncharacteristically looked at his watch twice. I did have formal meetings with him every three months, when the 1922 executive committee went to see him for a regular meeting, and I spent twenty minutes with him in his private office, arguing the toss about Chase Farm Hospital.

Not bad for a first-term MP. But best mates? Close colleagues? Not a chance.

Regular access to him? Over his staff's dead bodies.

The system existed to keep backbenchers away from power and, on the whole, that has worked quite effectively since just after the Second Reform Act of 1867.

The Cabinet were a different proposition, but only the most prolific of networkers (like my office colleague from East Anglia) could hope to get on close personal terms with all members of the Cabinet – then twenty-eight of them in total – within a parliament. Some ministers made it easy to get to know them, as they would often be in the Members' Tea Room, an exclusive MPs-only room, where the only rule was: 'What happens in the Tea Room stays in the Tea Room.' As a result, it was a very useful venue for exchanging views and lobbying on any subject of our choosing, though, to be fair, most of the chat was on topical gossip and the more outrageous commentaries and jokes from such established comedians as Sir Nicholas Soames and Sir Simon Burns.

Some Cabinet members started to run 'Tea Room surgeries', which became fashionable with a few of them when they thought David Cameron would lose the 2015 general election. Being supportive in the Tea Room and being seen to be 'approachable' would help, it was assumed, to rally MPs when these same Cabinet ministers came round begging for votes in a leadership contest.

The idea, on the face of it, was that if you wanted to ask about a policy you were concerned about, or you had a particularly difficult constituency case that needed ministerial intervention, then this was the place to do it and get the help you needed. Assuming they agreed with you, that is.

I never took advantage of it, for no other reason than it

wasn't necessary, but I did notice one afternoon that Theresa May, then Home Secretary, was sat at a table holding her Tea Room surgery along with her very loyal parliamentary private secretary, the MP George Hollingbery. At that moment in time, she had no takers, and having just had a constituency visit by her junior minister for Security and Immigration, James Brokenshire, who had hosted, quite brilliantly, a meeting on immigration, I dropped by to let her know how well it had gone. A perfect opportunity to exchange a few pleasantries, perhaps, and get to know the lady in person.

'Theresa, I just wanted to let you know that James was in my constituency yesterday evening and was superb. He gave up a lot of time, dealt with a huge number of questions and did very well indeed. I know these events can be quite demanding on ministers' diaries, but I wanted you to know how very grateful I am.'

I was standing by her table, not having presumed to take one of the two vacant seats.

'Thank you, Nick.'

Now, it just occurred to me that perhaps this was an opportune moment for her to say, 'Good to hear that, Nick. How are things in the constituency?'

Or, 'How are things, after the riots you had in Enfield?'

Or, frankly, anything to have the chance to spend a few minutes with a backbencher whom you don't really know well at all.

'That's a nice tie,' perhaps?

Nothing, not a sausage.

Maybe it is because some politicians – and Theresa is no exception – having spent so long in politics, forget that forging relationships beyond your immediate circle is to everyone's advantage. For the minister, it helps keep you in touch with what's going on beyond what your advisors want you to know, and it also helps build confidence and respect amongst people you may come to depend on at a later stage. After all, if the Home Secretary spends five minutes talking to you in the Tea Room one day, the chances are she will forget about it minutes after the encounter, and that's not unreasonable. But you won't, and that's what matters.

Given that we had just concluded working on a critical extradition constituency case where she had in fact tried to be very helpful, it was all the more frustrating how difficult it was to build any form of personal relationship beyond just 'doing the business'. Fine in some respects, but odd if you are seeking to win colleagues over to you as a future PM. Relationships and interpersonal skills matter in any profession, and are often the determining factor between success and failure. The miscalculation by No. 10 and Theresa May in holding the 2017 election was born in part from her relying on far too narrow a circle of advisors, and not having the good sense to listen to and trust her own MPs. If my experience is anything to go by, that would be difficult to do if you don't work at building relationships with them in the first place.

At a more parochial level, it also helps illustrate why it is so hard to live up to your constituents' expectations that you are closely allied to all the major power brokers of government, because sometimes that's not made an easy task for you to achieve.

Yet, while I may not have been as close to the power brokers as my constituents would like to think, I pretty much only had myself to blame for fuelling that impression in the first place. Let's face it, I was hardly going to parade down Enfield's main shopping district advertising the fact that I had no sway whatsoever.

Far from it. Instead, I did the complete opposite, and worked hard at trying to convince folk of my influence. And that, inevitably, meant that on occasion I had to deliver results for those very demanding constituents of mine. Which can be a problem when you have little clout and are up against a system that wants you to have even less.

So, after the riots in Enfield had wreaked their havoc, including the destruction of the Sony warehouse, which was set on fire by opportunist young thugs, it was easy to ensure the highest level of attention from our leaders. Within days, Theresa May as Home Secretary was on site, looking at the aftermath of the largest European arson attack on record. I had spoken with the directors of Sony the day after the fire and offered the full support of the government in helping to rebuild their warehouse and distribution centre on the same site, to avoid losing such an important company and employer in the constituency. David Cameron offered to speak to them if required. So far, so good.

I was hugely relieved when Sony decided to rebuild their facility in Enfield, at the same location. That is, until they tried to invite the Prime Minister back a year later to open the new facility.

I thought it a no-brainer. One year on from the ashes of the worst mainland riots we had ever seen, Enfield emerged stronger, fit for business, and ready for the future. At the helm to mark this momentous occasion would be the Prime Minister, the leader who had helped rebuild Britain after those tumultuous days in August the year before...

'Sorry, Nick, the Prime Minister's diary is somewhat committed presently. Do let us know if we can help another time.'

Seriously?

'Well, I'll let you know if we have another arson attack and, if so, when the second rebuild will be complete, and we can try and invite him up then?'

Didn't Bridget Jones have a pet name for people like this?

My frustration was evident.

Why does this place make it so damn hard to get even the easiest thing done? What's the point of being on the same team if it's a one-way relationship? You give (your vote), they take (your vote, your judgement, your right to think, and your right to have a visit from the Prime Minister just once in five years!).

Irrational of me? Quite probably. But that's what it seemed like, to me, at that precise moment.

Time to calm down.

Think. What options have I got?

1. Can Sony move the opening date to suit the Prime Minister? Probably not, as they wrote to him with a set date.
2. Does the Prime Minister even know about the invitation? Almost certainly not. The private office would have just put a line through it. So, find out why for goodness sake! After all, we all know that the private office exists to say 'No' to most requests, even more so from backbenchers. At least then you may have the basis for a good excuse for his lack of attendance.
3. Ask the great man himself if he wants to do it?
4. If all else fails, get someone else?

So, having got over my tantrum within about thirty minutes (a record time, I hasten to add), I set about once again trying to play the system to work for me, instead of whinging about it working against me. I was almost certainly not the first MP to face this problem, and I bet others had dealt with more difficult challenges.

A cunning plan began to take shape.

'Good morning. Nick de Bois, Member for Enfield North here. I spoke with you, or perhaps a colleague, earlier, about a possible visit by the Prime Minister to open the Sony factory in Enfield following its rebuild after the riots.'

My plan, such as it was, was to find out why David Cameron couldn't do it. Hopefully, he was on a major international
conference elsewhere in the world, or a summit meeting with
President Obama; anything that would be on the news that day,
so the good folk at Sony would at least know he was genuinely
unavailable and I could offer a substitute, whose attendance
might be easier to secure. Theresa May, maybe, or the Mayor of
London Boris Johnson, perhaps?

'Yes, you spoke with me, Nick. I'm afraid, as it's a Friday, he is
in his constituency all day.'

What?

I wanted to scream.

OK, Friday is the traditional day for MPs to be in the constituency, holding advice surgeries and attending local events.
That's expected for most MPs. But seriously, the Prime Minister,
faced with the opportunity to open a landmark international
business that had re-committed to the UK after the shock of the
riots, was instead going to be tasting overcooked jam at some
blasted Oxfordshire county fête or some such bollocks?

This, his private office thought, was a better plan?!

At worst, couldn't he detour via Enfield and then go to his
constituency and sup tea with the good folk of Witney afterwards? After all, I don't suppose his 22,000 majority was at risk.

Deep breath.

'I see, that's most unfortunate.'

Another deep breath.

'Perhaps you could, nevertheless, mention this opportunity
to the Prime Minister, and see if he could accommodate us?'

'There will be a letter in his weekend box [the file of documents the PM is expected to read over the weekend] turning
down the invitation, so I am sure he will be aware of the
commitments.'

Oh crap. That letter must not go, I thought.

'Thank you for your help.'

A politician's insincerity ringing loud and clear, I hope.

Perhaps I'm being harsh, because the civil service and the PM's private office are not there to help backbenchers; they are there at all times to serve their master and what they perceive is in his interests.

Opening a business's facility, unless it suits their messaging 'grid' at the time, is not going to even figure on their radar as remotely of interest or use. That, however, is not how your constituents will read the situation. Given all the pledges of support made by the government at the time of the riots, such a decision will seem inexplicable to the staff and directors of Sony; more so if the PM is busy judging the best homemade jam competition as opposed to attending a vital international summit.

And it would be me making that explanation unless I could do something about it.

It was Tuesday. The letter would be signed and sent by Monday. I had two parliamentary days before the weekend to turn things around.

For once, the whips came to my help.

That same day, it seemed we were in for a closely contested vote. A must-win vote in which the Liberal Democrats, with their characteristically pick-and-mix approach to the coalition, were threatening to withhold support for a government Bill, even though they were part of the government. Some Liberal Democrats were even threatening to vote against it, which meant the mathematics of the vote left the government vulnerable to a defeat.

The whips naturally cancelled all slips, asking all MPs to return to the Commons immediately (a slip being an authorisation previously given to an MP allowing him to miss a vote).

Threatening emails were duly despatched to the entire parliamentary party, warning of the tight vote and ensuring that all ministers cancelled any engagements outside the parliamentary estate. And, of course, that included the Prime Minister.

So, in a day of uncertainties, the one thing I could be sure of was that the Prime Minister would be voting, and therefore would be in the voting lobby, queuing up with all the other MPs to have his vote recorded. Which was his and his officials' bad luck, and my very good fortune.

Once again, tradition and archaic procedures were going to come to my rescue.

MPs are principally elected to vote on legislation, which means that almost every day, when Parliament is sitting, we all troop through one of two lobbies to cast our vote. We either walk through the 'No' lobby or the 'Aye' lobby. (The language, as you can tell, has not quite been modernised as yet.)

When we vote, however, a strict parliamentary process is always adhered to, which dates back to the early nineteenth century. It is designed to ensure fairness and accuracy by recording voting numbers, who voted and how they voted.

From the minute the Speaker calls for a division, a bell rings throughout the parliamentary estate, alerting Members that there is a vote taking place. From that moment, Members have eight minutes precisely to make their way to the voting lobby of their choice. The lobbies are to the left and right of the main chamber of the House of Commons, and if you arrive at the door to the lobby after the eight-minute period, and after the Speaker has declared, 'Lock the doors', you will not be let into the lobby and therefore cannot vote.

I have seen grown men try to use their full body weight to stop a doorkeeper shutting and locking the door, so that they can get in to vote. They rarely win, and the doorkeepers, the majority of whom have a military background, will stop at nothing to shut and lock the door.

Assuming you make it into the lobby, MPs are either still queuing up to have their names checked off against a full list of Members and have their vote counted as they walk through the exit doors of the lobby, or they have already been through that process and exited the lobby completely.

It is called a lobby for a reason. And it is for precisely that reason that I had pinned my hopes on nobbling the Prime Minister for a few minutes when he came into the lobby to vote.

Having made sure I was in place, inside the voting lobby and close to the entrance, I waited. Near me, loitering with some element of menace, were the whips, who station themselves near the entrance at every vote. They look as if they are chatting innocently amongst themselves, but I suspect their beady eyes are being cast over their flock of MPs, checking for signs of resistance or the whiff of independence over some impending controversial measure.

More usefully, two other whips are outside the entrance to the lobby, marshalling in MPs should they be in any doubt as to where they should be voting, as they are all too often.

With seconds to spare, the Prime Minister sauntered in. In an instant, he saw me as I saw him, and we both knew he was cornered. With his irresistible charm, he touched my shoulder in a collegiate fashion and steered us both to the voting desks.

His pace had picked up from a gentle saunter to a near gallop as he fulfilled his duty of trying to avoid being asked to do anything, whereas I all but dragged him to a halt, giving me time to deliver my 'elevator pitch' as to why he needed to come to Enfield. I blurted out some feeble exchange, hoping the key words would register:

'Riots.'

'Sony.'

'Promise.'

'Witney constituency day.'

'Marginal seat.'

'Please.'

I might well have thrown in a lost-puppy look for good measure.

'Ah, yes. I see the problem with the constituency day commitment that Sam [his wife] and I have agreed to do.'

'Sony will move the time to help meet your commitments, Prime Minister.'

'Ah, yes, right. Well, talk to my office and let's see what we can do.'

Bugger.

That might sound all right in theory, but it meant there was still a huge mountain to climb. Perhaps I should press him up against the wall and threaten him. After all, no private detectives are allowed in the lobby.

I settled for a more cautious approach.

'There will be 400 people there, and main board Sony directors. It really is a "phoenix from the ashes" good news story, and will help me in the constituency a lot, which I will greatly appreciate.'

Code for: 'I won't rebel again for at least the next year' (fingers only slightly crossed).

Then, music to my ears: 'Tell my office to see if they can work something out.'

Which is precisely what we did and, with great generosity, the Prime Minister did detour from No. 10 to Enfield and then, with some haste, on to jam tarts and tea.

When I first entered Parliament, I was convinced that voting should become electronic. The time involved in voting (approximately twenty minutes for each vote), the personnel involved, and the seemingly archaic method all point to modernisation. Yet in weeks I had changed my mind, simply because changing the process would mean ending the backbencher's ability to lobby the Prime Minister, or indeed any other member of the government.

In the lobby, senior ministers are not protected by officials. It is hard to escape our clutches or hide behind the parliamentary protocols that apply when asking questions on the floor of the House. It is a great system when used effectively and sparingly.

Lobbying may be a dirty word in the minds of the public, because of the perception that money can buy policy, but, for MPs, the ability to lobby directly and without interference at the heart of the Parliament is a precious tool that works for constituents.

So, while 'Billy No Mates' was a reasonably accurate description of my limited access to the senior bods in government, getting the Prime Minister up to Enfield helped fuel the view that I was not entirely without use for my constituents.

I rationalised that it therefore followed that getting more visits to the constituency would hopefully increase further my usefulness, and perhaps extend my political life beyond the one term.

The problem was I dreaded ministerial visits, particularly the fashion for 'walkabouts'.

The media, on the other hand, loved walkabouts. For them, every walkabout was an accident waiting to happen, which they could gleefully capture for posterity and the six o'clock news. Residents generally like the idea that where they live is drawing the attention of the powers that be, and my political supporters and activists enjoy it as they should.

But I most definitely loathed it.

As far as I was concerned, every single visit was a disaster waiting to happen. The press would be bastards, the visits you had set up would be hijacked by some action group, or some fruitcake would start hurling rotten eggs or worse at you and the minister. You might survive the day, but your reputation would be in tatters. And worse, no one would think you would ever again be able to count on support from the great and the good, having just subjected one of their kind to a right shambles.

None of this ever happened, but that never stopped my constituents from giving me periodic heart attacks whenever a visit took place, nor the local press from sapping some sort of sadistic pleasure at my expense from most ministerial encounters.

'Nick, this is the fifth bloody time I've been burgled, and the police do naff all about it. You get the bleedin' Home Secretary down here to my shop, and I'll show her what's really going on. They know sweet F all about what we have to put up with.'

Theresa May, then Home Secretary, was visiting Enfield to meet with anti-knife crime campaigners and to publicly show her support for my proposed law to introduce mandatory custodial sentences for carrying a knife. This, despite the government not being able to support the Bill formally because of the opposition from those flaky Liberal Democrats, with whom we were in coalition.

I was very grateful to the Home Secretary for her efforts, and it seemed that I was about to reward her with a right ear-bashing from shopkeepers on the Hertford Road.

To be fair, they had a point. Shop burglaries had rocketed and, from their point of view, nothing effective was being done to protect their shops and their livelihoods.

'Colin, if I bring her to the shop, you will do your best to make your point without assaulting her ears too much, won't you…?

'I'm not gonna punch her, Nick. It's those thieving little bastards I want to give a good hiding to. What do you think I am?'

'I don't mean physically punch her ears, Colin. I mean, don't assault her ears with too much verbal abuse.'

'What the fuck you on about?'

'Please don't swear at Theresa May, will you?'

''Course not. She's a lady, she's all right. It's you I swear at, Nick, until you do something!'

'That's why I've asked her to come here, Colin.'

'Well, we'll see about that, won't we, mate.'

Then, with perfect timing, the night before her visit, Colin was burgled again. It set us up for an interesting meeting with Theresa, which she took head-on, listening carefully to what he and other shopkeepers had to say. After all, she was in fact visiting a crime scene, which Colin was quick to capitalise on.

'One thing you could do for me, Home Secretary, please.'

A wary look crossed Theresa May's face, as she asked, 'What's that, Colin?'

'I've never seen as many police here as we have today. Can you leave some behind to clear up here and catch the buggers who did this?'

That visit left me perplexed further about Theresa and the relationship she engendered with colleagues. Her main purpose of the day had been achieved with her visit to shopkeepers and meeting with a knife crime campaigner, but I shall remember it more for her bizarre treatment of my colleague and neighbouring MP David Burrowes, who also accompanied me during her visit.

As we made our way back to her official car, she summoned David over and gave him a perfunctory and, I am afraid, public dressing-down.

'I don't appreciate the way you have treated my immigration minister, James Brokenshire.'

David was perplexed, and a little startled. He had been publicly urging the government to relent on its stance on the forced
deportation of a young girl back to Mauritius in the middle
of her A-levels. That the government were not prepared to
delay so she could complete her exams struck most people as
pretty obtuse, whatever the rights and wrongs of the decision
to deport her. David put up a strong case both privately and
publicly, trying to minimise the disruption to the young girl's
A-levels and introduce a level of common sense.

David's job, like any MP's, was to make his constituents' case,
and he did that robustly. Theresa felt her duty was to protect
her minister from public criticism, and that's why she publicly
rebuked David that morning, which was completely unnecessary. It's one thing being loyal to your minister, but it's blatantly
absurd to reprimand a colleague for doing his job. Some might
respect the fact that an ambitious Cabinet minister would not
worry about irritating MPs whose vote for leader she might
wish to secure one day. On the other hand, to do so in public,
and when it was utterly insensitive to the strength of local feeling, is just plain bonkers.

Ministers expect to get a bashing if an MP is standing up for
a constituent. It does not mean they will change their mind, but
equally, no one expects the MP, regardless of whether he is from
the same political party or not, not to create a fuss. No one, that
is, except Theresa.

By contrast, my dealings with her when the Home Office were
trying to reform the European Arrest Warrant were perfunctory and efficient. My constituent, a young man named Andrew
Symeou, had been banged up in a Greek jail for a trumped-
up charge that took over two years to come to court. He never
should have been extradited in the first place, as the evidence
was deeply flawed. Theresa recognised the failings and agreed

to try to redress them. Andrew was there because of the flagrant misuse of the European Arrest Warrant, which turned a young man's life into hell and put his parents and sister through an exhaustive, financially burdensome and emotionally draining fight for their son. That the European Arrest Warrant was misused to hold Andrew in jail and not bring him to trial was a disgrace. During my representation to Theresa and her ministers, she went some way to preventing such future abuse. The change she introduced was dubbed the Symeou clause.

But even with that high-profile issue in common it was remarkably hard to get to know Theresa and, as her taciturn Tea Room surgery showed, it is difficult to avoid concluding that she is uncomfortable with people she does not know. It is an odd characteristic for a Prime Minister. If the public want a PM who works bloody hard then Theresa is that person – in fact, she would have given Margaret Thatcher a run for her money when it came to work ethic. The role of Prime Minister, however, often demands more than that.

On the other hand, I could be misjudging her entirely; perhaps it was simply that she didn't think much of me and was getting on famously with everyone else. My level of influence remained well below average, and it was only the more sensational events that were confined to my constituency that drew her attention to Enfield. To many, I probably looked well connected, but looks in this case were very deceiving.

In contrast, Boris Johnson needed no excuse to visit Enfield. People were drawn to him, and I happily tagged along in the hope of some of his stardust rubbing off on me. He came to Enfield on at least ten occasions, and each time he was mobbed. Quite literally.

Our press, of course, were always hoping for a Boris-ism, where he might allow a local reporter to earn some extra cash by saying something they could syndicate to the nationals. He managed to avoid doing that, however, and so the *Enfield Advertiser* resorted to ridicule, which wouldn't earn the journalist any extra cash but would make them feel better.

In Boris's case, I had the job of escorting him to the Johnson Matthey plant in Brimsdown, Enfield, where precious metals worth huge sums of money are smelted. As a result, extremely vigilant security measures are taken when entering and leaving the site, including removing your shoes. I then discovered that Boris and I shared something very personal in common. We had socks with holes in them.

And, naturally, the *Enfield Advertiser* devoted several column inches to that fact alone. Still, at least the public got to see that I was close to Boris on a number of levels.

If visits were not enough to convince Enfieldians that they had elected a man of influence then there were other means to do just that. Statements in Parliament from other MPs, reminding my constituents of what a resourceful and committed chap I was, were easy to negotiate and it was standard fare for a minister to heap praise on a backbencher in his own party.

In fact, not to do so was regarded as pretty bad form.

But I could count on the fingers of one hand the number of constituents who watched a parliamentary debate or questions (with the exception of PMQs), and even fewer watched anything that I happened to be speaking in. While still in the grip of Marginal Agitation and Despair syndrome, in desperation, I produced video clips for my own website that, unsurprisingly, carried reasonably flattering edits of my efforts on behalf of Enfield North.

Looking back, I like to rationalise that having influence, or at least being seen to have influence, was important for my constituents. However, the evidence suggests otherwise. After all, I was inundated with visits, changed laws and met with the Prime

Minister every three months when secretary of the backbench 1922 Committee, but it mattered not one jot to my constituents. They either didn't notice or remained distinctly unimpressed, as demonstrated by their votes in 2015.

And they were right. It strikes me that all of this seemed less for their benefit and more to satisfy my own politician's ego and sense of worth. After all, I was in an institution in which it was extraordinarily hard to 'do something', so that elevated the importance of being 'seen to do something'. Quite a different proposition. Indeed, on those rare occasions something was achieved, the contrast could not have been sharper.

Sitting at the heart of my constituency office was, of course, Helen, about whom much has already been written. Not only did she and Leanne deliver extraordinary results for constituents in real need, but Helen herself was at the centre of one of the most significant moments during my time in Parliament, though it was a moment that truly had little to do with me, and all to do with Helen and her son Jack.

Rifleman Jack Otter was twenty when he lost both legs and an arm when the Taliban detonated a bomb while he was on patrol in Helmand Province in September 2009. It would be impossible for me to capture his story and do it any justice, but the improvised explosive device that changed his life was really only the beginning of a chain of events that is unimaginable for most people to comprehend.

At the time of writing, Jack has undergone more than thirty-five operations arising from complications following the initial surgery and efforts to save his life. He has faced many setbacks, as well as navigating considerable personal successes, each with the same stoic determination characteristic of our servicemen and women. Jack would not want me to dwell on that side of his life, so I won't.

Jack is remarkable in many ways, not least his strength of character, wit and charm. His mother, however, is at pains to point out that nobody should think he is, by any means, a saint.

'Oh, Jack bloody annoyed me today,' would be a familiar refrain on some mornings in the constituency office. 'I saw Jack yesterday, and can you believe what the silly buggers were doing?'

She was of course referring to Jack's fellow injured soldiers at the Armed Forces' medical rehabilitation centre at Headley Court.

'He was bloody well showing off his new electric wheelchair to his mates, and decides to tow one of them who's still in a normal chair around the building.'

Sounded reasonable to me.

'Then they end up in fits of laughter, because Jack hadn't mastered his new toy very well, resulting in his shoelace from his one "good" leg all tangled up in the mechanics of the brand-new electric wheelchair, which caused it to break down.'

'Honestly,' she finished, 'grown-up bloody kids, the lot of them.'

But when Helen sat me down to talk about the problems Jack and other amputees were facing over the quality of the prosthetic legs they were being fitted with, I was left in no doubt that this was serious.

For a young man to lose any limb must be hugely debilitating, even more so for an active young man as you would find in the army. The quality of the prosthetic replacement is crucial to achieving any satisfactory level of active life that a young man in his early twenties would want. The problem was that the government was not providing them with the best available, and the soldiers knew it.

Afghanistan was a combined mission with other NATO

allies, including, of course, the Americans, and it was from their American counterparts that our soldiers knew that far superior prosthetics were being given to US troops. They were known as Genium Bionic Prosthetic System legs, developed by Ottobock, a highly advanced prosthetic engineering company based in Germany. The challenge for the government was that the cost was roughly £80,000 for one leg.

To the soldiers and, I expect, most reasonable-minded people, the government's covenant with the armed forces was simple. The soldiers put their life at risk at your bidding; the government should fulfil their promise of providing the very best of care and recuperation.

That's how the soldiers saw it, and that's how I saw it after listening to Jack's story. The question was: what to do about it?

It was 2012, and I knew by now that I could do the usual things such as raise the issue in Parliament, challenge the ministers, the Prime Minister even, at Question Time and so on. I could go nuclear and involve the press if I had lame responses to those questions, but that was not something I was keen to do. Getting the papers involved could be very counterproductive with colleagues, putting the government on the defensive over such a sensitive issue. That, I calculated, would be a measure of last resort, not least because I felt we could achieve a good outcome through persuasion, so I dug in for a long campaign.

Which, remarkably, proved unnecessary, thanks to Jack and Helen.

'Let's put Jack in front of the Minister of State for Defence.'

'Hmmm.'

'Why not? Let them explain to a multiple amputee why he can't have the best replacement leg because of austerity.'

'I think we need to approach this from a friendly, constructive position, rather than all guns blazing from the start, don't you?'

I was treading on thin ice here. Helen was fed up with delay and obfuscation.

'Well, it's not as if they are unaware of the problem, and they have had plenty of time already to do something about it.'

'Absolutely. Why don't we ask for a meeting during Defence Questions?' I suggested. 'That way, it is pretty hard for the minister to say no.'

'Will you warn him about what you are going to ask before you ask the question?'

Still somewhat feisty, Helen was not convinced by my approach.

'Yes, I will.'

'What if he palms you off?'

'Then I shall ask the same question of the Prime Minister, and maybe we won't warn him.'

Somewhat mollified, Helen gave me the all-clear to proceed. That was 12 September 2012. The very next month, I was listed to ask a question of the Minister of Defence, Mark Francois. Hansard, the official parliamentary record, reflects it this way:

Nick de Bois (Enfield North) (Con):
Does the Minister share my concern that multiple amputee UK soldiers are not receiving the Genium X2 product, which is generally accredited as the best available in the prosthetics field and is used by the US? Will he agree to meet triple amputee Rifleman Jack Otter, who is my constituent, to understand the difficulties and worries that such people have?

Mr Francois:
I am familiar with the issue that my Honourable Friend raises. The Ministry of Defence has made considerable investments at Headley Court to provide a world-class service for those

with prosthetics. I was present when His Royal Highness the Prince of Wales opened the new £17 million Jubilee rehabilitation wing, which was paid for by the Ministry of Defence. The Secretary of State has recently announced a further £5 million of investment.

I am familiar with the case of my Honourable Friend's constituent, and will agree to meet him. However, I must enter the caveat that I am not qualified as a doctor, and that I will have to take clinical advice on what decision it would be best to take following the meeting.

Progress, but clearly, from his answer, he was not able to commit to use the Genium X2 products.

Helen was very cross with me.

'You didn't ask for him to meet a delegation.'

I hung my head and tried to charm my way out of it with the overused sad-puppy face.

'No, I didn't,' I confessed.

She was, rightly, having none of it.

'It's not fair for Jack to do this on his own. There would have been a huge impact on the minister and his officials if more than one injured soldier went to see him. You ducked that one, didn't you?'

To be fair, she wasn't exactly cross with me, but she clearly felt I had not lived entirely up to expectations.

I genuinely believed we would be better off with just Jack, not several colleagues. Naturally, I would join him, as would his mother. She was right that one person, Jack, would be centre stage, and a lot depended on how effective he could be in making the case on behalf of himself and his injured colleagues. But it would be more powerful for just that reason, rather than a group of colleagues all trying to give the same message.

And anyway, with Helen coming to the meeting, my main job would be to see that she, like me, kept quiet and let Jack do the talking. No easy task, as constituents, colleagues and I have learned over the years.

In April 2013, the three of us, Jack, Helen and I, met at the entrance to the imposing Ministry of Defence building on Whitehall. If the building was designed to intimidate, I must say it did rather a good job.

A huge, bustling foyer greeted us when we'd negotiated our way in past the inevitable security checks. Military personnel hovered all around us, intermingled with civil servants all charging around across the marble floors sweeping the entire length of the building. We were promptly met by an aide of the minister's and whisked upstairs to the relative calm of the ministerial floor. We were asked to wait in the anteroom to his office, which presented me with my most important task of the day.

'Helen,' I ventured, 'you know I do as I'm told, most of the time?'

'Most of the time… why?' she asked suspiciously.

'I just want to stress how important it is that Jack does the talking. I will say a few brief words of introduction, but then it's up to him. Can you do that?'

'Do what?' she asked.

'Shut up throughout the meeting?'

I could see that Helen was chewing over precisely how to respond to such an audacious, and frankly near impossible, challenge.

She was about to speak when Jack laughed.

'Oh, shut up Jack,' she said. 'Don't you start.'

But that did the trick. Jack had laid down the gauntlet, and Helen was going to prove him wrong.

'Fine,' she said.

The deal made, we were shown promptly into the minister's office.

Mark rose from behind his desk, oblivious to the negotiations that had just taken place, and welcomed Jack and Helen to his office as I made the introductions. He, in turn, introduced a flank of senior military brass, including the top military medical man and the head of Headley Court. No pressure on Jack, then.

'I am very sorry,' Mark began, 'but we have a probable vote coming up, so I may have to leave this meeting, as Nick will appreciate.'

Bugger – that I did not know. This only fuelled the demands on Jack to make his case, and the need for Helen to honour her pledge and remain uncharacteristically quiet. This was Jack's show, and it was entirely conceivable that he may only have ten minutes to make his point.

And off he went.

Jack set out why the Genium prosthetic leg mattered, and why it was vastly superior to the current models used by the army.

It comes down to this, Minister.

Geniums can sense different surfaces, because they have adaptive stability, which means I can actually stand still. With the current prosthetics we have, I have to keep moving to ensure I am stable and don't fall over.

The Genium is the nearest thing to 'real legs', because they have microprocessor knees and ankles, which are programmed specifically for me by computer.

This means, with adaptive swing, I can step back, sideways, and I could even run. That's just not possible with the old ones, and will make a profound difference to my quality of life.

And that is just a summary of what Jack said.

As Mark started to ask questions and dig deeper into the subject, I could sense his understanding and enthusiasm for the idea was gaining ground. Here, in front of him, was a real person, with real experience, who was plainly and simply making the case for how the government could make a huge difference to the lives of critically injured soldiers. There was no obvious emotional play by Jack on his own circumstances; he was simply a soldier, making a case to some of the most senior men in the forces, and there was not a creased brow in the room. They were spellbound by his concise, articulate presentation, underpinned by the fact that a triple amputee was sitting in front of them, having given his all for his country, making an unimpeachable request.

'Minister, sorry to interrupt, but there is a vote in the House now,' said an aide who entered the room.

I held my breath. From where I sat alongside Helen, like two naughty children squashed on a sofa in a corner, I was praying she would not be tempted to say anything at this point to break the mood and, likewise, that the military bigwigs across the room would not seize the opportunity to close the meeting.

'Thank you, but never mind, I will miss it,' replied Mark.

I breathed a silent prayer of thanks, and saw Helen give the glimmer of a smile. She knew how well this was going, and that my fears were groundless.

Mark Francois had been a whip before becoming Minister of State at the Ministry of Defence, and his decision not to vote spoke volumes about his level of interest in Jack's case.

As the meeting concluded, it was clear that Jack had made his point very effectively, but it was not until his summing up that he landed his most powerful point. Jack said that he didn't regret joining the army and he wasn't bitter about what had happened to him, but he and his colleagues did expect the government to look after them for the rest of their lives.

No one in the room was going to argue with that.

Mark insisted on accompanying us all the way back to the entrance when we left. True, we did not have a commitment at that stage, but I was very optimistic. And rightly so. Within a few months, the armed forces started to use the new prosthetics following new funding from the government.

I always believed that the government would have introduced the Genium product at some point, but I am also convinced that injured service personnel would have been waiting far longer had it not been for Helen lobbying her boss, who in turn lobbied the minister. If this was indeed a case of 'It's not what you know, it's who you know that matters' then that is fine by me.

Jack did the rest, and the minister, Mark Francois, delivered. Indeed, he spoke to Jack about attending the press conference, and underlined the point himself, making it clear that his meeting with Jack had clinched the decision to fund the new prosthetic legs.

In this case, 'Who you know' mattered, but the 'What you know' that Jack delivered was some of the most powerful evidence I have ever heard, and this was all down to him.

My biggest contribution to this achievement was keeping his mother Helen quiet throughout the meeting, so that Jack could do his bit.

Job done.

18

ONLY AS GOOD AS THE COMPANY I KEEP?

When I was six, I wanted to be a long-distance lorry driver. When I was fifty-six and turfed out of the House of Commons, I wanted to be a tour guide for the same place.

Whether it was describing the assassination of a Prime Minister (in somewhat embellished and theatrical terms, I admit) or explaining the power of the voting lobby and why we should defend the antiquated but highly effective system rather than submit to the digital age, I loved doing personal tours of the Palace of Westminster for constituents.

Whatever you may think about the politicians who work in Parliament, the fact is it is one of the most historic buildings on the planet, and one that has not just seen great moments in history played out on its remarkable stage, going back over many centuries, but has also been the setting for many personal dramas, such as the resignation speech of the Secretary of State for War in 1963, Jack Profumo, who resigned after a sexual relationship with the nineteen-year-old model Christine Keeler, who in turn was sleeping with a Russian spy. Profumo had lied to the House of Commons about his relationship, a unforgivable misdemeanour and one that seemed to crystallise the problems of the then Conservative government. Having already suffered the loss of one Prime Minister months earlier, the government was soon to lose the next general election. The Profumo affair, as it became known, was captured in the 1989 film *Scandal*. More recently, of course, great speeches have brought down great leaders, as did the resignation speech of Geoffrey Howe, one-time Chancellor and Foreign Secretary to Margaret Thatcher. His withering attack on her leadership style at yet another time when the Conservative Party was engulfed in a crisis over its relationship with the EU, led to a challenge to her leadership and her eventual resignation.

The toppling of the Prime Minister began from the floor of the House of Commons, and for political enthusiasts such drama is enthralling, more so because Margaret Thatcher had to sit and listen to the damaging speech from her seat in the Commons as it was delivered by her bitter former Cabinet colleague. Gripping stuff, or at least for me it was, which is perhaps why I always did the tours of Parliament personally if time permitted. I am convinced that I could eke out a living after Parliament as a Palace of Westminster guide.

There is so much to tell and so much to learn.

We have, in fact, only had one Prime Minister ever assassinated, and it took place in the lobby of the House of Commons, when it was situated in the present-day St Stephen's Hall.

Spencer Perceval was a decent enough chap, now best remembered for the fact that he is the only British Prime Minister ever to be assassinated. He was promptly despatched to a greater place because a grumpy citizen, John Bellingham, who thought the Prime Minister had not done enough to release him from prison in Russia, decided to sit out the afternoon in the lobby of the Commons and fire the fatal bullet when the Prime Minister turned up to a debate in the chamber.

Despite the high drama of the event, and the loss of what most contemporaries considered to be a man of great talent, Spencer Perceval was not given a state funeral.

Unlike for the US Presidents John F. Kennedy or Abraham Lincoln, there is no memorial of any national significance. Even in death, we Brits expect most of our politicians to just go quietly, without much fuss.

This struck me as surprising, since one of the first things I learned as an MP is that if you die in the House of Commons you are entitled to a state funeral. I liked that idea, should it ever come to pass.

Sadly, any such visions of grandeur and legacy were swiftly dealt with when it was pointed out that, to avoid the expense of a state funeral, an MP's untimely passing would always be recorded as happening at the nearby St Thomas's Hospital, not in the Palace of Westminster. No one, it seems, is allowed to die in the House of Commons, thanks to austerity.

See how badly MPs are treated – we even have to lie about our own death.

On digging deeper into the subject, there appears to be little evidence to support any of this anecdote, although it has gained sufficient credence across the parliamentary estate to be considered true. I must confess to being very disappointed that, in the event of an untimely death, I could not have one last splurge of taxpayer money by being wheeled from my birthplace in Ely, down the A10, through Enfield, and on to Westminster Hall for a grand lying in state. Nothing IPSA could do about those expenses, I thought.

True, I think the turnout to pay respects would be quite unimpressive, but I reckon I would have increased my Twitter following because of the event, albeit a little late to fully appreciate the fact.

But back to reality, and the tours. We do have a far more credible wealth of history captured in the beautiful but, it should be noted, rather bland setting of Westminster Hall. This palace was once an indoor tennis court for Henry VIII. It was also the setting for the law courts during the age of Samuel Pepys (where a very questionable level of justice was handed down by today's standards). In more modern times, we have seen great figures of history who did receive the honour of a state funeral lying in state, including wartime leader Sir Winston Churchill and every senior member of the royal family.

The Palace of Westminster embraces Big Ben at one end and the Parliamentary National Archives at the other and, sandwiched between them, the House of Lords, the House of Commons and, of course, Westminster Hall. It is an astonishing national building, maintained by the people, and should always be open to the people. I did my bit by hosting tours whenever I could, which threw up some interesting and entirely unexpected encounters.

The Hatton Garden robbery is still fresh in our minds, and two films have already been made to keep the 'Diamond Wheezers' (average age sixty-five) held in curious, if not quite affectionate, regard by many, with the exception, I imagine, of their victims. For me, however, I can speak with some personal knowledge of one of the thieves, Hugh Doyle, a local constituent and member of the Hatton Garden gang. Three members of the gang were in fact from Enfield. Another dubious first for my constituency.

Hugh Doyle was not party to the planning of the burglary and never went to Hatton Garden, but was contacted by one of the gang when they needed somewhere to exchange the stolen loot. He offered up his workshop, and ended up rightly being prosecuted. On conviction, he had a suspended jail sentence handed down by the judge.

Long before these events, Hugh came to see me in his capacity as a plumber running a successful small business. He was outraged about a scam to defraud the taxpayer by what he believed was an abuse of a free boiler fitting scheme run by the government called the 'Green Deal Improvement Fund'. He displayed an extraordinary passion for the subject and, after I was satisfied he stood to make no commercial gain from pressing the matter, we began work on the issue. We spent days going through his evidence, preparing parliamentary questions and building a case that would stand the test of examination.

In the meantime, he had joined my local constituency's Businessmen's Club, which was essentially a lunchtime dining group of small to medium-sized businesses, where we would do question-and-answer sessions with a variety of speakers from the party along with myself. He faithfully coughed up his membership fee, which went to supporting local campaigning and paying for the lunch. A touch ironic, of course, that he was in effect supporting the campaign for an MP who happened to be a member of the Justice Select Committee and a believer in more robust sentencing from the courts. Hugh, it seemed, focused more on the self-help and enterprise side of Conservative politics.

Hugh ran a successful small business, which he was very good at, and, as with all small enterprises, his was one of many I tried to support whenever I could. With that in mind, when he insisted I took part in his company's free monthly draw, where he was himself giving away a free boiler upgrade to the lucky winner, I was asked to draw the winning ticket. It remains amongst my MP memorabilia, the photograph of me outside Enfield Library with my arm draped around Hugh Doyle, drawing that ticket. That was in March 2015, just before the notorious robbery took place.

Hugh's enthusiasm and support did not stop there. He was also generously buying raffle tickets – all, I might add, before he had any proceeds from the heist of the century. The more you bought, the more chance you would win, and that's precisely what happened with Hugh when he won a tour of the House of Commons with me and a friend or partner. He also went to extraordinary trouble to see if he could bring his eight-year-old son with him, which, of course, I was thrilled to encourage. The more young people who take an interest in where our laws are made, the better.

With this tour came an offer for me to host them for tea and cakes on the terrace of the House of Commons, which I was thrilled to do. Hugh's young son turned up in a very smart jacket and bow tie, along with Hugh and his partner.

I could not have imagined that this very respectable, enthusiastic and, from what I could tell, very hard-working individual could soon become involved in the biggest diamond theft on record, and that the goods would be exchanged only half a mile from our local party HQ in Enfield. At the time, I had shown Hugh and his guests some of the most valuable and treasured items held within the Palace of Westminster, including the Sovereign's Throne in the House of Lords, which, I am sure, could have been reached by drilling underground. Hugh might know more about that than me.

So, in summary: my local party took cash off him, showed him around Parliament and hosted him on the terrace of the House of Commons just weeks before he took part in the notorious Hatton Garden robbery. You couldn't make it up. The plumber, the MP and a £15 million jewellery heist. What would *The Sun* have tried to do with that!

'MP sinks to new low in cash for tea scandal'.

But is there much to choose between a member of a jewellery

heist gang and a former mobster lawyer turned Mayor of Las Vegas?

A year into my life as an MP, I formed the All Party Parliamentary Group for the UK Events Industry, which is the sector I worked in before coming to Parliament. It is also an industry that, at the time, had difficulty in being heard in government, hence the formation of an all-party group. As the chairman, I drew the attention of other international cities that promote the hosting of conferences, which is why Oscar Goodman, three times Mayor of Las Vegas, and his wife, the current Mayor of Las Vegas, wanted to meet with me at the House of Commons.

It also seemed a very fitting way to celebrate the halfway point of this first parliament. We might not physically have had a party, but we had the spirit of the biggest party city in the world with us, at least, and they wanted to take me and my staff to the very nice Roux at Parliament Square restaurant. My staff, naturally, insisted I accept the invitation.

Las Vegas is well known for gambling and shows, but it is also one of the most successful destinations for conferences, run by businesses and trade associations from around the world. It has done well to escape its shady and ugly past of being run by organised crime syndicates, with contracted killings, drugs and tax avoidance. This era was brilliantly captured in the 1995 Martin Scorsese film *Casino*.

What I didn't know until five minutes before I met Oscar and his wife was that he played a cameo role in the film as himself, the mob lawyer.

In fact, as my researcher, Jack Hart, was whispering in my ear as we waited in Westminster Hall for the delegation from Las Vegas to arrive, Oscar had defended some of the most notorious (alleged) leading figures from the mob scene in Las Vegas. Remarkably, and perhaps only in Vegas, Goodman was then elected mayor of the city in June 1999, receiving 64 per cent of the vote. He went on to be re-elected three times, the maximum permitted for any mayor under city law. He increased his vote share to 85 per cent.

That's a record I envy.

He then made the most spectacular entrance into Westminster Hall I have seen that did not include royalty. In many respects, he and his wife Carolyn were second only to royalty at home, but on this day, they both arrived through the magnificent entrance to Westminster Hall flanked by three stunning Las Vegas showgirls in full show outfits. I, along with about fifty other people who were in the Hall at the time, watched them proceed with a touch of star quality across the historic stone floor of Westminster Hall. Henry VIII himself would have stopped playing tennis to witness such an entrance. He might even have tried to marry one of them, judging by his record.

Their brightly coloured, glamorous outfits, proudly showing off the brand of Las Vegas with considerable effect, lit up what is, after all, the rather drab, dull grey interior of Westminster Hall. I shook Carolyn's hand, then Oscar's, and then, with considerable self-consciousness, gave a welcome kiss to the three ladies, Portia, Jennifer and Mercedes.

Rarely have I glimpsed so many camera flashes going off. I apologise for ruining the photos that excited male staffers were trying to take of the showgirls that day.

During what was one of the most enjoyable tours of Parliament, peppered with a vast number of questions from my very enthusiastic guests, I couldn't help reminding myself that I was in the company of someone who knew far more about criminal behaviour than I could ever expect to know from sitting on the Justice Select Committee. Equally, I kept seeing images of

Marlon Brando, Robert De Niro, and a horse's head in my bed if I annoyed the guy.

Over lunch, while my young staffers made complete fools of themselves trying to impress the Vegas showgirls, I tucked into a conversation with Oscar about crime. He could not believe how tolerant we had been on knife crime, and enthusiastically embraced our ideas of automatic jail sentences for the possession of knives. I asked him what he thought about the government's 'war on drugs'.

'War on drugs?'

'Yes. Can we ever defeat the scourge of drugs?'

He leaned over and held his face very close to mine. If this had been in a bar in Vegas, I would have felt a cold chill go down my spine. Instead, I spilt my wine over him as I leaned forward to listen.

'Bugger. Sorry.'

Something of a Hugh Grant moment, from a less threatening Mafia-based movie called *Mickey Blue Eyes*. There was a red stain spreading over the tablecloth. At least it was wine and nothing more sinister.

With immense good grace, he barely mentioned it, and then leaned in to speak to me again.

'Legalise them.'

'What, marijuana?'

'Legalise them, all of them. Control the supply, pull the rug from the criminals, control them.'

I guess if anyone is qualified to advise governments on drug policy, he is.

I don't think this last visit entirely reflects the character of the first half of my tenure in Parliament, but marking the occasion with a visit from a former mob lawyer turned highly successful politician seemed appropriate nevertheless. He was different.

He was candid, radical and came from the most unlikely background to succeed in politics. I think there is something to be learned from that, even if, to some, it was a very unparliamentary way of marking my halfway point in this, my first and only parliament.

19

PLAIN STUPID

Speaking of drugs.

'What do you think of the plain packaging of cigarette cartons to reduce smoking?'

'Codswallop. Why, are the silly buggers going to introduce it?'

My staffer James Roberts, an arch-libertarian, was showing an unhealthy interest in the subject and clearly wanted to prompt me into action.

'Looks like it. And it's crying out for someone to knock it on the head.'

'We will lose.'

'It's better to try than to do nothing.'

'So, you want me to align myself with big tobacco companies just before an election and try to overturn something that most people will agree with?'

'I thought you had principles.'

'We are eighteen months from an election. There is only one principle: don't piss off your voters.'

'You know it's a daft policy. You should at least go on record, if nothing else, to shame the Department of Health and warn the Treasury that they are about to lose huge chunks of tax revenue.'

Hmmm.

'Or, I could just do nothing controversial for the next eighteen months and nurse the constituency?'

Now, that might sound like we just made up policy issues on the back of a fag packet, but, in fairness, that brief conversation did sum up my feelings at the time. The policy, I thought, was daft, but why take on a fight I would lose, one that would earn hardly any support across the constituency in the run-up to an election? Why not just put a sock in it, stay low and nurse the home patch to help me secure re-election?

Everything pointed to doing just that.

I was going through a rather dull period in the Commons, as not a lot was happening. Knife crime legislation was pretty much sorted, and there was hardly any legislation of interest going through the House of Commons because the coalition could find nothing to agree on. Things were ticking along, but there was nothing remotely exciting happening. It was the perfect time to stay out of Westminster and spend more time in Enfield.

It's also quite easy to set your own pace in the Commons and quietly sink into a period of oblivion if that's what strikes one's fancy. I needed only to make a few appearances in the chamber itself, asking minimal oral questions but submitting endless written ones, to keep my Hansard record above average.

Attending votes, of course, was imperative, but there was no need to sit for four or five hours in the chamber beforehand just to make a contribution of no great significance. Time could be better spent in the constituency, drumming up a few votes. All I had to do then was make sure I avoided meetings and invitations to speak outside the constituency. No one will notice and no one will mind.

'Terribly sorry, Mr de Bois's diary is full for the next six months, including many constituency engagements that he just cannot move.'

Who, really, is going to question that?

'A complex constituency case means he is unable to be on your panel that night, and I'm sure you understand that his constituents must come first.'

Impossible to challenge.

And if I wanted to remain completely off the radar for a while, I only had to avoid saying anything remotely controversial.

Like, 'If this government is stupid enough to waste time on plain packaging of cigarette cartons, I will fight it all the way.' Which is precisely what I told *The Sun* newspaper, who also thought plain packaging was bloody stupid.

The point is, if you want to have a quiet time, you can. If you are like me, though – and it seems I am genetically engineered to make it impossible to avoid taking on issues, however hopeless they may be – then life is rarely quiet and certainly not dull.

Now is not the time to rehearse the arguments on whether plain packaging is a good thing or not. The legislation has passed, the policy is in place. Time will tell if it has any impact.

Back then, when it was being lobbied for, and it looked like the government was thinking of caving in, there was no evidence to support the case, and I was instinctively unconvinced of the merits of the plan.

Yet what could I reasonably expect to achieve on a subject that would, through a sheer gut emotional reaction, have the overwhelming support of most of the public (including my constituents) and the tacit support of most MPs? Faced with these overwhelming odds, why on earth would I lead the opposition to this proposal and, by doing so, be seen to align myself with big tobacco firms? Ultimately, wasn't I just wasting everyone's time? I was going to lose, so surely I should not get involved?

Of course I bloody should. Otherwise, what's the point of Parliament as we know it? Why should any government be able to unquestioningly rely on a democratically elected chamber to rubber-stamp their plans, be they good or bonkers?

That's what they do in North Korea, and I was reasonably confident that in Enfield North they expected a little more from their MP, whom they had elected to the genuinely democratic House of Commons rather than the Supreme People's Assembly of the Democratic People's Republic of Korea.

All right, I exaggerate a bit, but you get the point.

Being awkward, and even being the odd one out, is a strength, not a weakness, for our democracy. Although, I must confess, it didn't always seem like that, particularly when I tried to rally support for the issue.

First, though, I needed to do my homework; if I was going to lead a charge on opposing this measure, I would at least need to have some facts to back me up. So, where else should I turn but to my constituency?

The key objections to plain packaging were that counterfeit cigarettes would be easier to sell, and that illegally imported, untaxed cigarettes would increase at a faster rate, costing us, the British taxpayer, a large chunk of income because of these so-called 'illicit whites'.

I was, I confess, inundated with written evidence supporting these points from big tobacco companies keen to furnish any data to make the case against plain packaging.

Now, again, I am sure anti-smoking campaigners will be tempted to reach for their Twitter accounts and trash me as being a lapdog of British American Tobacco, Imperial, Philip Morris International and so on. Well, to be clear, as an MP, I was assiduous in making sure I never accepted so much as a coffee from them. As tempting as it may have been to solicit the odd jolly to Monaco, say, for the Grand Prix, or the tennis, that was neither on offer nor asked for. I was doing this for lots of reasons, but a free dinner and tennis match were not amongst them. Anyway, I don't like the game very much.

What's more, reported data was all very well, but I wanted to see things for myself.

'So, how widespread is the selling of fake cigarettes, and how do they sell them, and to whom?'

'Well, for example, 114 million counterfeit cigarettes were sold across south London last year,' claimed a tobacco company representative with whom I was speaking.

'Seriously? Who says so?'

'The councils of Southwark, Bexley, Bromley, Greenwich and Lewisham.'

'Not you, then?'

'No. And there is more data from more councils.'

'Jeez. And why is it so dangerous, as you claim?'

'Because counterfeit cigarettes are more toxic than ordinary cigarettes. More tar, more arsenic, more lead, more nicotine.'

Eww… arsenic? I was recalling all the cigarettes I had smoked between the ages of fifteen and thirty-five, and feeling quite ill. Yes, arsenic is in the legitimate fags as well.

'Frankly, they even found dried faeces in some of the packs.'

'What?'

'Dried dog shit.'

'I know what it is, I just didn't know where it was found!'

Too much information.

'But have you any packs to show me?'

'We can do better than that.'

And that's how I found myself going undercover with a team of private investigators to buy illegal cigarettes. I am hoping there is a statute of limitations on any prosecution for doing this.

The morning in question arrived, which I had been eagerly anticipating and planning for. First, I dressed down to what I thought an undercover investigator should look like. An old pair of jeans, a tatty worn sweater, unpolished boots and un-combed hair all formed part of my disguise. In fact, so ignorant was I of this practice, it seemed I had assumed that what most respectable people wear to do the gardening was the perfect gear for undercover work. Second, I practised in front of the bathroom mirror my shifty, dodgy look. Narrow the eyes and look down. Easy stuff for an MP.

Too much imagination and a poor diet of bad spy films meant that I completely missed the point about who was buying these illegal cigarettes: schoolchildren in uniform, manual workers, office workers and more. Ordinary folk, not the shifty, badly dressed down-and-outs I had somehow convinced myself were most at risk from these illegal sales. Pretty much everyone, it seems, is buying either counterfeit or non-duty-paid cigarettes in our pubs, our shops and online.

I could have worn whatever I liked, without all the theatrics. Still, the other three members of the professional investigation team were polite enough not to laugh at my efforts when we met in the Tesco car park on Southbury Road in my constituency.

'Right,' I said. 'Where are we going today?'

'Not far. In fact, we are staying in your constituency.'

'Really? There's no need for that. This can be London-wide as far as I am concerned.'

'Oh definitely, sir, but the borough of Enfield is one of the most lucrative areas for counterfeit and non-duty-paid cigarettes.'

'Oh.'

Another disappointing first for Enfield.

Our first purchase was at a block of flats. We parked up across from the entrance in our white transit van, having made the call an hour before. The team showed me the adverts on the net. We could pick up a carton of legit Marlboros for £5 a pack, instead of the UK retail price of £9. These had been brought in illegally from Poland, where they presently sell for about £3.15. They are the genuine product, just smuggled into the UK.

Our operative jumped out of the van at the arranged time and stood by the door to the tower block. As quick as a flash, the door opened and a hand slid out, grabbed his money and pushed the carton of ten-packs into our man's hand. I never saw the face behind the door.

This is going on every day across the country, costing the taxpayer about £2 billion a year. With plain packaging, identification of the cigarette brand would become meaningless and smuggling become even more attractive to brand-conscious smokers, the young in particular.

More worrying, though, is that the more dangerous 'illicit whites' would be easier to sell in plain packaging. For the brand-conscious, counterfeit cigarettes in packaging that closely mimics the brand of well-established cigarette products will almost certainly flourish. That will threaten the health of smokers even more than normal cigarettes.

So, next time you are outside a café, pick up the packets of empty cigarettes on the floor and you will find that a high proportion are likely counterfeit. Of those that are genuine, more will be non-tax-paid brands. That's not just our tax pounds being robbed from us, but increased health dangers to our smokers.

Which was precisely the point made by the investigation team as we continued our undercover work. By mid-afternoon, I was getting into my stride. We had just purchased some fake Marlboro Golds in a shop on Ordnance Road, after a lengthy exchange with the man behind the counter, who was clearly suspicious of us. He kept saying he could not understand what we wanted, but the team had watched him sell from his back office to other people the day before, so we were definitely on to something. Finally, he produced the goods and we purchased a couple of packs. The undercover team left.

I returned to the shop, irritated with the shopkeeper, because minutes later I had seen some youngsters go into the place and come away clutching cigarettes. I had no idea whether they were dodgy or not, but I wanted another word with him anyway.

'Hello, sir, you forget something?'

I gave him my card.

'Yes. I forgot to ask you why you are selling illegal cigarettes from this shop. I am the MP for this area and I would like an explanation, please.'

'No, sir, not here. We have cigarettes, you can buy,' as he waved at the range of legal tobacco products behind him.

'You just sold my friend two packets of illegal cigarettes, didn't you?'

'No, sir. They are not mine.'

A blatant lie.

He then lapsed into the old 'Sorry, my English is no good' routine and tried to wave me away.

'Boss not here. Boss not here.'

It was a pointless exercise. I admit, I was powerless to do anything there and then, but at least I had the satisfaction of reporting him to Trading Standards.

'Next stop, chaps?'

'Hertford Road, sir.'

'Right. Ready when you are.'

'Well, you might not want to go to this one. He sells quite a few and we spent an hour watching him yesterday.'

'That's awful. Of course I want to see him in action myself.'

'That might be difficult, as he will probably recognise you. His shop is right next door to your constituency office.'

'Seriously?'

'He is one of the biggest suppliers.'

Now I know why the bugger keeps trying to give me my Diet Coke and wine gums for free!

After this brief journey of discovery into the world of undercover operations, two things emerged. One, I was convinced I could not have followed my father into the undercover intelligence work he so skilfully did. Two, I was much more confident about making the case to ministers and Parliament about the downsides of their proposed plain packaging policy. That was, assuming I could get to speak to anyone, or rally enough parliamentary support to show that there was indeed some momentum behind my proposed rebellion.

Where better to start, I thought, than with my colleagues on the backbench 1922 Committee.

Sure enough, I found sufficient support at the officer meetings, principally because the proposal was seen as an unnecessary and as yet unevidenced intervention in a marketplace, which reeked of gesture politics and nanny state government.

With his usual courteous and diplomatic style, Graham Brady, the distinguished chair of the 1922 Committee, even raised the matter with the Prime Minister, whose response gave me no encouragement whatsoever as he sought to play down concerns that his government would bring in plain packaging, saying that it wasn't 'presently' an issue.

Loosely interpreted, this meant it was on the cards that the Prime Minister would allow the legislation to go through. I was well and truly shafted, it seemed.

Despite misgivings about the issue, not least the time being devoted to it, my colleagues generally felt it was not an issue worth going to war on. Even with the support of *The Sun*, I was not on to a winner here. I did enjoy the robust support of a couple of colleagues, Philip Davies and Sir Gerald Howarth, but the signs of a defeat were all too clear.

The question was: would I go out with a glorious bang or a pathetic whimper?

The Department of Health came to my rescue. Having failed to engage with me on the subject, they clearly felt that if the policy was introduced as legislation on the floor of the House in a conventional manner, it would be open to debate and questions from all MPs. They believed they would get substantive flak from Conservatives, even though they would likely have their votes in support of the measure.

So, in a sneaky but, to be fair, rather clever move, they had a very junior minister announce it in what's known as an adjournment debate, held at the end of a full parliamentary day but after all the formal business has ended and MPs have gone home. The only remaining MPs are the Member who has 'won' the right to speak in the adjournment debate of their choice, the minister who must reply and, if you are lucky, a mate might hang around to sit near the proposer in a looser version of the doughnut.

In this case, a Labour MP had won the right to a debate on plain packaging, ready to accuse the government of doing nothing, so the government decided, shamefully, to announce their intention to introduce the policy in response to the Labour motion. I had been tipped off about this a few hours earlier, and went to the debate, so there were five of us in the chamber plus the Deputy Speaker in the chair. These debates are limited to thirty minutes. Convention dictates that only the proposer speaks and the minister replies. Interventions from MPs are rare and frowned upon. It is also highly irregular to announce government policy on a controversial issue in an adjournment debate, as it means that MPs cannot question it at the time.

When it became clear that the junior minister was announcing the policy, Sir George Young was in the chamber, ready to praise the government. So, when he asked to intervene (to do so, the minister speaking at the time must agree to let you intervene), he was duly granted permission and gushed forth in praise of the policy. Not unreasonably, I tried to intervene with a counter view, but was not invited to do so by the junior minister.

I tried again.

She still said no.

I tried again and promptly got told off by the elegant and very headmistress-like Deputy Speaker, Eleanor Laing. I duly sat down, and grumbled to myself about freedom of speech or some such nonsense.

I had been successfully outmanoeuvred by a very dodgy tactic, but it was satisfying to know that the government clearly feared problems on the floor of the House and knew that they could not answer all the questions that challenged their plans, hence the decision to announce the policy in an adjournment debate. At least the Health Secretary had the good grace to apologise at the next 1922 Committee full meeting for the way the legislation had been introduced.

Ultimately, the Bill was brought into law through a technique called secondary legislation, permitted because an earlier vote, many months before, had allowed the government to do this. Secondary legislation is introduced through a Bill Committee, and time-limited to a debate of approximately ninety minutes. The junior minister still failed to answer the questions put to her on estimates on tax losses, cross-government support, health implications of increase in 'illicit whites' etc. etc.

But so what. They won. And in Parliament, winning the vote is what counts for the government.

Winning the argument is a subjective verdict often delivered by the losers to each other, but it was one I clung onto regardless.

de Bois 0, government 1.

20

BACK OR FRONT, SIR?

Just over halfway through my term!

Like most mid-term MPs, I was confronted by a sudden attack of 'What have I achieved?', which, fuelled by the ever-present MAD (in case you forgot, Marginal Agitation and Despair syndrome), meant a bout of self-doubt. Massive self-doubt.

What could I point to that would help motivate my constituents to re-elect me?

Knife crime sentencing?

Maybe, but that was ages ago.

Ten Minute Rule Bill?

Hardly anyone had noticed, despite all those bloody press releases.

Secretary of the backbench 1922 Committee, the trade union, if you like, of Conservative backbenchers?

Not a chance. Who even understood what the hell the 1922 Committee was?

I should have been a minister. People notice that. That makes people think you are useful, I bet.

We were halfway through the parliament. It was not too late. I could let the whips know I was keen to be considered for a ministerial job after all, promise to behave impeccably, speak on command and never miss a vote. Then I could at least point to something, and maybe even do something?

That is not precisely the conversation I was having with myself, and neither did it take place all at once. But it had been playing on my mind. Maybe, I reflected, I should see if it might be more productive seeking out ministerial office.

At least, that was the case until matters were taken out of my hands.

'Nick... how are you, dear fellow? We don't talk enough.'

'Very good and it's good to hear from you. What can I do for you?'

It was another MP on the phone, who at the time was one of several advisors to David Cameron.

He would possibly be described as 'avuncular' by some, in that he always appeared to have your best interests at heart in a genial, family fashion. Your friendly uncle, indeed. With a strong commitment to sartorial elegance. I was once in a radio interview when he was described by Paul Ross on talkRADIO as a 'dandy' because of his attention to his wardrobe, a job made harder by the fact that he was not very tall.

Often at the despatch box in the House of Commons, what he lacked in stature he made up for in wit and charm. I always, however, felt the urge to grab him by the feet and head, and stretch him out from within his snugly fit suit to add a few inches. Irrational, I know, but better than stretching his neck.

'You are listed as Question No. 1 to the Prime Minister on Wednesday and, traditionally, this is always a soft-ball, support-ive question.'

'I know, and I guess you have seen my note to the PM's private office about my question on Chase Farm hospital and the death of a young boy. I think, on this occasion, it's right that I raise the issue with the Prime Minister. It is just unfortunate it is listed as the first question.'

Sadly, some parents had taken their sick child to Chase Farm in the mistaken belief there was still an A&E unit there. Although they were seen by a doctor, tragically, there was nothing that could be done to save the little boy. Notwithstanding my opposition to the changes at Chase Farm, I believed it was vital that NHS London increased their communications with the public so that people, particularly at a time of intense emotional stress with a sick family member needing urgent care, knew where they could go for the most appropriate help. That was the point of my planned question.

'Nick, this is quite a tricky one for the Prime Minister to respond to as a first question, and we wonder if you could be a little more helpful. Obviously, I can fix it for you to see the Prime Minister privately on this issue, another time.'

'Look, there here is huge public interest in this, as well as the family wanting lessons to be learned from their loss. I am going to ask the question.'

'Righto. I just thought I would check with you.'

'Thanks.'

It's odd, really. Even though the public believe, as backbench MPs, that we enjoy unparalleled access to the Prime Minister and his senior colleagues, the truth was dawning on me that this access is often limited to when you pose a threat to the cosy status quo. It seems then that taking time out to listen to you is never a problem.

One hour later, phone call no. 2.

'Nick, have you a few minutes to discuss PMQs again?'

'Of course.'

'Have you had time to consider what you are going to do? I have assured the PM that we can work something out.'

You probably have, I thought to myself, but I bet he doesn't know the detail and wouldn't worry at all about answering it if he did know.

'Well,' I continued, 'I don't think we can work anything out. And, to be fair, the Prime Minister will understand and will deal with it very well, I am sure.'

'Fair enough.'

Pause.

'On another subject, Nick, you came up with a brilliant idea a year ago on the appointment of trade envoys and, as you know, the Prime Minister has already made several appointments.'

'I know. I was a little surprised I was not asked to undertake one of the roles, given I had worked up the whole idea for him and presented it in person.'

That was an understatement. I was mightily pissed off about it.

'Well, we can do something about that now, I think.'

That struck me as ultra-convenient.

'This Friday, we are about to make a second round of appointments, and you are top of the list.'

'That's great news. I am delighted to hear it.'

'It is, yes. But, obviously, this could be a little awkward if you have a difficult exchange with the Prime Minister.'

No shit. This really did happen. Bribery, patronage... maybe I should hold out for a Cabinet post. I was, I have to confess, rather taken aback that a question I was convinced the Prime Minister would both understand and deal with respectfully was leading to a covert job offer.

'Can you clarify what you mean, old chap?'

'Oh, I don't want you to mistake this conversation in any way. Obviously the two things are not linked.'

Amazing. That had never crossed my mind.

'I think we can settle this right here and now,' I concluded.

'Wonderful. I knew we could reach agreement.'

'You can offer me the post of Foreign fucking Secretary, but I am asking the bloody question.'

And that's precisely what I did. Ask the question, that is, not become Foreign Secretary. David Cameron dealt with it by both answering the question and agreeing to meet with me. Thoroughly professional, as I would have expected, and precisely what I had told his special advisor would happen.

The temptation to revisit his neck and stretch it was growing.

In truth, I reasoned he was just doing his job as he saw fit. It was my misfortune that he saw a legitimate question as a threat and that, because of that, I was never to have the chance to sample life as a parliamentary trade envoy, something I genuinely would have loved to have done. The offer of the role turned out to be genuine, as I found out when the then PPS to the trade minister at the time came up to congratulate me as she had seen my name at the top the list of next appointments. She was quite taken aback at the decision to remove me from the list because I insisted on asking a question deemed unhelpful.

However, the brutal truth is that at some point in your parliamentary life, you have to make a decision: either be a backbench MP and prioritise wholeheartedly your constituency needs and demands, or try to make it to the front bench and enjoy the opportunities and pitfalls of being a minister, with the high chance that you will compromise both in how you vote and in how much time you will be able to commit to your constituents.

That choice, however, is not one entirely of your own making, as the many twists and turns of parliamentary life, patronage and deals conspire to shape your future.

Your chances of success rarely depend on your level of competence. Much like school, where competence was not an ingredient for being made the class monitor, house prefect or even head boy, nor does it necessarily qualify you for a role as a minister in Her Majesty's Government. (Demonstrating incompetence, on the other hand, can be fatal to the health of your ministerial career, but by then you have tasted life in the back of a ministerial car, which is more than most.)

The fastest route to the front bench, in addition to behaving yourself and performing reasonably well in the House of Commons, is being favoured by the Chief Whip or No. 10. Preferably both. The former is important to understand, because the power to recommend and even appoint junior ministerial posts gives the whips the means to exercise control over the ambitious.

In short, Parliament is not a meritocracy, and it's up to you to figure out what route you want to take.

I was encouraged to abandon any thoughts of a ministerial career by two very good friends of mine.

The first, Stewart Jackson, the then MP for Peterborough, bluntly told me early on in my parliamentary life that my career prospects were limited.

'Why?! I have not screwed up in the chamber; OK, I had a small rebellion, but I have sat through endless dull Bill committees and asked lots of decent questions. Is it perhaps my questionable intellect?'

'You are a middle-aged, grey-haired white male.'

'So, none of that is seen as a mark of distinction then?' I asked, hopefully.

Apparently not.

I had no idea if Stewart's assessment was correct; I will leave others to work that out.

Charles Walker, however, provided the clincher on my first day in my new office in Portcullis House, having escaped the testosterone-fuelled office of my early years. Charles was my new neighbour, as our two offices were separated only by a common secretarial and admin team room for our respective staff. He came bounding across from his office to mine and, with his customary loud, eloquent and cheerful delivery, said, 'Mate, mate, great to have you as a neighbour. This is fan-tas-tic. Mate, listen.' (You don't have a choice but to listen, along with most of the corridor outside our office). 'Mate, you are an MP! You are in the Premier League. You have arrived. This is it, mate. You are at the top of your profession. This is where it matters! Enjoy every day, don't waste a single moment!'

Great advice, so motivational. I was beaming.

'I won't, I promise you!'

'Excellent, mate, because we both know you're going to lose in 2015, so just bloody well enjoy it while it lasts.'

Crushed. Totally.

Carol, his wonderful PA, came in as he bounded out, bringing tissues and wine gums to help me recover.

For the record, I reckon Charles is the parliamentarian of the decade. And, as you can tell, he is incapable of telling even a white lie.

So, armed with this advice, and having already calculated that there was little chance of a quick rise in the ranks given that I had rebelled early on, ministerial advancement seemed doomed.

Having found yourself in that situation, there are two emo-tions: relief, and then a huge bout of post-rationalisation that you have done the right thing in abandoning all hope of becom-ing a minister, despite the fact that being a minister is a pretty good way of bringing about change, and, who knows, you could have had every chance of ending up in the Cabinet.

Relief, however, is what I focused on. Relief at not being plunged into the generally thankless first job on the ministe-rial ladder of being an unpaid parliamentary private secretary to a relatively junior minister. As a PPS, you spend most of the time running around amongst colleagues, persuading them to submit friendly parliamentary questions so that the minister has less chance of humiliating himself at the despatch box when he answers questions from MPs once a month. When you're not doing that, you have to try to rally the troops to attend Parliamentary Urgent Questions, which your departmental minister has to answer, and which are designed by the opposition to heap as much embarrassment on the minister as possible and illustrate his or her incompetence, be it genuinely deserved or not.

And on it goes. In return for this, you get no ministerial pay rise, and yet you are a formal member of the government and share collective responsibility for all the unpopular decisions made by the government.

At the end of it all, you might, just might, become a junior minister for one of the many departments in government about which you probably know diddly squat. But you will have made it onto the ministerial ladder, and rightly so, if not just as recognition of the sheer effort made!

It is, nevertheless, a curious way to run the country when it is entirely possible, even probable, that because you have won an election and have not annoyed too many people in your early years in the House of Commons, you can, overnight, be put in charge of a huge department that runs some of our key public services. This, despite the fact that you personally may have never run anything more challenging than a bath.

And yet we have produced ministers who founded the NHS, transformed homeownership, negotiated international agreements and treaties, launched space programmes, helped make the City of London the best in the world, and secured peace in Northern Ireland.

Does patronage work? Of course it does. It's a hugely

successful tool to keep MPs in line and get government legislation enacted. The smaller the majority of a governing party, the
more susceptible are the whips (the government managers) to
resorting to all the tactics they have at their disposal. In desperate situations, the whips are more likely to use more aggressive
tactics. This, however, should not be mistaken for the old-
fashioned attempts at bullying that pretty much ended after
Tony Blair came to power in 1997. In fact, in all my dealings
with the whips, they have been nothing but courteous, if at
times somewhat forceful. The idea that the present Chief Whip
(at the time of writing, Julian Smith) could be anything but
courteous is laughable, yet he will be steering the government's
legislation through some of the most difficult parliamentary
arithmetic since the 1970s. I suspect that when he bares his
teeth, colleagues will soon learn that he has a spine of steel.

The whips, however, have an Achilles heel. If you don't seek
ministerial office, they have very little influence over you. Prior
to David Cameron coming to power, the most difficult of MPs
could be bought off with the chairmanship of a Select Committee, or even a seat on a Select Committee. That all changed in
2010, probably against the advice of all the parties' Chief Whips
at the time, when Select Committee members began to be elected, rather than appointed by the whips.

If the troublesome MP is minded to travel at taxpayer expense,
the whips have the power to put you on such innocuous groups
as the OSCE (Organisation for Security and Co-operation
in Europe), where I myself spent a few days in both Ankara and
Monaco representing the UK Parliament in what was quite possibly both the least influential and the most costly international
parliamentary assembly ever.

Somehow, the whips have been able to retain the power of
appointment on that one, but I think for me it was meant as a

punishment for voting against an increase in the EU budget. They sent me packing for a week, to sit in endless meetings voting on motions that were duly ignored by every government we voted to censure, which, in this assembly, consistently meant Russia and Belarus. (No wonder they vote for each other in the Eurovision Song Contest every year. It's their chance to get back at the rest of us.)

Ultimately, however, and with a staggering sense of disbelief, I learned that the system actually works. It works because, the people having elected a government on the basis of a manifesto, that government's legislative programme needs to be passed into law, and that cannot happen with a bunch of independent-minded individuals wishing to constantly push their own agenda rather than the one they were elected on. To ensure the legislative programme passes, we need the whips. And for the whips to function, they need the power, as well as the personal charm, character and determination, to get their job done.

As Enoch Powell once remarked, 'A Parliament without whips is like a city without sewers.'

Equally, there is always room for taking an independent stand where there are matters of principle or matters close to the heart of a Member's constituency.

And, truthfully, most – but not all – whips get that.

But I never did become a trade envoy.

21

TRADING VOTES

'**N**ow I can speak the truth,' commented Gyles Brandreth, celebrated author and one-term MP. 'Let's face it, the people have contempt for politicians, but it is as nothing to the contempt we have for you.'

Ouch!

It is funny, I grant you, but rather harsh. It's hard, after all, to have contempt for the fellow who wanted to discuss his haemorrhoids with me. I can think of lots of other words to describe our relationship, but not contempt.

To help me empathise further, he insisted on clarifying matters for me.

'Well, son, it's like riding a bike without a saddle.'

What he expected me to do about it, I still don't know, but when he was not discussing the problems with his backside, he regularly popped in to discuss his benefits situation and whether we could help him out. Fair enough, but he would spice up these sessions by bringing aspects of personal hygiene into play.

Helen would run through his list of essential expenses, as we always did with benefit claims. Electricity, gas, food, transport, deodorant.

Deodorant?

Helen had not seen that one before.

'Why did you single that out as essential?' she asked, as I looked on, a little bemused.

'Well, if I'm going to improve my circumstances, as your boss says I should try to do, then I need to stand a chance with the ladies, right?'

He looked straight at Helen, and I am certain he winked.

I left them to it. How could anyone, Gyles included, possibly have contempt for piles and romance?

Irritation, on the other hand, was a frequent sentiment of mine, and sometimes that irritation morphed into frustration, which, rather worryingly, I did let show on occasion. What drove that frustration was that some visitors to my advice surgery would rather have me try to get more taxpayer money coughed up to sort out their problems than get off their (hopefully haemorrhoid-free) backsides and try to do something to help themselves.

But letting this frustration show is not so wise. While it did give me a moment's satisfaction, it is not in the best interests of my electoral prospects or, indeed, to the benefit of the individual constituents.

But it happened, and happened more than once, often over unreasonable claims for more money from our hard-pressed taxpayers.

As we know, those same taxpayers dish out about £140 billion quid a year in benefits, excluding pensions. That's about 40 per cent of the total income tax and national insurance take, or, for every pound of the hard-earned cash that you hand over in tax from your pay packet, 40 pence of it ends up in state benefits. You can decide if that's a good thing or a bad thing, if it's too much or too little.

Over five years, about 800 of my constituents had already made up their minds, evidenced when they came to see me saying that they didn't get enough cash from the taxpayer... sorry, from the government.

Before some political opponents get hysterical and reach for their Twitter accounts to trash me, no, I don't mean everyone, I mean some. I don't mean the disabled or the sick, I mean the able-bodied and the mentally fit. I don't even mean those who have tried to sort out their own problems first, before turning to me. I am talking about 800 people who believed they were being short-changed by the state when they came to see me or contacted my office. Few were being reasonable, and few had tried to do anything about their problems first before they presented themselves at my office demanding an extra wodge of cash.

'Mr de Bois. My daughter and grandchild have come to see you, because she is finding things very tough right now and she needs your help.'

I was faced with a young mum, let's call her Tina, and her five-year-old son, who, not unreasonably, looked and behaved as if he did not want to be there, but consoled himself by eating my wine gums. All the talking was being done by his grandmother.

'You see, Tina, my daughter, had to leave my home when young Darrell started growing up, as there really wasn't any more room for them in my place. And now she's in a small two-bedroom apartment, which is all right, I mean it's not great, and she really needs a bigger place, but anyway, she's getting no help whatsoever from the government, which is why we need your help. She has no money.'

'I get nothing from the government at all,' added Tina, helpfully.

'Gosh. No help at all? That doesn't sound right. Let's see what we can do about that then, shall we, Helen...?'

Helen, my constituency caseworker, had devised a simple process to deal with the question of benefit entitlement. It was aimed at weeding out the unrealistic, the delusional and the uninformed from the genuine hardship cases where the system had failed them.

So, as I let Helen off her leash, she produced a sheet of prepared questions aimed at getting to a simple list of Tina's income and expenditure. According to Tina and her mother, there would, when completed, be a very full expenditure side, but nothing, not a penny on the income side. As it happens, we rarely get to expenditure except with the genuine cases.

'So, where do you live then, Tina?'

'Just off the Hertford Road.'

'And whose place is that? A friend's?'

She looked at me as if I was the one in need of help.

'No, it's my place. My mum has just told you.'

'But how do you pay for it?'

'Well, I don't. The council does.'

'Ah, I see. So what is it, then, two bedrooms? That's about £900 a month in housing benefit, right?'

'Well, I dunno, but I don't pay it.'

Helen noted the first figure in the income column: 900 quid.

'Now, I know that in these circumstances you might find it hard to feed yourself. Have you been referred to our local food bank at all, or does your mum help out with the bills?'

Tina's mum came to the rescue here.

'I can't afford to do that. I do babysitting, though,' she added helpfully.

'So how do you and Darrell eat, Tina? Have you ever been referred to a food bank?'

'Oh yeah, once, when my benefits were stopped for a while.'

'What benefits are those, Tina?'

'Well, I get…' and on it went, 'jobseeker's allowance, income support, child benefit, council tax support.' In fact, in addition to her rent being paid, there was approximately another £740 a month. Coupled with the housing benefit of around £900, Tina had an income of £1,640 a month, or £19,680 a year, net.

Tina's issue was not about getting nothing from the government, but perhaps not having much left over after the essentials. That's a completely different issue, and not one for her MP. She was receiving everything she was entitled to. It was not for me to find her more money than that from the taxpayer.

'How about Darrell's dad? Is he able to help you out with a little more money? Does he work?'

I expected her to say that he was no longer around and had shirked his responsibilities.

'Oh, he does do some work, odd jobs for different people and his mates, mainly. So he really doesn't have any money to spare.'

Translated, we think the taxpayer should sub me some more for my little boy, rather than his father supporting him.

'Here's an idea, Tina.'

She looked hopeful.

'Did you pass the newsagent's next door to this office on your way in?'

'Er, yeah.'

'Lovely Kurdish fellow who runs it. Works all hours of the day and keeps me fed with Coke and wine gums. Pop next door and ask Mehmet to give you some money. I'm sure that won't be a problem, eh?'

'What?'

'Seriously, Tina. How do you justify coming here, to ask me to get the taxpayer to give you more money for your little boy, when his own father won't dig deep for him? It's like asking that shop owner to work all the long hours of the day and night he does, just to hand more of it over to you. This meeting is finished. Talk to Darrell's dad, not me.'

Helen showed them to the door. We never got to the expenditure column.

Angry? Frustrated? Irritated?

All of the above, but, truthfully, I knew I was targeting my feelings at the wrong person. We, the political classes, have spent the past thirty years inventing a tax and benefits systems that has become so ingrained in both our behaviour and our expectations that some people do not even realise that it is working taxpayers who fund benefits and, worse, some do not even recognise the scale of the benefits they receive. Worse, and deeply worrying, is that, having developed this system, some people now look to the state first to solve their problems, without making any substantive effort to sort them out themselves. Just like Tina and her partner.

While Gyles Brandreth is right to some extent, he, like me, will have enjoyed some very rewarding moments in his constituency during his tenure. When your constituency team do get some wins, you know you're making both a small and a big difference to constituents who first appeared to be on a hiding to nothing.

When we won, we shamelessly stuck the generous thank-you cards and letters on the wall, a reminder when things were not going our way that it was still a very worthwhile job to do.

And when we had outcomes that were life-changing, it was a spectacular feeling. Like the day in May 2017 when I was stopped in Enfield market by a young couple clutching a two-year-old. I had not been their MP for two years, but they recognised me.

'You won't remember us, Mr de Bois.'

They were right, I was embarrassed to admit.

'We came to see you about the dreadful delays and problems we were having with the adoption authorities, and you and your team got on the case. Your help was magnificent.'

'Well, thank you for stopping and letting me know. How did it work out?'

Probably one of the dumbest questions I had ever asked, given they were holding a young lad in their arms.

'We wanted you to meet him. Thank you so much, your help was crucial, and look, here is our little boy.'

I must confess, as someone who dotes on his own children and now grandchildren, for a brief moment I was caught completely off guard and I did well up for a moment. To think we had made a difference to this young family was a unique feeling, and to meet them all together was something I will never forget.

Clearly, Gyles Brandreth was not thinking about the successes when he lambasted his constituents, but he may have been thinking about the curious logic that comes from many when they are speaking with their MP.

'If you want my vote next time' is the most common introduction to an exchange with a constituent. We have, it seems, unwittingly developed a transactional relationship with politicians, with the result that just about everyone ends up disappointed, including the MP.

And I am just as much to blame as the constituent.

We ran a constituency office as effectively as we could, and we plonked it in the heart of a Labour stronghold in the constituency, with the key purpose of helping people in exchange for their vote.

'Right then, before we get down to whatever the problem is, Mr Jones, I want your assurance that if we sort it out, you will vote for me at the next election, right? Deal?'

'Well, I have always voted Labour, but if you sort out the vandals at the end of my street, you can have my vote next time.'

'Sign here, please, thank you... Right then, let's see what I can do, eh?'

Of course not. If only.

But that was the unsaid proposal. 'Unsaid' being the key word, which is why it was so bloody irritating when so many people opened the conversation by breaking the code of silence and offering their vote in return for help.

When that happened, I was obliged to reply, 'When you step across this office door, I want you to know that how you vote doesn't matter. I represent everyone here in this constituency, and my job is to help you regardless of your voting intention or allegiance.'

I rather hoped that the pleading look in my eyes would leave the visitor in no doubt that I didn't mean a word of it. Of course I wanted their vote.

Now, I am confident that I never won Tina's or her mother's vote at the subsequent election and, to be fair to them, they did not offer it as a trade for a successful outcome. I am, however, also convinced that absolutely no one who makes that offer ever votes according to the outcome of their problem.

The reality is that few people vote on whether you are a good or effective MP. At best, an MP can hope to get a personal vote of 1,000, and that is quite extraordinary. The vast majority vote for a government of the day; a Prime Minister and whoever has made the best 'retail offer' of manifesto pledges that might plonk a few extra quid in the household income. So, the offer of a transaction to win their vote if you do repair their drains, fix the street lights or sort out their neighbours is, at worst, an idle threat should you fail or, at best, an attempt to ensure you listen. Either way, it pissed me off from the start.

Occasionally I would respond with, 'I may not be standing at the next election, so your vote may indeed have to go elsewhere.' As it turned out, that's precisely where many of their votes did in fact go.

Not all these offers to trade their vote came in person. As a nation that is digitally switched on, unsurprisingly, I received offers via Facebook, Twitter, texts and, in extraordinary numbers, emails, of which a large proportion carried the direct or indirect trade-off proposition of a vote for support or help. The unspoken trade was not just spoken a lot; it appeared in writing far too often.

Some seemed to think they had more than one vote, given the regularity of their correspondence on one subject or another, all offering the same exchange. Take one of my most regular campaigners, let's call her Esin, who wrote to me, it seemed, on any subject worthy of the remotest protest.

I have never met Esin, and I am unlikely ever to do so. I imagine she is a very angry or possibly a very lonely person, judging by the extraordinary amount of communication she had with me during my time as her MP.

To begin with, I had a few well-written emails that touched on subjects clearly of importance to her, or so I thought, but, to be frank, of very little interest to me. Saving this or saving that was worthy, but I never felt the urge to take the action she often suggested, which was to lobby MPs for a law change, sign a pledge card (absolutely not, we had seen what trouble they could get you into!), or make representations to the Chief Minister of some remote island to free the blue-winged Iberian spider from captivity in a zoo. I always wrote back. All constituents deserved that, or at least I thought so.

Then along came 38 Degrees, which most people will not have heard of. They were essentially set up in response to the coalition government, and promptly set about campaigning against everything from selling off the forests, to the Health and Social Care Act, and of course any cut worth mentioning.

Their technique was simple. They wrote a campaign letter,

you clicked a button having shared your postcode, and off it went in your name to your MP. The idea being that the more letters an MP got, the more responsive he or she would be to the demands of whatever campaign it might be.

And my God, it worked. At first.

Marginal-seat MPs like myself are generally quite neurotic about public opinion during their first few months, if not the whole first term, so to receive a barrage of letters on a particularly hot topic of the time, all demanding you defy the party, is not good news. Marginal Agitation and Despair syndrome (MAD) feeds off this stuff. It does not matter that the letters all say precisely the same thing, or that they have been fired off simply by pressing a button on the laptop. I couldn't help thinking:

These people care enough to write to me!

That means they care enough to vote!

And they will hate me if I vote for this!

They will tell all their friends what a bastard I am and not to vote for me!

There must be hundreds of them!

Worse, some of the early campaigns run by 38 Degrees reached epic proportions. In one case, I had over 700 emails on the Health and Social Care Bill. On saving the forests from privatisation, I received over 400 emails. I didn't even have a forest in the constituency. I barely had any trees.

I don't know about other MPs, but I was not remotely qualified or knowledgeable enough to write to people on every aspect of government policy. If, as I had done on some occasions, I had gone into the voting lobby as directed by the whips, without anything but a vague notion of what we were voting on, it was perfectly logical that I was poorly qualified to respond in detail on every aspect of government policy. Or have the time to find out.

That's why the very helpful Conservative Policy Response Unit (PRU) was worth spending about £3,000 a year of taxpayers' money on, as they produced standard policy reply letters for MPs like me to use. And, with the emergence of the 38 Degrees campaign organisation, use it we did.

Notwithstanding the fact that I would never send out a standard reply without having read it, amended it and personalised it, the fact is, there was something deeply satisfying about sending a standard reply to, well, a standard campaign letter. In the early days of panic and worry, this was extremely efficient, and helped ease the self-doubt that I was, in fact, a heartless uncaring bastard whom no one would ever vote for again, as each letter I received implied.

Over time, I became somewhat sceptical about the true nature of the 38 Degrees campaign letters. It was becoming increasingly evident, judging by the replies I began to receive, that not everyone was even aware of what they were signing up to when they visited the campaign website.

Dear Nick,

Thank you for your letter on reforms to construction site hazardous materials management regulations [I made that up, incidentally]. I must confess, whilst I welcome what you are doing, I don't recall ever writing to you in the first place.

Aha! Someone pressed a button not really aware that they were about to launch their MP into action…

But the best letters were the ones complaining about my inadequate response to their original complaint. These invariably had extensive use of capital letters to make it clear that the author was shouting at me because I had apparently disrespected them.

Dear Mr de Bois,

Thank you for your STANDARD LETTER reply, which shows just how much you care about the issue, NOT!!!!!

It is disappointing to KNOW THAT MY MP does not care enough about SAVING THE PLANET... that he just presses a button to send me a PARTY WHIP LETTER!

Yours sincerely.

To which the only possible reply was:

Thank you for your reply.

I think I care as much about the issue as you do. Isn't that why you sent me a standard template campaign letter from 38 Degrees?

Yours faithfully,

Nick de Bois

Maybe Gyles Brandreth had a point after all.

Nevertheless, in an age when data matters more and more, 38 Degrees did more for the circulation of my newsletters than any other device. Each campaigner would receive my automated reply within seconds of hitting their own 'Send' button. Buried within the text of my automated reply acknowledging receipt of their email was a small data protection note asking them to opt out of future communications and warning them that if they did not, they would be subject to lots of useful updates from me. (Unfortunately, the law is changing to stop that easy harvesting of email addresses. I think I foolishly voted for that as well.)

See – don't get mad, get even.

In the digital age, standard letters at the touch of a button, and endless tweets and Facebook messages, simply create one big negative echo chamber. The same people making a dispro-portionate amount of noise on a single issue, or even multiple issues. Sitting behind a desk dealing with them would leave any sane and rational person with the distinct impression of utter failure. It was important to get out of the echo chamber, out of Westminster, and just talk to people, where the chances are you will be able to make more sense of what is going on and what people do actually think and want.

Refreshingly, the vast majority do not want a handout, or for me to save the planet, or even to make a deal with me in return for their vote.

Unfortunately, that cut both ways when, having successfully helped many people, they took my refusal to barter at face value and never felt obliged to vote for me.

22

ASK THE PEOPLE

Knocking on doors and asking people how they are going to vote is quite rude.

A stranger bowls up on your doorstep and within fifteen seconds he is asking you how you are going to exercise your secret ballot. It is to the credit of the great British public that we don't have more candidates and MPs with black eyes.

Of course, some residents don't mind you knocking on their door, some quite like it even, but most don't care, and definitely most forget about it by the time they have ventured back from the front door to their living room or garden, from whence I had disturbed them.

Knocking on doors often carries risk. You are there for one purpose only: to find out if they will vote for you. They, however, have plenty of other plans for you, and that's if they welcome your call. If they don't, be prepared. Be flexible with the first, and mitigate the possibility of the second.

When I first started out in politics, there were some fairly accurate indicators of voting intention before you got to the doorstep, thus reducing the risk of an unwelcome response. For a while, neatly turned-out gardens pointed to a more

Conservative-minded voter, for example, but those days soon passed. The best indicator remains a poster in the window supporting you. That often means just a quick courtesy call to thank the owner, because you could mark them down as a Conservative voter without troubling them if you wished, given they were happy to advertise their support for you in the window.

Or so I thought.

Way back at the 1997 general election, when Conservatives were broadly loathed by a larger than usual chunk of the population, anyone brave enough to wear a Conservative rosette was effectively pinning a target to their lapel inviting both physical and verbal assault. At least, that was what it felt like in the no-hoper Labour safe seat of Stalybridge and Hyde, which I had been selected to contest.

Somewhat ominously better known as the home constituency of the notorious child killer Myra Hindley and later for the killer Dr Harold Shipman, this seat had been returning Labour MPs since 1940 and it's the one in which I plunged into the task of door knocking with a complete lack of self-awareness.

Posters promoting Conservative candidates were few and far between then, simply because many of the dwindling band of Conservative voters thought having one in your window or garden was tantamount to an invitation to have a brick thrown through your window. If we were lucky enough to have one put up, it was invariably torn down by our opponents' more enthusiastic activists. It was therefore with immense surprise that, as I drove past a small, neat terraced house on the Back Moor Road near Stalybridge, I saw a poster for me in the upstairs window.

A rare sight indeed, and a most welcome one.

I pulled up, parked the car and near galloped back to the house, keen for once to knock on a door confident of the outcome. These people deserved a thank-you from the man himself. I even took out my rosette and pinned it on my jacket.

Standing outside the door on a narrow pavement on this busy road clutching my election leaflets, I unsurprisingly received a horn blast from a passing motorist with the now customary two-finger salute as the driver spotted the rosette. No matter, this house would more than make up for it.

The door opened to reveal a huge individual, half-open shirt displaying a neck as thick as a wrestler's and biceps that matched the size of my thighs.

Worse, his expression changed from one of curiosity to downright astonishment as he took in my blue rosette and cheery smile. Something was wrong and instinctively I took a step back, which was unfortunate given the narrow width of the pavement, as I was in danger of stepping into oncoming traffic.

At least that's what the householder thought, so he reached out to steady me with his right arm, which I naturally took for an attempted right hook to my face. My instinctive coward-ice meant I flinched, ducked and dropped my leaflets, which started to distribute themselves across the road and pavement, inviting more car horns.

'You all right there?' he snapped.

Dignity gone, leaflets going all over the place, I gave up scrambling after them and stood up.

'Now what the hell are you doing here?' he barked. 'I don't want a bloody Tory on my doorstep, I can tell you!'

'But...'

I feebly pointed up to the window, now utterly confused.

He stepped out and looked up.

'Why, that little bugger,' and he took off back inside the house, striding upstairs to the offending window.

It turned out his son, angry with his dad for some unknown

reason, had put the poster there to annoy his father, rather than displaying it as a positive endorsement of me. Where he had got it from confounds me. If, to annoy his father further, he buys him this book, please let me know.

I left (somewhat chastened and certain that no votes would be forthcoming from that household) to continue my journey towards a huge thumping at the ballot box that year.

So much for the reliability of posters, which frankly dimmed my enthusiasm for door knocking.

On the other hand, if I didn't knock on doors it was certain that I would be charged with going AWOL.

'I never hear from my MP' is a common enough complaint.

'We never hear from you except at elections' is another – uttered even, I may add, when there are no elections pending.

Or:

'You are never around this part, we never see you' – when in fact that's precisely what is happening at the time we have that exchange.

It is a hopeless situation for both the constituent and the MP, and some management of expectations would definitely help matters, so let me have a go.

In my constituency there were approximately 40,000 households. In a five-year parliament there are roughly 260 weekends. Assume three hours a day canvassing with a small team of, say, five volunteers: that's a combined fifteen hours' work a day. In fifteen hours, one can certainly knock on a lot of doors, perhaps thirty an hour, making 450 a day. Walk up the garden path, knock, wait, no answer, bung leaflet through door, back down garden path. Of course, you would not get to speak to anyone at that rate, because that's simply knocking on doors. And knocking on doors when no one is in is not going to help very much apart from a leaflet saying I called.

In reality, myself and a team of five probably spoke on average to forty, maybe fifty people in any one session if we were lucky. Theoretically, repeating that every weekend over a five-year period it would have meant we chatted to 26,000 people. Not bad!

Well, not bad in theory, but completely wrong.

Contrary to popular myth, MPs and volunteers are normal people, and in Enfield North we were no exception. Taking into account that not one of us is completely mad, we didn't want to spend every weekend for five years canvassing opinion, marginal seat or not. Despite this, and despite my voters having normal busy lives working, shopping, visiting family, friends, going to the cinema and having holidays, over the five years we knocked on about 25,000 doors and probably had a conversation with 8–10,000 people.

Sadly, most will forget it ever happened, and another 20 per cent of those we called on will move during the five-year period and not be around when it comes to voting.

So perhaps strictly speaking and to cover all bases a voter would be more accurate to complain along the following lines:

'I personally have not seen you in this area, and you may very well have called on me but the chances are I was out because I don't spend my weekends waiting for you to pop round.'

Defensive?

Yep.

So why bother?

Because it sort of works, and oddly it keeps morale up because, for once, I feel as if I am doing something. On rare occasions it can have profound effects.

It was during a pre-election canvassing session in 2010 that I knocked on a door in Turkey Street ward, Enfield. The lady who answered shaped a huge part of my political life thereafter. Her name was Yvonne Lawson, and her son Godwin had been stabbed and killed in a senseless random attack in March 2010. I had knocked on the door of a grieving mother with the intention of asking how she might vote. I left with a mission to campaign with her to tackle the root causes of knife crime and to ensure that David Cameron delivered on his manifesto pledge to introduce automatic jail terms for those caught carrying a knife.

I have already told how that was achieved, but what I have not told is how Yvonne went on to lead the way in ensuring her awful experience was used to help youngsters understand the appalling consequences of gang and knife crime culture. The Godwin Lawson Foundation went on to focus on implementing programmes to help vulnerable youngsters aspire and achieve positive outcomes, thereby transforming young lives. Yvonne faced huge challenges in getting this work off the ground, not least in accessing a little bit of seed money to fund such effective work. I often went into battle alongside her, whether it was to convince reluctant head teachers that she should be allowed into their schools to tell youngsters her powerful story, or just to beat on doors to get a little bit of financial help to deliver her mission. She was always so gracious to me for my help, but frankly I was honoured to have known her and she remains, for me, a quiet hero whose voice should be listened to at the highest levels.

And all that came from knocking on doors, which made every contrary or awkward encounter I went through nevertheless very worthwhile. And that's why our system is still one of the best on offer when it comes to MPs representing constituents.

Unlike many other European countries, we have a constituency system where we elect an MP on the first past the post system, which means whoever gets the largest number of votes wins. My constituents chose me, they have a relationship with me, and if they like what I do they can vote to keep me; if they don't, they can vote to sack me at the general election.

The alternative proportional representation system widely favoured in Europe means a voter votes for a party and the party choose the candidate from a list of candidates. The more votes a party gets, the more candidates from their list get elected. The voter may sack the party, but not any one individual. He could be corrupt and lazy, but if he or she is in with the party hierarchy then they could still be on top of the list and duly elected.

There is less incentive for the MP to have a direct relationship with constituents, therefore less door knocking, with the side effect that the politician is quickly out of touch with what is happening on the ground. On a visit to the German Parliament, we met with members of their equivalent of our Foreign Affairs Select Committee, who were astonished at David Cameron's 2014 pledge to have a referendum on EU membership. They asked us why we supporting this move.

'Because many of our constituents want it,' was the universal reply. 'We know that because we canvass their opinion regularly on the doorstep.'

'What do you mean?' one member asked.

'We go out regularly between elections and knock on doors to introduce ourselves and seek voter opinions.'

I don't know who was more surprised: the German MP elected by proportional representation that we went out regularly canvassing opinion, or me and my colleagues when it became clear that little if any canvassing was undertaken by German MPs except at elections.

Canvassing between elections fuels that relationship by listening to key voter issues and priorities and responding to them. During the election, though, door knocking is less about listening and more about identifying your vote and making sure your supporters turn out on the day.

'Good evening, Mr Oliver, my name is Nick de Bois and I am seeking re-election as your MP on 7 May.'

A straightforward enough pitch.

'Oh hello, I have been hoping you would call as I wanted to share with you my disappointment about the government and its pay restraint policy, and why I won't be voting for you at this election and will be again voting Labour.'

At this point I have everything I need to know. He is against us – fine, mark that down and move on to the next dwelling.

But no such luck. He wants to chat and explain why he won't vote for me. That's tolerable in between elections, but very counterproductive during elections. At this point I don't care why he is voting Labour, but I do care about finding those who might vote for me and getting them out on the day.

So, what I should have said at that point was: 'Thanks for the voting intention, but I don't give a toss at this precise moment why you are going to do that. Bye.'

Or, perhaps more reasonably, add some explanation:

'So, Mr Oliver, I won't waste any more of my time being nice and polite by listening to you, and will instead move on to the next door, where there is still hope of finding a Conservative voter. You see, at this precise point in time I am not at all interested in your views. And we both know you won't change your mind. Had you bothered to turn up at any of my surgeries or open meetings or sent an email, we could have chatted, but you never did then and I don't have time to do so now.'

But, of course, I don't say that.

I would love to have said it.

It would have given me immense satisfaction to say it to a few particular people who enjoyed torturing me on the doorstep, but I am just not made that way.

Trust in politics and politicians is still low, and ruthlessly turning your back on people only reinforces that impression – but unfortunately that doesn't help when trying to win an election. I spent far too many minutes talking to people who were going to vote against me. What's more, I heard countless stories from residents about my opponent turning around and walking away, not wasting any time. She won, of course.

Then, just to rub it in, young Tom, my campaign manager, has to chip in after I have spent ten minutes with Mr Oliver.

'You do of course understand what a waste of time it is having a discussion that is pointless and won't earn you a vote, Nick?'

Tom is clutching the canvass board that records the voting intention of every person we call on. He has clearly heard enough of my conversation to pass judgement on the spot.

'Hang on, Tom, next time you are stuck in a boring conversation going nowhere, see how quickly you can get out of it without being rude or offensive. And then imagine your job depends on it.'

A moment's silence as he thought about that. He ended our conversation perfectly, of course, not caring whether he offended me or not; his job depended on it.

'Next house for you is Mr and Mrs Okran, No. 27.'

Point well made. As I noted earlier, he is insufferably smug at times, but right.

'I don't know why you canvass at all, I would just lie to you,' notes my wife Helen rather too bluntly.

'That says more about you, darling, than my other constituents,' I respond somewhat defensively.

'Rubbish,' she taunts.

'Every election I have been with you, you always came back from canvassing saying you would win, and you didn't, so it stands to reason I am right.'

I do love my wife, she is an extraordinary woman, but that was brutal.

Despite the odd canvassing skirmish with the enemy voter, she does have a point. There is a big drawback to relying on a personal canvass to identify your voters. It's that we Brits are basically really nice people.

Admittedly, there are some vile, odious idiots on the fringes who are consumed by hate and have targeted politicians recently, but the clear majority of us Brits are a courteous bunch.

'This meal sucks, doesn't it, darling?'

'My chicken was dry as bark from a dead tree and the mushrooms were raw.'

'Well, I had to drop ice into my white wine as it was warmer than the bloody midday sun on the Costa del Sol!'

And with perfect timing the waiter would appear: 'How was your meal tonight, sir, madam?'

'Wonderful, thank you so very much,' we both tell him, and we almost certainly end up leaving a tip. It's not his fault, after all, just the chef.

That's us Brits: polite, don't make a fuss, but we would probably never visit the restaurant again.

Much like canvassing voting intention.

'Hello, I am Nick de Bois and I am seeking re-election as your MP on 7 May.'

'Thank you for calling.'

'May I count on your vote?'

'I think that's quite possible indeed.'

Watch the eyes, watch the eyes…

And there they go, drop down of the eyelids, starting to close the door on me. The body language saying what the lips won't, which is: 'No chance, sod off, you wicked Tory.'

The door bolt being firmly slammed into place after the door has shut leaves you in no doubt where that vote is going. They hate you, and the chances are all you have really done is remind them to vote for the other lot.

Experts tell me that the more data I capture on voters before an election, the more chance I have of converting undecided voters into votes for me. Further, if used correctly, the data captured on voters who have decided to vote for me will help ensure that they do vote, either on the day or by postal vote. The object of door knocking is to help gather that data.

Of my last two election results, one was a narrow defeat after five years as the MP and one was a trouncing in the Corbyn-mania that swept across London. That aside, I am none the wiser about what the majority of voters are actually voting on or for. Me, the party leader or the party? Are they voting for policy, change, stability or hope?

All I can do as the local candidate and incumbent MP is influence one thing, which is what I say about myself. I therefore also saw door knocking as the opportunity to form a relationship with the voter and thereby increase my chances of their vote. I suspect, sadly, that the experts are right: forget the relationship, personal votes are insignificant.

If people are not, as seems to be the case, voting for a local MP, then what is the point of all this campaign work we are doing in the constituency? How many visits from me made a difference to how people voted? Did any letter or leaflet targeted at key voters make one jot of difference?

Tom, my campaign manager, ensured I was sent packing across the constituency within days of winning the 2010 election. He had me and my merry band of volunteers knocking on some 25,000 doors to seduce voters into giving me another five years in Parliament at the 2015 election. As you can tell – much like my youthful efforts at trying to win girls in the past – my

242CONFESSIONS OF A RECOVERING MP

seduction of voters was at times clumsy, funny and depressing, but ultimately futile.

On Election Day 2015, my wife and I were knocking up Conservative-pledged voters as late as 9.30 p.m., half an hour before the polls closed. A lady stopped by a house where I was trying to encourage some voters to get to the polling station.

'I think you are the best MP we have ever had, you are an amazing local MP,' she said as we started to move on to our next house.

'Thank you, that's very decent of you to say so.'

'I really hope you win, you have been so good for the town.'

'Well, your vote for me is the only way I can win. Have you voted?'

'Yes, I have. I didn't vote for you because of that David Cameron.'

'I see...'

'I couldn't vote for Cameron.'

'But you wouldn't have, you would have put your X by my name, not his.'

And, rather loyally but undiplomatically, my wife added: 'Otherwise you get the MP you deserve.'

Being a good MP didn't do the trick for that voter, who merrily trotted off thinking she had done her best to get me re-elected by simply speaking to me but not voting for me.

And there was my dilemma. Divorce myself from David Cameron and try to win an election on my record and reputation, or hope the choice between David Cameron and Ed Miliband would be enough to win the seat for me.

The Prime Minister's decision to close the A&E despite promising not to do so seemed toxic locally, so it was an easy enough choice to play down Cameron and rely on my record.

Yet every campaign expert will tell you an MP does not win on their record, which left me with Hobson's choice.

In fact, that's precisely what the head of voting strategy said to me in no uncertain terms at CCHQ days before I was re-selected to fight Enfield North in the snap 2017 election.

'See her up there,' as he pointed to a television monitor in CCHQ showing the last Prime Minister's Questions, where Theresa May was on fine form.

'This election is about her, not you, so don't fucking well put out leaflets about your opponent's expenses and failings when she was last an MP, don't go on about the hospital. It's all irrel-evant and that's why you lost last time. This time it's all about her, Theresa May.'

That strategy went well, then.

I am looking forward to seeing him again to chat that one through.

The irony is that in 2015, my local team and I airbrushed out David Cameron from our literature, choosing instead to focus on me and my record. He promptly went on to secure a mag-nificent victory. My campaign, meanwhile, secured a glorious defeat, narrowly losing that election by roughly 1,000 votes.

So with the lesson learned, in the subsequent 2017 general election I did as I was told and we led with Theresa May, ensur-ing I was relegated to the fine print. Her team snatched defeat from the jaws of victory; I got trounced.

So much for experts.

23

OUT OF ORDER

I only confessed this once, perhaps twice even, during my time in the Commons.

I like the Speaker.

As a statement, that usually brings forth a bucketload of abuse, or embarrassed chortles of laughter from many of my colleagues on the Conservative benches. True, John Bercow has chosen to allow his own ego to get ahead of him on many an occasion, but there are very few politicians who cannot be charged with that crime, me included, so he is in good company. Of course, his troubled relationship with his wife has been plastered over the papers far too often, but that's not his fault. It took a court action, after careless and libellous words on Twitter, to put a sock in his wife's mouth. Huge sighs of relief all round.

When it comes to ego, none of us could compete with Sally Bercow.

But what matters to me is that John is bloody marvellous at getting backbenchers heard in the House of Commons. The Speaker's formal role is as the chief officer and highest authority of the House of Commons, a position he is elected to by MPs. In reality, although he has a considerable number of duties, most MPs have most contact with him when they are in the debating chamber and he is chairing debates, questions to ministers or, of course, PMQs. To do his job he must remain politically impartial at all times, and that is where the present Speaker draws most criticism, principally from Conservative MPs, many of whom feel he favours the Labour Party. Given that John Bercow is a former Conservative MP, this rankles some even more.

For me, none of this mattered because I knew that he was delivering on the one pledge that counted when he sought election as Speaker in 2009: namely, he would ensure more backbenchers got to speak and hold ministers to account. His predecessor had shown little respect for backbenchers' wish to be heard and John Bercow wanted to put that right.

He delivers that by ensuring that ministers at the despatch box do not waffle on endlessly just to avoid having to answer other questions from backbenchers by eating into the time allocated for departmental questions. He is intolerant of such behaviour, and a determined champion of getting as many backbenchers as possible into the daily, hourly departmental question times. Good for him, and many a time I have had cause to be grateful for his approach.

Of course, none of that stopped him doing some daft things at times.

I know how irritating MPs can be. I was one of them. But, unfortunately, the Speaker invariably let his irritation show to such a degree that he often ended up looking more like the antagonist than the guardian of the House of Commons; more so when he regularly picked on a select few, such as the then PPS to the Prime Minister, Gavin Williamson (now a senior Cabinet minister), Karl McCartney, Jason McCartney and the dapper

Chris Pincher and Alec Shelbrooke. Because of the regularity with which he singled them out for reprimand, they formed the elite BBB club, Bollocked By Bercow.

All right, slightly childish, I grant you, but it did catch on and become something of a badge of honour, such was the deteriorating relationship between the Speaker and a number of Conservative backbenchers.

Karl, for example, was known by his colleagues to ask particularly well-aimed questions at PMQs, not least because he often shamelessly targeted both Ed Balls and Ed Miliband at any opportunity. (Incidentally, Ed Balls was quite capable and effective in dishing it back as well.) When it came to PMQs, however, the added challenge for Karl, and indeed any backbencher, was to keep their question pithy and easily understandable. Karl was generally quite good at this, but on one of these occasions, when he rose to ask his PMQ, he was given an unusually resounding and lengthy welcome by his backbench colleagues before he could begin, no doubt in anticipation of another cutting dig at the opposition leaders. Always good for morale, but not welcomed by the Speaker, who probably saw it as just more time being lost unnecessarily.

I don't quite know why the Speaker chose to reprimand Karl on this occasion, but he promptly seized the opportunity to take the sting out of Karl's effective dissection of the opposition. Instead of letting the Prime Minister answer, and thereby maintain the flow, he intervened with his own thoughts on the length of Karl's question, thus depriving him of the opportunity to take another whack at the opposition.

So what's unusual about this particular telling-off?

Simply that in the same Prime Minister's Questions five Labour MPs and George Galloway all asked longer questions, both in the number of words they used and in the time it took to ask them, far longer than Karl ever did, but without the un-welcome intervention of the Speaker.

But despite this inconsistent treatment, I happily confess to respecting how the Speaker otherwise protected backbench Members' interests, and, on a personal, one-to-one level, I always found him a decent chap.

And let's face it, he was only trying to manage an unruly mob. That his behaviour to a select few only encouraged more unruly behaviour is of course another matter. The principal agitator amongst them at the time was the little-known parliamentary private secretary to the Prime Minister, Gavin Williamson, who of course is currently the Defence Secretary, following his speedy promotion to Chief Whip. Clearly being a victim of the Speaker's acerbic comments was not harmful to his political career.

Gavin was regularly and not unreasonably castigated by the Speaker for shouting across the floor of the chamber during Prime Minister's Questions as he loyally flung 'challenging propositions' at the Labour front bench. Most of these propo-sitions were respectable in choice of words if not in the tone of delivery. Some were less so. Inevitably, Speaker Bercow would bounce up on his feet and admonish poor old Gavin, often being rewarded with more cries of derision from Conservative backbenchers as he occasionally let his irritation show.

Every Wednesday lunchtime, I was whisked back to my school classroom as we backbenchers produced collective childlike cries of, 'Ohhhhhhhh! Temper, temper!' Not quite the tone of a national legislative chamber, I agree. More Frankie Howerd and the *Carry On* cast than Francis Urquhart in *House of Cards*.

'Order, order!'

Bercow again, with familiar chant.

'It does not matter how long it takes, or how much complaining there is from Members on the government benches, the Leader of the Opposition will be heard. Mr Ed Miliband.'

More lengthy cries of derision as we backbenchers rained down sarcastic cheers of welcome for the now much bemused Leader of the Opposition, who had stood up to try to press on with his point.

'Order, order! The behaviour on the back benches is tiresome,' he would begin, while looking directly at the principal Conservative troublemakers. 'Members should consider the public, who witness this spectacle with the utmost and wholly justifiable sense of disapproval. Members would do well to reflect on the impression they also give to distinguished guests in the House today, as well as the public we all serve,' he rather grandly reminds us.

Utter tosh. The public love it, and I have yet to meet a visitor to the public gallery who has complained about either the confrontational or the theatrical nature of the event. On TV, 1.1 million people tuned in to watch Jeremy Corbyn's first PMQs against David Cameron. That's on a par with BBC One's evening programme *The One Show*. It's more than watch *Songs of Praise*, more than watch *Gardeners' World*, and more than watch all but the top fifteen Channel 4 programmes. In 2016, the Parliament channel recorded 2 million viewers for the first time, showing an increase of 150,000 each month compared to 2014.

The visitors Speaker Bercow worries about are, I believe, looking to be entertained, not informed. After all, we Conservative MPs rarely learned anything at Prime Minister's Questions, because the whole point was to avoid answering questions and to taunt the opposition – something that Gavin Williamson managed with consummate skill. He continued to barrack and heckle the opposition without further interruption from the Speaker, because he wisely enlisted the support of my good friend Andrew Bingham, former MP for High Peak.

Andrew routinely sat behind the Prime Minister at PMQs. He did so by being first into the chamber on Wednesday morning to reserve his seat for Prayers, which take place moments before the day's parliamentary session begins. In yet another quaint but bizarre custom of the House, we are not permitted to reserve places in the chamber, but we can reserve places for Prayers, which basically amounts to the same thing; a process Andrew ruthlessly exploited by reserving the seat next to Gavin, who, as PPS to the Prime Minister, always occupied the seat directly behind the PM. To his left was Andrew.

'Bingham, lean forward so that your nose is almost touching the Prime Minister's back when he is sitting down.'

'Why?'

'Put your phone down as well.'

'OK, why?'

'Bercow won't be able to see me, and I can continue to heckle.'

As I said, some schools train you perfectly for the job, including mine.

I think Andrew's services would, by default, make him an assistant to the Assistant of the Prime Minister. A glittering career beckoned, perhaps?

In fact, Andrew served the PM in another way at PMQs, by acting as his unofficial comic. Now, maybe you did think the gags were all off the cuff, and indeed, on rare occasions they were, but by no means was this always the case.

Andrew and another notable wit, the MP for Daventry, Chris Heaton-Harris, formed the unofficial joke department for No. 10. No pun intended.

Andrew was sitting harmlessly in the Tea Room one day, along with a few colleagues, chatting about Labour's links with unions, which at the time were back in the news. In keeping with the tradition of the Tea Room, Andrew cracked: 'The opposition do not speak in unison, but they do speak for Unison.'

Someone told Andrew to feed that joke into No. 10, and a new part-time unpaid career was launched for Bingham and Heaton-Harris. Not quite at the Jimmy Perry and David Croft level of partnership, which produced iconic comedies such as *Dad's Army* and *Hi-de-Hi!*, but certainly from the same era. Chris, incidentally, continues to share his witticisms on Twitter, should you like to see what you may have been missing.

So, are we all kids in a playground, and is the Speaker right that Parliament should behave better?

The short answer is no, because it does behave better.

PMQs is plain theatre, a chance for all MPs to let off steam for thirty minutes in every parliamentary week if they wish to do so. Much like spectators at the Colosseum, we heckle and we cheer the two main gladiators in the ring. It's horribly childish, but bloody good fun and jolly good for morale if you are on the winning side.

Our Parliament, unlike many around the world, is designed to be challenging and confrontational. Yes, it is pure entertainment at the weekly PMQs, but the process at all other times can ruthlessly exploit policy weaknesses and also expose underperforming members of both the government and the opposition front benches. The alternative is a Parliament that is less effective in holding its government to account and which has the added disadvantage of being desperately boring.

That we have an open, transparent Parliament is a credit to our democracy, and while millions may not tune in to Parliament TV every week, it is good that people have the choice to watch their legislature at work in a challenging and engaging fashion. Try watching C-SPAN and the US Congress in session, and you will see what the alternative could look like.

Although Parliament TV can have its downside.

At the same time as Andrew was being used as a shield for Gavin Williamson, I was rather keen to be seen – by my constituents, that is.

Parliamentary TV is, as I have said, a mixed blessing, not least because it is far too easy to forget it is there. Obviously, you don't forget when you are speaking, but you are quite likely to do so when just lolling around on the benches, whether waiting to speak, doughnutting someone, or just doing your job and listening to the debate.

I have been caught out on rather too many occasions, when I have been attending Question Time to ministers and have been distracted by an email, possibly important, possibly not. During that time, some eager bugger next to me stands up and rattles off his question. Too late for me to drop the phone and look fully attentive. Sure enough, within seconds, Twitter captures the moment, and my constituents are duly informed that I am not paying attention. There will always be someone prepared to remind you of your poor performance.

Annoying, but not fatal.

Unlike when I was caught out by a lip-reader.

Fortunately, a decent bloke as it turned out.

It was the same night that Ed Balls kept us late in the House, which led to me taking a taxi back to my constituency and ending up on page 3 of the *London Evening Standard* as a prolific waster of taxpayers' money, and that was not the only hiccup that evening.

In the early days of the 2010 parliament, it was still quite a novelty to have late-night sittings, and not too much of a chore doing so during lovely summer weather. Not surprisingly, many of us took to the Terrace Bar and sank a few drinks to pass the time. On this rare occasion that I drank in the Commons (most nights, I drove home), I returned to the chamber for the closing speeches feeling slightly light-headed.

The House was full. The opposition had done a very good job of keeping us up late, and Ed Balls was not unreasonably questioning the stamina of the new Conservative intake as we all looked thoroughly fed up and knackered. A colleague close by me was intervening on the shadow Chancellor and asking him a long, drawn-out question.

I, at the time, was ignoring him, while looking across the chamber at the opposition members. And – with absolute good taste, I hasten to add – I remarked to my neighbour how lucky Ed Balls was to be married to Yvette Cooper, who was looking far too bright and presentable for those early hours of the morning. Very fetching.

OK, this was laddish, and by today's standards not very cool.

So I was a little concerned when my parliamentary email flashed up an alert from someone who said, 'Just caught you on Parliament Live TV saying you fancied Yvette Cooper. Not very parliamentary!

'PS: Remember, lip-readers are out there!'

My first thought was: why was someone watching Parliament TV at this hour?

My second thought was:

Oops.

I wondered how this would play out on Twitter, but, fortunately, I did not have to find out.

Ping.

Email.

'Gotcha. Now, behave, or I will have fun at your expense.'

And with a final flourish, he added, 'Who says "fetching" these days?'

Well, I certainly won't again.

This transparency should have limits, I think. Being in the chamber and being visible to constituents is one thing, but family members seem to take a perverse delight in checking up on their dads, mums, wives, husbands and partners. Surely that is asking too much of our representatives?

While Andrew, for example, may have enjoyed the gratitude of the Prime Minister's PPS when he helped Gavin hide from the Speaker, he simultaneously received a text from his mother telling him: 'Sit up, Andrew. You look a mess all hunched up like that!'

He took that rebuke on behalf of his party and his Prime Minister, but failed to convince his mother.

And then there is always the danger that you sit there not really listening. All it takes is a moment or two when you let your mind wander and you can find yourself on screen grinning vacantly as the MP next to you refers to the death of a constituent. It's unlikely a fellow MP from any party would pick you up on that, as we all understand the consequences of a momentary lapse of concentration. But your constituents won't forgive you so easily.

My phone buzzed.

'I see you have a new friend.'

It was my wife, Helen, passing judgement on me one evening in the Commons. No little kiss after the message, which, as we all know, implies huge problems.

I had just sat down next to someone in the chamber who had been caught up in relationship issues that were currently splashed all over the newspapers.

It is very difficult to take your place on the green benches when you have been involved in a tabloid 'scandal' of whatever sort. The victim of the tabloid frenzy will always feel that everyone in the place has read the details; this is almost always hugely inaccurate but, nevertheless, they do feel exposed for all to see. To then have to walk into the chamber, in front of colleagues across the House, feeling that all eyes are on you, is, I think, a time when you find out who your friends are. In this case, I was only too pleased to walk in with this colleague and sit with them in the chamber, chatting away.

And that's precisely what happened. In fact, a couple of other colleagues offered to join us, which was even better.

As we gathered behind the Speaker's chair, where there is an entrance into the chamber, one of those colleagues went to pull open the large swing door and ushered the rest of us in. He was, fortuitously, left to follow on behind us. Way behind us, as it turned out.

Meanwhile, my other chum, who had ventured to join us by escorting our wounded colleague into the chamber, offered up a magnanimous bow and invited me to be the first to follow our tabloid victim into the chamber. After his gallant bow, I noticed he moved silently to the row of benches behind us, sufficiently divorced from me and my colleague, who were now alone together.

Which was exactly the moment that my wife turned on the TV and drew her own conclusion: that I was clearly a close collaborator who had been fortunate enough to escape the attention of the tabloids. Guilt by association. That's when my phone buzzed.

Very shortly afterwards, the division bell rang and we all made our way to the chamber, duty happily done. I thought no more of it and, after the division, returned to the chamber and sat with some other colleagues.

My phone buzzed again.

'I see I touched a nerve. You moved. Guilty as charged.'

As is becoming increasingly apparent, there is no right of appeal with Helen.

Late-night sittings do have the effect of undermining rational thoughts and behaviour. Inside a relatively small chamber, built for maybe 450 people, late-night sittings at voting time mean the place is packed tight with over 600 MPs. All knackered, all irritable, and most wanting to go home.

The opposition front bench, whose only sense of achievement lies in how many times they can force a vote, and thus keep the government MPs up as long as they can, do relish these moments. It's what they do, and it makes them feel effective, as if they really are doing something.

Into that toxic environment I wandered, shortly before a series of votes were expected which would finally allow us to go home.

'Nick. Over here a sec.'

It was my whip, Bill Wiggin, plotting some mischief.

Do you fancy shouting one word at the Speaker?

Too many ideas flooded my head, and I resisted the temptation to make a suggestion.

'All you have to do is shout "Object!" when he asks the House to formalise the appointment of Labour MP Cathy Jamieson to the Department for Culture, Media and Sport Select Committee.'

It was 1 a.m. and I was utterly pliable.

'Fine.'

'Do you want to know why?'

'Go on then,' I yawned.

It's a way of getting back at them for all these late nights, and it doesn't really matter because she will get on the committee tomorrow anyway.'

'Fine. Just nod at me when you want me to object.'

Utterly oblivious to the Select Committee's agenda for the following day, I duly shouted 'Object!' at the appropriate time.

It should have rung alarm bells when the Speaker looked across at the benches and said, 'Do I hear an objection...?' sounding genuinely puzzled. I assumed he was surprised by this unwarranted intrusion to a normally straightforward procedure.

'Object!' I repeated, just to make sure none of the 600 or so Members in the House were in any doubt as to what was being said and which silly bugger was saying it. I really wanted to go home.

Controversial? Yep.

Not least because the very next day, Rupert Murdoch and his son were about to be humbled before the Select Committee for News Corporation's disgraceful conduct in the hacking scandal exposed early in the parliament.

And yours truly had foolishly submitted to a request from those cunning whips, having failed to put two and two together.

I should have known something was wrong when it emerged that the whips had asked Kris Hopkins MP, a big, tough-looking bugger from Yorkshire, to accompany me out of Parliament. Apparently some Labour Members were so bloody furious they wanted to have a pop at me; physical or otherwise, I have no idea.

Even then, I was blind to the sense of fury at my one-word contribution to Parliament that day. What I had done was block, albeit temporarily, the appointment of a Labour MP to the Select Committee that was interviewing the Murdochs the next day about the hacking of private mobile phones in search of tabloid news stories.

Rupert Murdoch's News International group was on the defensive. Labour were on the front foot and the government was on the defensive. The left went mad, and went mad at me specifically. The ugly side of social media came out of hiding and let full rip at me. I wisely failed to respond to that and every other journalist enquiry that day. Mind you, I added a few followers that night.

Controversial? Definitely. Stupid? Absolutely.

I had broken a cardinal rule. Don't do what the whips ask you to do, and certainly don't do anything last-minute and late at night.

In the House of Commons, it is not just the Speaker who can do daft things.

It was a sharp reminder that even someone I like to think of as relatively independent-minded and reasonably bright can make a complete fool of himself through a momentary lapse of judgement, which is precisely what I had just done.

Later the next day, I caught Cathy Jamieson being interviewed. Not unreasonably, she commented that she wasn't sure what she may have done to cause me concern about her appointment. She had a point.

Sorry, Cathy.

24

DO AS WE SAY,
NOT AS WE DO

Imagine this on your ten o'clock news.

'Today's lead story is that a 62-year-old man has been fired from his job as a Minister of State because he must make way for a younger person. The minister was not found to have been grossly negligent, been in breach of contract or been guilty of having sexually harassed or bullied members of staff. He was sacked to give someone younger a go.'

In other news…

If only that had happened to me, the subsequent law suit would have meant a luxurious retirement beckoned, wouldn't it? Well, it might have done had I been working anywhere but in Parliament as a minister. In fact, there never was a chance for it to happen to me as I never became a minister, but it did happen quite regularly to my colleagues, and will almost certainly happen again.

The irony is that in a place that has produced enough rules and regulations on employee rights to make employment law one of the most lucrative branches of the legal profession, the House of Commons and governments of every colour pay precious little attention to them when it comes to managing their own affairs. In other words, they fail to practise what they preach.

It is well accepted in business that it is not easy to sack someone these days, except perhaps for gross negligence. Parliament has seen to that. In fact, we have passed endless regulations ensuring consultation periods, career advice and wider personal support are made available to those who lose their jobs.

So it strikes me as a touch ironic that Prime Ministers routinely sack their own ministers for no other reason than they are fed up with them and want to give someone else a go. I well remember during David Cameron's first reshuffle, meeting in the corridor outside the Tea Room in the House of Commons a much shocked and unsurprisingly miffed junior minister from south of the Thames who had just come from the Prime Minister's office a few yards away.

'He told me it was time to let someone else take the reins and give younger people a chance, never mind whether I had been doing a good job or not!'

So, ageism, no formal consultation period and a process of no-fault instant dismissal. I suspect an employee tribunal would take a rather dim view of this example in the unlikely event that they were ever asked to pass judgment.

Of course, in most workplaces, when someone does actually leave the company having been dismissed or made redundant, they are rarely ever seen again on the premises. In Parliament, however, not only is the now former minister still very much in the House of Commons, he or she is also free to lob unhelpful questions at the Prime Minister or any other member of the government from their new place on the back benches. And of course many in this position know where the political bodies are buried, which could be embarrassing to the government should they wish to expose them. He or she may have been summarily dismissed as a minister, but not as an MP; that is something even Prime Ministers cannot arrange.

As a result of this rather awkward situation, the dismissed minister is given lots of loving care and attention from the whips, who constantly hint that their future is by no means all doom and gloom. David Cameron and his Chief Whip would try to soften the blow with the swift application of a gong of some sort. The most popular of these was being made a member of the Privy Council if you were not already one, and therefore earning the right to be known as the Rt Hon. Joe Smith until you draw your final breath. Even more welcome would be the more highly prized award of a knighthood for men or a damehood for women. Quite a few of these were dished out by Her Majesty on request of No. 10 in order to soothe bruised colleagues. And for those unlucky enough to get none of the above, there was always the old favourite of the whips, the prospect that you may return to the front bench at some future date if you behave yourself. You were after all, still 'in the club', and they still needed your votes and your loyalty, even if the latter was not entirely deserved in some cases.

To be fair, MPs well understand the ministerial working conditions that they are entering into when they run for Parliament. Few MPs, if any, would really welcome the idea that a Prime Minister must go through a statutory consultancy period before they could fire someone from their Cabinet, be it for incompetence, bad behaviour or just to give someone else a turn. Of course not, and anyway, I suspect some of the public quite enjoy a little bit of comeuppance for senior politicians every now and then when a Cabinet reshuffle takes place. Assuming they notice, that is.

The MPs' staff, however, deserve better.

In the semi-detached world that Westminster can be, some 3,000 people who work for MPs do so in an employment bubble that can be the most exhilarating, challenging and rewarding of careers but also carries hidden dangers and vulnerabilities, of which only some have come to public attention in the autumn of 2017. My first introduction to the matter came about because of a pair of brogues back in 2013.

'I wish he would stop throwing his shoe at me.'

My head jerked up from the rather dull briefing I was reading. 'Sorry?'

I was listening to a conversation taking place in my outer office, and at the time couldn't recall throwing my shoe at anyone.

One of my team wisely shut the door, confining me to my room, so I was unable to interfere any more.

'It wasn't your shoe,' was the parting shot.

Why an MP was throwing their shoe at a member of staff, and apparently doing so on repeated occasions, is unclear but it is most definitely a touch bonkers as well as potentially dangerous. I have size 11 feet and a shoe thrown from me would hurt.

I needed to find out more.

It turned out that, along with shoes, this particular MP shouted extensively at his staff, threatened them with dismissal on a regular basis and worked them all unreasonable hours. He was, I believe, the exception rather than the rule, although he was by no means the only one, and he is no longer in the House of Commons. The staff who could not put up with this had nowhere to turn to make a formal complaint or even a simple plea for help, so a community of self-help grew up amongst the staff who worked for MPs, which is how I came to overhear talk of the flying shoe.

I decided not to raise the subject with my parliamentary

assistant again as she would probably just throw a shoe at me, so I went chasing after her visitor.

She didn't hesitate to put me right when I suggested that she should raise it with the whips.

'Don't be daft, if someone complains to the Whips' Office all that will happen is that the whips benefit by having more info on a misbehaving MP so they can make him vote for the government if he ever wants to rebel.'

'Really?'

'True or not, that's the perception.'

'Even so, can't they take the MP to task and sort things out?'

'They could, but then the chances are I would lose my job at some point, and probably struggle to get another one here again.'

'That's wrong and probably illegal. Would you like me to help?

'No.'

And, on that occasion, I didn't.

But now I did want to speak to my own parliamentary assistant, Maddie.

'No, I think you should tell the whips, but that's simply an option, not an established process that's in place. Look,' she went on, 'if you throw a shoe at me what options do I have?'

'Throw it back at me?'

'Yes, apart from that, and even if it did shut you up, you are my boss and I have nowhere to go to report you and hold you to account for gross misconduct. You are untouchable because you don't have a boss.'

'Newspapers?'

'Seriously, what professional working here would want to do that? We leave that to the MPs. Anyway,' she added, 'even if I did do that, I wouldn't work again, and why should I not have the same rights and protections from you that the rest of the country have!'

I sensed she was in danger of beginning to think I had thrown a shoe at her.

'Maddie?'

'Yes?'

'Just to remind you, I have not actually thrown a shoe at you.'

'Yet,' came the reply.

Her point was well made.

Clearly, we need to take steps to create a formal complaints process so staff can be confident that issues will be handled professionally and without harm to their career prospects. However, we also need to make sure MPs understand that they are not above the law and they have a duty of care to all employees.

We want a Parliament made up of representatives from across the country and from all different walks of life. No longer are we a House of Commons packed with lawyers and former public school boys. We have former miners, union leaders, teachers, doctors, nurses, soldiers, business people, self-employed workers, tradespeople and more. Yet not all MPs have experience of employing people before they come to Parliament. Some will never have worked in a professional institution before, and many will not have a clue about management practice or their responsibilities to staff – which go way beyond just authorising the monthly pay packet.

Within days of being elected, and without any training or formal mentoring, the newly elected MPs are expected to recruit and manage a new team as well as handle the ongoing constituency and parliamentary work required from an MP's office, which in reality they themselves have little understanding of at that stage.

In my first week in Parliament, the only help I got from the

House of Commons authorities was an induction on how to manage the new expenses system introduced after the expenses scandal. That was important but, frankly, had I not had the advantage of having run my own business and managed staff, and I had not understood employment practice, budgeting, staff appraisals, property management to help secure a new constituency office, and the need to have a motivated team, I would have struggled from the very first day. In all likelihood I would have struggled to keep up with the requirements of the job thereafter.

Throw an inexperienced person into this and you have a recipe for chaos. Add in the kind of pumped-up ego that fuels some, but by no means all, MPs and a toxic relationship can form between the MP and his or her staff. And sometimes, albeit far less often than the media would have you believe, this produces dreadful staff management, unprofessional behaviour and, in extreme cases, bullying.

The staff have nowhere effective to turn should they not feel confident enough to take the matter into their own hands. For a few, the dream job of working in Parliament becomes a nightmare. And on the one occasion I took the matter up with the whips, I left the meeting deeply unsatisfied that they themselves were adequately equipped to tackle the problem I raised, not least because they themselves were after all MPs with mixed ability and skills in human resource management. That was not their job, and, worse, there was nothing else was in place to deal with these issues.

It is little wonder, therefore, that when it came to the much-reported sexual harassment of staff by some MPs, it was inevitable that a toxic combination of ego, power and lack of accountability meant yet another Westminster scandal, and some quite distressing circumstances were laid bare in November 2017.

My early political days were spent in the shadow of the ill-fated 'back to basics' campaign that the then Conservative Prime Minister espoused in the early '90s. He meant hard work, enterprise, reward for efforts and, of course, family. Unfortunately, the tabloids had other ideas and interpreted it to mean a return to clean living and the upstanding credentials of the Conservative Party. Which in turn meant they promptly exposed every sex scandal they could lay their hands on, bolstering sales by focusing on a few cheating MPs. There were carefully planned honey traps, as in the case of the relatively little-known MP Piers Merchant, who was the object of not one but two tabloid newspaper stings in 1997 which pictured him in activities such as an 'open-air sex romp' with a seventeen-year-old Soho night-club hostess. In fact, it was far less tantalising than it sounds, but that didn't matter. The headline 'Sleaze Merchant' proved irresistible to several newspapers.

At the time, the Conservative government was going from one sleaze scandal to another, be it over sex or money. I don't recall drugs, but there probably was some of that as well for all I know.

While extramarital sex was an obsession with the tabloids at the time, it later seemed to die down for a while as the public seemed to accept that what consenting adults get up to in their bedrooms is nobody's business but the participants'. It might still make for good headlines, but it rarely leads to resignation.

Quite what the tabloids would have made of a parliamentary assistant in 2014 coming across an empty carton for a vibrator in the ladies' loo on the ground floor of Norman Shaw North is anyone's guess. More so because it was apparently far from being the kind of cheap model one might buy for a Secret Santa gift. I didn't really know what to say or where to look when I was told about this out of the blue over tea in Portcullis House one afternoon.

On the other hand, when I heard tales of the latest goings-on from colleagues or staffers, I was still mildly surprised that while extramarital affairs were not considered particularly interesting, suggestions of prolific sexual activity were considered fair game for speculation. That any MP managed to be so prolific amazed me, in part because I couldn't figure out how they found the time and in part because I was brought up in an era when sex and politics didn't mix all that well.

'What do you mean, he doesn't wear a condom?'

'Apparently safe sex for him means ensuring he gets a regular supply of antibiotics.'

'Seriously, why are you telling me this?'

'You're a gossip, you like to know these things.'

I blanched at this evident misrepresentation of my character (obviously).

'But he is not married; he can have as many affairs as he likes. What I don't get is why people sleep with him in the first place?'

'It's a power thing and he casts his net wide.'

'He's a backbencher! We have no power.'

'Most people think MPs are all a step away from the Cabinet, and that's intoxicating.'

'Really?' That was definitely not my experience. 'I bet this isn't true.'

'You wait and see.'

•   •   •

Workplace relationships, eh? Who would ever be so daft as to get into that?

Except for me, that is. So let me confess.

I approached her, touched her hand, made eye contact and then kissed her.

She worked at my company, she was single.

I did not put my hand on her knee.

I was her boss.

I had never attempted to do this before, and would have backed off had she told me to do so. She didn't, and we were married in 2009. We are still married and I am very happy; I hope she is.

This happens across workplaces all over the UK. Unsurprisingly, this also happens in Parliament, and I hope it continues and that people enjoy fantastic relationships.

I don't see an alternative way of taking a relationship to that level – that is, unless we resort to a regulated Tinder- or Grindr-style platform on a mandatory basis. (True, that may help mitigate some of the clumsy initial steps people make when they want to develop a relationship with someone they fancy.)

But thank God for human interaction.

So, as Parliament catches up with the rest of the world and introduces credible processes for dealing with sexual harassment and bullying, I do hope a sense of proportion is maintained. There are, after all, about 7,000 people who work in the Palace of Westminster. There will be lots of happy, fruitful relationships, and no doubt plenty of consensual sex.

I can't help wondering: if I had first approached Helen in 2017 and she'd told me to hop it, would she consider it harassment? I suspect not, simply because touching her hand was a relatively small step, and it is not that hard to judge whether a kiss would be welcome or not. However, someone persisting beyond that first step with unwanted sexual advances is a more serious matter.

Having declared an interest, it's almost certainly true that people in positions of power, including a few MPs, have presumed far too much, probably intoxicated by their own position, and have harassed staff members entirely inappropriately. It is also true of many other companies and organisations across the country but, unlike every other institution, Parliament has no process for anyone so treated to seek help and hold their boss to account. As it was put to me in 2014, 'People love this place, they have got their foot on the ladder of a serious political job and then a total dickhead comes along, screws it all up for them and they are left with a choice. Comply, or complain, crash their career and give up on their dream.'

At the time of writing, if someone in Parliament does want to report their boss for harassment, where do they go? The answer is: if it is not a crime, they have nowhere they can take their complaint.

So, with incomprehensible irony, for years we have made the laws to protect everyone but our own. And we knew that. Which makes it more stomach-churning that some people had to put up with sexual harassment.

In effect, until now Parliament has been saying: do as I say, not as I do.

So when we hear some politicians say that we must learn lessons from the scandal of sexual harassment and bullying of staff, and that political parties must do more to protect staff interests, I don't disagree, but I am irritated. All political parties have known there is no process in place for fair and independent support for employees. Every Member of Parliament would know within months of starting their job that the protections they legislate on for others do not exist for their staff. The good news is that the vast majority of staff and MPs have no cause to miss them, but for the minority who do there is nowhere truly effective to turn. Once again, Parliament is playing catch-up.

For all the grandstanding we have witnessed on this issue from both the opposition and government parties, from the Speaker of the House of Commons and indeed the House of Lords, the truth is they have all been aware of the shortcomings for many years.

25

'ENFIELD 'TIL I DIE'

'**Y**ou do realise, lad [I was forty at the time], that you may not win this seat first time round?'

It was 1999, and I was meeting with the executive of the Enfield North Conservative Association for the first time, seeking selection as the candidate for the 2001 election. They looked thoroughly fed up, and not overly impressed with my efforts. Either that, or they had not recovered from losing what was considered a safe Conservative seat by a thumping 6,822 votes two years earlier.

Worse, they had got to know, like and trust their new candidate in that election, Mark Field, who, much to the regret of the Enfield North Conservative Party, had wisely gone on to fight the safe seat of the Cities of London and Westminster, vacated by Sir Peter Brooke just before the 2001 election.

Enfield North's MP until 1997 was Tim Eggar, who had held the seat since 1979. He had wisely chosen to stand down before the wipeout of the 1997 Labour landslide.

Frank Thacker, who had just informed me I would not win in 2001, was then the chairman of the association; a blunt-speaking Black Country Conservative who is one of the

Conservative Party's local heroes. He has spent a lifetime with three loves: his work as an engineer, his family and his work for the party. He won't mind me saying this, but he is well into his eighties and has only just put his feet up.

Never shy of an opinion, he, much like his formidable wife Audrey, who ran the local Conservative office and was a former Enfield councillor, were vital to keeping things going locally as the UK Conservative Party collapsed in the aftermath of New Labour's 1997 victory. CCHQ would do well to remember these folks when they next dish out the honours.

Anyway, Frank was proved right about 2001. In fact, it took eleven years to win the seat; the win, when it came, was down to some bloody hard work from the local party volunteers and, in part, because I refused stubbornly to give up. I sense that the electors had worked this out by 2010, when I did win, and had calculated that they would see less of me if they packed me off to Westminster to stop me hanging around the constituency and bothering them so much.

My stubbornness, however, while well-motivated, was perhaps not my brightest decision.

At the 2001 election, I achieved a decent swing and cut Labour's majority from 6,812 to 2,291. That's when I should have left and gone off in hunt of a nice safe seat. At the time, that was the typical game plan of most candidates: do a tough one, then wait for the 15,000-majority constituency to come knocking. But no, I had to be stubborn.

Enfield Conservatives wanted me to stay. I thought we had a decent chance of winning in 2005 and, all in all, I had become very fond of all the members and the core team of helpers. However, I was completely oblivious to how fast the local demography of the patch was changing, and how that change favoured Labour, not me. Equally stubborn candidates like

Robert Halfon in nearby Harlow took the same approach and are still in Parliament, having turned very marginal seats into very safe seats. Good for them. And Parliament is better for it.

Looking back, I can genuinely say the same thing except, unfortunately, by 2017, I had turned Enfield North into a stonkingly safe Labour seat.

When the *Daily Mirror* labels the Conservatives Tory toffs, or when *The Guardian* implies we are all selfish, tax-dodging brutes, not only do they insult the millions who vote for the Conservatives, they also forget the thousands of party volunteers across the country who could not be further removed from that stereotypical image that opponents try to paint.

The local party is, essentially, a campaign organisation made up from the likes of you and me. Perhaps they're a little bonkers, to give up so much time for a party whose values they believe in, and to back candidates time after time at elections, but, nevertheless, they do just that, as do volunteers for all parties.

For some, it is more a vehicle for social events. For others, it is about policy. But, in the main, it is about campaigning. At least it was in Enfield. And some local members were far too enthusiastic about their campaigning methods.

Andrew Nicholas, my local chairman in the 2005 election, was the most ebullient of them all. I was with him when he parked a country-style Land Rover in the middle of a very non-Tory-leaning housing estate that had apparently not seen a Tory since 1979. Using the megaphone, he promptly announced that the Conservative candidate was waiting in the car park to meet people. Some of those potential voters clearly thought Christmas had come early and took the opportunity to perfect their vernacular English vocabulary on me. He, meanwhile, stayed with the car to protect it from young buggers who might have been looking for spare automotive parts, while he sent me packing.

'They will probably vote for you, though, Nick,' he cheerfully announced, as I eventually sought refuge back in the car. 'After all, they can now put a face to the name.'

He was wrong, of course.

Andrew's very polished manner, impeccable presentation and natural authority hide a ruthless streak, both in the execution of our campaigning and in making difficult but necessary personnel changes within the local party.

He never allowed me to be tarnished by any of the fallout, and where Audrey and Frank brought stability at a crucial time, Andrew set a path for the future through change. It should come as no surprise, therefore, that, for fun, Andrew drove tanks across the fields of Normandy once a year, and I can only imagine he had political leaders who had failed his high standards, or posed a threat to his values, firmly in his sights as he thundered across the northern French plains.

For as long as the party hierarchy fails to embrace the pockets of expertise within their own party, it will be difficult to sustain a significant campaigning organisation at a local level. What will inevitably happen is that the energy and ideas at this level will look for other ways to be heard, as happened with Labour and Momentum, the grassroots campaigning network that evolved out of Jeremy Corbyn's 2015 leadership campaign. On the other hand, maybe that's just what is needed after the debacle of the 2017 election.

Andrew's successor as chairman was Matthew Laban, a head teacher and author of the very authoritative *Mr Speaker*. Matthew brought a very different style to the local party, but no less enthusiasm than his predecessors.

Having witnessed the challenges of working through committees, which is the mainstay of local party organisations of any political colour, Matthew would act first, then seek approval. Behaving much like a General Secretary of the Communist Party would have done in pre-1990 Soviet Russia certainly had its advantages and, surprisingly, no one in the local party objected. He was blunt, with the added benefit of knowing precisely what he wanted to achieve, and, where necessary, he would win by force of argument, such as the rallying call he gave to members at my adoption meeting just before the 2017 election: 'If you managed to get here for this meeting, there is no reason why you can't get off the sofa and campaign with Nick on the streets of Enfield.'

Much like his predecessor, Matthew took the view that there is no such thing as a no-go area for seeking out voters. He was equally blunt when sharing his opinion with voters as he was with party members.

'Oh no,' said one ostensibly comfortable middle-class lady from the door of her very nice house, 'I couldn't possibly vote Conservative. After all, Boris Johnson as Mayor of London never did anything for me.'

'Well, madam,' responded Matthew, with only a marginal hint of disdain as he surveyed the grand exterior of her house, 'living in a £1.5 million home, I don't suppose you need a lot of help!'

She pursued him down her driveway with some very unlady-like language.

It is frankly amazing that people come out onto the streets and help campaign time after time after time. More so when you are in some politically tough areas. Many of these volunteers are rewarded with quite the welcome: a slammed door in their face, the odd obscenity, a few tirades and the occasional threat.

'Knock on my door again and I'll set my dog on you' was one of the charming greetings that Lindsay Rawlings, my agent, received in one campaign.

Unfortunately, in Lincoln Crescent in the south of the constituency, I caught up with Lindsay standing stoically in a layby clutching her hand, wrapped in a blood-soaked tissue. She was waiting for a car to pick her up and take her off to hospital for some urgent repair work. A vicious little canine had bitten through a fingertip, severing it from her hand. So much for responsible dog ownership, to leave the little bugger free to terrorise postmen and -women, as well as leaflet distributors of any kind.

Lindsay, a former police officer, was much braver than me and she knew it. Familiar with my inability to cope with the sight of blood, she quickly despatched me elsewhere, assuring me everything was in hand. A poor choice of words, I thought at the time, but I was very grateful for her insistence, as there is no doubt I would have fainted at the sight of blood and severed fingertip. Pathetic, I know.

No band of political volunteers is complete without a political dynasty, a First Family, if you like, and Enfield was no different. Matthew Laban's sister Joanne is, at the time of writing, the leader of the Conservative group on the local council, having set a work ethic in local campaigning second to none. She completed the line-up of constituency political leaders who all had one thing in common: their huge belief in our ability to win whatever the prevailing odds. This was matched by their unconditional support for me, though that never held them back if they thought I was screwing up.

'That interview you did on BBC London about the hospital was awful. What was wrong with you?'

Ouch. That was blunt from Jo.

'You sounded defensive.'

'I was! We had just announced we were closing the A&E.'

'You looked defensive. You looked like you were hiding; all

very shifty! You kept looking down, your eyes were all over the place, and you looked like you wanted to bury yourself in your own overcoat.'

'I wanted to hide. Just like I want to hide from you now, incidentally,' I added, none too helpfully.

'You should come out fighting in future, and say things like "I will chain myself to the gates of the hospital rather than let the bulldozer in", or "They will not close this A&E so long as I am around!"'

She had a point.

I was rather feeble, but then the leftie reporter from the Beeb used all the tricks to make me look shifty, and in doing so, taught me a lesson.

I was sharing my misfortune with Tim Donovan, the very same Tim Donovan who had managed to skewer me in a joint-piece interview with Sadiq Khan – though, to be fair, that was due to my lack of grasp on the issue rather than any premeditated plan of his. I listened gratefully to his advice, if not with a little bemusement.

His lesson was simple: 'If the reporter interviewing you is shorter than you, don't look at them when answering the question. Look above their head, and that way, you avoid looking down (and shifty), and avoid your eyes looking narrow or closed (downright criminal), which will happen if they bring the camera right up to your face, which of course they do if they think you'll be on the defensive.'

In this case, the interviewer had been a short arse.

'The alternative', continued Tim, 'is to spread your legs.'

'Pardon?'

'Spread your legs apart, so that you drop your height to his height, and then look him in the eye.'

Clever.

'Also, take off your coat, even if it is bloody freezing. Then you don't look like you're in a hurry to leave.'

Advice duly noted, and several reporters over the next few years have enjoyed the sight of me straddling College Green in Westminster, where many MP interviews take place, looking like I have just stepped off a horse after a ten-mile gallop.

Mercifully, not all is politics with the local party association. Helen and I always tried to attend as many social events as possible, except on one notable occasion.

The Annual Quiz.

I am making a confession in writing, because I never had the nerve to disabuse the organiser of the dreaded annual quiz, a chap called John Boast. As the organiser and question master of the annual quiz it is not surprising that he was extremely knowledgeable, certainly on politics and electoral constituency history. I think he would have smashed *Mastermind* if his chosen subject had been 'Constituency Election Results since 1931'. John Boast was part of that history, having stood in 1966 and again in 1970 in the seat of Stoke Newington. A safe Labour seat, he nevertheless came second on both occasions with a respectable 28 per cent share of the vote in 1966, which he increased to 34 per cent in 1970 – a vote share increase that I failed to match.

John was one of my most committed supporters, a former councillor in Enfield, and always on hand with sound advice, whether to help guide me through tough local issues or when wrestling with the prospect of defying the government, on those limited occasions I felt it necessary to do so. That advice would often be compared to or drawn from a political precedent over the past century, thanks to his extraordinary depth of knowledge.

Unfortunately, his extraordinary depth of knowledge was

not limited to politics, which is why he proposed, designed and delivered the annual quiz. Every year, I would fork out for a dozen bottles of wine as the top prize, which would be shared amongst the winning team, generally made up of six people. The only year I won was the first year, so, naturally enough, I took back two bottles of my own wine.

Sadly, when I say my own wine, I really do mean my own wine. As a result of a long lunch in a Provence vineyard with friends of my then wife's family, I foolishly took up an offer to own two humungous rows of vines. In return for a relatively modest fee – well, it seemed so at the time – every year for the next five years I received 400 bottles of the ghastliest vin de pays you can imagine. For those of us who survived the original Liebfraumilch and Blue Nun days of the '70s, trust me, they were a connoisseur's dream compared to the gunk I had signed up to. It wouldn't pass as vinegar in a fish and chip shop, it was that bad.

To my huge embarrassment, I had offered up the first prize from that year's collection of wine having not yet tasted the delivery. These wonderful volunteers were being badly treated by the very same man they worked so hard for, and yet I knew they would be too polite to say anything to me after I had stripped their insides with this grape juice special.

From that moment on, I always bought decent wine for the top prize, in the hope that I might win some of it back again. Unsurprisingly, I never did.

John devised questions that few could answer. Few, that is, who were born after 1959, like me. If you were born before then, most of the questions were straightforward. Even the music clips were from His Master's Voice archive collection (HMV to you younger ones), and could only be played on 75rpm record players, generally only found in antique stores.

With Helen being born in the late '60s, between us, we stood no chance.

But it's part of my job to just grin and get on with it and, to be fair, I do like some quizzes, though I prefer ones where I have a reasonable chance of getting the odd answer correct. Helen never hesitated to extract a heavy price from me every time she came along. Even her huge affection for John did not outweigh her sentiments towards this otherwise popular annual event.

One year, however, she just refused to go.

In fact, she organised an event for us to attend that clashed with the quiz, that's how determined she was to win a reprieve that year.

Realising far too late that I could do nothing about it, I had to apologise profusely that we could not come. Worse, that year the number of tickets sold was relatively low, and I was asked if I could send two people along in my place.

Never wanting to let my fabulous party members down, I agreed immediately, without any idea of who I could ask.

I tried my good friend and neighbouring MP, David Burrowes.

No joy, and anyway, he had still not forgiven me for setting him up at the Turkish Cypriot dinner.

I tried Charles Walker MP, next door in Broxbourne.

Nothing.

I tried my neighbours. Not a chance, but that's how I came to find out that they didn't vote for me anyway, so the good news was there was one fewer house to canvass.

Then I tried Leanne and Helen, my staunchly loyal constituency office team, who lived in Enfield.

Surely not a problem.

'Nope, I'm doing my hair.'

'Rubbish. Please don't be difficult.'

'Well,' chipped in Leanne, 'I'm under thirty, I'm young and I'm not giving up a Friday night for a quiz night that you are not even going to attend.'

'But it's fun, and you will know so many people there.'

'You don't mean that and you don't want to go, so it can't be that much fun.'

'I'll pay for the tickets.'

I was beginning to plead, and they sensed this could work for them.

'What about drinks?' chimed in Helen.

'OK, a tenner for a couple of drinks.'

'A tenner?!'

'It's cheap at the club.'

'We need time to get ready as well.'

'Seriously? You leave here at 5.30, and it doesn't start until 7.30. It's not being held in the West End!'

Big intake of breath from Leanne.

'You should', she quietly intoned, with a hint of finality, 'let us leave early to get ready.'

'OK, how about four o'clock?'

'Lunchtime,' stated Leanne.

'How long do you need to get ready?!'

'Half a day, take it or leave it,' said Helen.

Totally had.

'Deal.'

The taxpayer would never know how I abused their money on this occasion, I thought.

To this day I am uncertain if John ever suspected my reluctant participation at the many quizzes he organised, and sadly, now I can never be sure. I received a call from John when I had just completed the first draft of this book, and, with his characteristic understatement about the life-threatening illness he was undergoing treatment for, he asked me if it would be possible to read my draft as he didn't think he would be around for publication. I spent two lovely hours with John and his wife Jean when I dropped the manuscript round to him and we agreed to meet up again a week or so later so I could get his advice and of course judge his reaction to my confession. That was sadly not to be. I never saw him again. We shall both miss him.

Unsurprisingly, he left me one bequest, which his daughter shared with me: a long list of notes, corrections and advice on the manuscript, all of which I have included in the final version. But I am still not sure what he thought about my views on the quiz.

As she had stoically accompanied me to many of the quizzes, I was always relieved to have the opportunity to take Helen to many of the fabulous social events that took place across the borough. I knew how much Helen enjoyed balls, in particular. We didn't get many in Enfield, but I would always ensure we attended whenever invited.

So it was with immense pleasure that I accepted an invitation from David Burrowes when he rang to invite us to join him and his wife Janet at the annual dinner of the Cypriot DISY political party, sister party to the Conservatives.

This was, of course, a good local event to attend, because so many north London Cypriots would be there, along with a cross-section of local councillors and MPs. Greek Cypriots are wonderful hosts, with very generous amounts of food and drink laid on, often followed by some traditional dance performances and then the rest of the night to add one's own personal dance style to the evening.

The event was being held in David's constituency so, mercifully, there was no chance that I would be invited to speak, as he would say a few words on behalf of us all. I checked the final arrangements a few days before, including the dress code: black tie for gents, and 'long' for the ladies. Helen was looking forward to a good night and we seemed set for a bit of fun. What could possibly change that?

Two things, in fact, that both changed the whole dynamic of the evening and caused a distinct cooling in relations for the de Bois marriage. The first event was one I couldn't really do anything about.

Glafcos Ioannou Clerides, a much-revered President of Cyprus from 1993 until 2003, died. He was also the founder, in 1976, of the DISY political party, whose annual dinner we were attending. Clerides also temporarily took over the reins of power after the brute Nicos Sampson was swept from power eight days after he led the coup in 1974. His death was indeed felt very hard by Greek Cypriots, nowhere more so than the expat community in north London, who chose the night of the ball to publicly honour and remember him.

'Hi, David, just checking arrangements for tonight. All set?'

'Yes, we will be there for 8.00.' A total fabrication from David – he never made it anywhere on time, bless him – but by then I always discounted fifteen minutes for an accurate estimation.

'Great,' I replied. 'Black tie for us and long for the ladies?'

'Absolutely. I won't make that mistake again!'

'What mistake?'

'Seven years ago, we went to the same ball, which was then being held in the West End, and I thought it was lounge suits.'

'And…?'

'It wasn't. It was black tie and long dresses. Unfortunately, Janet was in a trouser suit.'

'Ouch.'

'Precisely – so don't worry, I have checked! And one other thing,' he added. 'Don't forget that Clerides' passing will be mentioned at some point, but you won't have to say anything as I will mention it in my vote of thanks.'

'Who's died?'

I was oblivious to the news.

'Former President Clerides...'

'Right.'

'See you later.'

A quick brush-up on Cypriot history on the web was called for, but I thought nothing more of it in respect of the ball.

Fully confident that I would be earning some much-needed brownie points from Helen for this party, we arrived, most unusually, at precisely the same time as David and Janet, and all four of us made our way through the front door into the lobby area. David and I were immediately taken off to one side for photos. Janet and Helen, who were quite used to this, happily made their own way through to the ballroom in search of a gin and tonic.

Photos done, and, enjoying the lovely warm reception David and I got on arrival, we slowly made our way through the packed ballroom searching out our wives. The atmosphere was wonderful, and, although the passing of former President Clerides was in many people's thoughts, it appeared not to have dampened anyone's spirits. The right tribute, I felt.

Surprisingly, as we fought our way through the densely packed room, we spied Janet and Helen at what must have been our table. Strangely, they were seated already; from the look of it, quite possibly the only two people seated in the whole room.

David Burrowes is one of life's natural enthusiasts, and rarely have I seen him anything but good-natured and jovial even under the most pressing of circumstances. He bounded up to the table. 'Hello, ladies. I see you've found a drink then!'

His customary charming boyish smile accompanied his

welcome, though unfortunately it was unmatched by either
Helen or Janet. Completely failing to see the warning signs, I
plunged in, matching David's good humour.

'Hungry, are we? Already seated, I see.'

'Well, given that we're the only two people in the room in
long ballgowns, I don't suppose we're going to be standing up
very much.'

Oh.

I just don't notice these things. Clearly, neither did David.
A panicked glance around the room confirmed matters. Long
dresses were definitely not in the dress code.

I always think honesty at this point is very important, so,
with what was a familiar trend during our time together in
Parliament, I firmly laid the blame at David's door. Shamelessly
once again. But, on this occasion, accurately.

'David...?'

His good nature and honesty means that he is utterly incapable of being disloyal, whereas as I was more than willing to
place limits on my loyalty when absolutely necessary. Tonight
was one of those necessities. With zero help from me forthcoming, David settled for a guilty plea. As a practising barrister,
no doubt he calculated he could negotiate a plea bargain.
Meanwhile, a brief exchange with Janet confirmed that, on this
occasion, I was innocent, but Helen practised her customary
'guilt by association', which ensured that David and I were banished to sit together on one side of the table, while Janet and
Helen remained seated on the other, presumably conferring on
what sentence to hand out to both the guilty and the innocent.

Despite the dress code cock-up, dinner progressed well, and
I even promised to dance later, not something I do easily, or,
as the children in Dhaka had found to their great amusement,
with any style at all. As coffee was being served, things were

looking better – that is, until the lights dimmed and a large screen dropped from the ceiling. At a stroke, the atmosphere cooled, the chattering died out and the principal host took to the microphone.

What followed was a passionate tribute to the late Glafcos Clerides. At least I think that's what it was, as the whole tribute was in Greek. It also lasted for about fifty minutes.

We then had another speech, and another tribute. Also in Greek.

David then stretched his legs, as he got up to give a mercifully short speech. His, I am pleased to say, was in English.

One hundred minutes in total so far. One hour and forty minutes.

David's vote of thanks marked the end of the speeches. However, there then followed a long film tribute to the late President, with whom Helen and I were now very firmly acquainted. No subtitles, regretfully, and again all in Greek.

Another twenty minutes in total.

My phone buzzed.

'I don't love you any more.'

I think she really meant it.

26

THERE IS NO ROOM IN THIS MARRIAGE FOR A THIRD PERSON

There are few MPs who will express anything other than love for their constituency and, in particular, their constituency party. That's not entirely surprising, given that the latter can de-select you as their candidate at any point in the run-up to an election, and the former are hardly likely to vote for a candidate who says he doesn't love them.

I loved mine, warts and all. Which is exactly the relationship they had with me: warts and all. I wouldn't have had it any other way.

It may well have been a tactical mistake for me to stick with a marginal seat for all those years because I never ended up with a safe seat. But, while politically we may not have been the most successful partnership, we are, I suspect, both richer in experiences than we would have ever have been had I been given a quiet, safe seat.

And then, suddenly, it was all over. In 2015, after five years as MP for Enfield North, it came to a very abrupt end. In the early hours of 7 May, in the huge counting arena at Lea Valley Park, the result was declared. I had lost to Labour by 1,086 votes.

A tiny, 1.7 per cent share of the vote. But it might as well have been thousands of votes that had defeated me, because it made no difference. Losing that night hurt like I'm sure Hell would hurt on its hottest day.

And, to rub salt into the wound, more people voted for me that time round than when I won in 2010 – but no matter, it was over. And when it's over it is over very publicly, in front of your political opponents, and, more acutely, in front of your supporters, your friends and, most difficult of all, your family. Not to mention the television and press media.

It was bitterly hard to see the disappointment on the faces of the wonderful volunteers and friends who had put so much into my campaign. But it was unbearable, and utterly heartbreaking, to watch my children in the early hours of that morning as they witnessed their father get sacked very publicly, and my wife as she saw her husband lose a job that he loved. Above all, I knew they felt, rightly or wrongly, a deep sense of injustice at the outcome.

I was helpless, however. Nothing I could say, no amount of hugs, no brave face would make it any better. I was powerless to change a thing.

Any family would feel the same. The democratic process I love and value so dearly can be a very tough mistress. I knew that when I went into politics; my family didn't. I don't think there has been a single other occasion when I have felt more proud of them, while simultaneously feeling so gutted for them. But that doesn't make it any easier for those closest to you to accept democracy's verdict.

For me, it just added to the shocking sense of having let everyone down so badly by losing.

Meanwhile, across the rest of the country, David Cameron was winning a majority. It was definitely party night for the Conservatives; we just weren't invited.

It did not take me long to conclude that it was time for me to leave Enfield, after sixteen years of political campaigning and following the verdict of the voters.

I felt that a new candidate should have the chance to oust Labour and win back the seat for the Conservatives in perhaps four or five years' time, when the next general election was expected. We had a cracking farewell party and I never lost touch with anyone during the next two years. I did, however, think that if I was going to try to get back to the Commons and complete some unfinished business, I should look for a safe seat.

And that's what I began to do.

Which basically means you have to attend all sorts of social functions in seats you think will become vacant. You also have to make sure you support them on local campaign days by turning up to canvass, deliver and, when invited, speak at functions. I did all this and more, and then some fool in the Prime Minister's office convinced Theresa May she should call an early election.

'So Nick, obviously we think you would be best placed to win Enfield North back for us at the general election.'

I was talking to the London election co-ordinator at CCHQ, listening to a pitch as to why I should return to Enfield North.

'It's a very hard seat to win, you know,' I announced with unintended foresight.

'Yes, of course, and we would love you to fight it, because you have the best chance.'

'I have told everyone that I would not be back.'

'These are special circumstances, and you know that the local party would have you back.'

'What about other seats, like Hornchurch?'

Hornchurch had a Conservative majority of 12,000 and I had invested days of canvassing and relationship building over the previous year.

'There will be a shortlist put up by CCHQ for Hornchurch.'

'Will I be on it?'

'Well, yeeeees. But you would make our day if you stood again back in Enfield.'

My contact at CCHQ, a lady of immense experience and devotion to election campaigning, was using superb subliminal tactics to nudge me or, perhaps more accurately, kick me back into Enfield North.

I promised to think about it.

Enfield was starting to look the most likely option.

Gentle but firm pressure from CCHQ, combined with my own sense that the right thing for the party was to maximise our chances to win in Enfield North with an established candidate, edged me to saying yes. The clincher was that we had a convincing twenty-point lead in the polls. With a national lead like that, we could scrape through even in tough seats.

It's just unfortunate that the polling figures were wrong. That, of course, and a bloody awful manifesto from No. 10 presided over by the Prime Minister's joint chief of staff Nick Timothy, who along with his co-chief of staff Fiona Hill jointly held the reins of power up to the doomed election. Overnight, these two powerbrokers of British politics went from being the Francis and Claire Underwood of Downing Street to the clueless George and Mildred from the classic 1970s British comedy farce of that name. Someone had to carry the can, after all.

While they had the luxury of resigning and fleeing the political scene in a manner of their choosing following the election, I, along with many fellow unsuccessful candidates, had to undergo a very public thrashing.

Much like the Romans enjoyed pitting Christians against lions, the British public like to flay their politicians on election night, lining them all up on a stage, often in the full glare of the cameras, while the result is read out to a highly partisan audience of party workers, friends and family. Then, while you're still trying to work out just how many thousands you've lost by, you have to muster something decent to say about your opponent, which is bloody hard to do at any time, let alone when they have just kicked your butt all over the election playing field.

But at least this time round it came as no surprise on the night. Unlike 2015, the 2017 count was all over before it began. The TV pundits had produced the one accurate poll of the election, and it predicted a wipeout in London. This was announced within minutes of the polls closing at 10 p.m. on Election Day, and was subsequently evidenced by the huge pile of Labour votes stacked up on the counting tables that greeted Helen and I as we once again entered the vast arena at the Lea Valley Sports Centre in Picketts Lock.

No shocks here, no job lost, just the rather embarrassing defeat by several thousand votes.

That did not mean that my thoughts were not, once again, with the huge number of volunteers who had traipsed the streets of Enfield tirelessly for weeks and, in many cases, years. Unsurprisingly, many had become good friends, and without them we could not have fought a vigorous and, I must confess, fun campaign in 2017. Not just with local people, but with the hundreds who poured in relentlessly from neighbouring seats such as Broxbourne, Chingford, Barnet and of course Enfield Southgate. Some volunteers who attached themselves to us had come from the north-east or from Bristol, and one regular trooper made the trek from Richmond to Enfield North almost daily to come and pump out leaflets or knock on doors. One glorious, super-fit councillor, Glynis Vince, even fed me regularly with some of the finest fruit cake I have ever had. Made to order, I hasten to add, and with unbroken regularity. Except, that is, when she took time out to wash and iron some of my shirts, much to Helen's despair.

Heroes, the lot of them.

Bonkers? Absolutely. But some of the most devoted and committed people I have come across in any profession.

And they deserved a speech from the podium that meant we did not go out with a whimper, with our tails between our legs. This was a time to thank them, congratulate the victors, and go with both grace and good humour.

'Most of you know that I have, sadly, one divorce behind me.'

There was a heavy intake of breath from the assembled throng of party activists below the podium. It was the early hours of 9 June 2017, and I had lost again in Enfield North by several thousand votes, in what was a bad night for the Conservatives. My principal opponent had been returned as MP and had made her speech, truthfully not saying very much, as, after all, the voting had said all that needed to be said.

There was a pause as my opening statement silenced a rather rowdy room, full of excited Labour activists who knew that they had also just taken the scalp of my good friend and colleague David Burrowes by winning Enfield Southgate. That count had taken place in the same venue as mine.

'But you may also know that I am very happily married again, to the most wonderful and supportive wife any politician could have.'

OK, even my wife was looking confused now. What was I going on about?

'The time has come', I continued, 'for me to make very clear that there is no room any longer for a third person in this marriage.'

Now Helen was looking at me very strangely, as indeed were most of the room, which still remained ominously silent.

I turned and looked directly at Joan Ryan, my Labour opponent and the victor on the night, who was looking sceptically at me.

'This relationship must end. We cannot go on meeting like this.

'This is the fifth time we have met on this stage, the fifth time we have spent weeks passing each other in the streets and, of course, endless encounters at public gatherings.'

Here, I was referring to the fact that the 2017 election was the fifth general election we had fought; a record, I expect.

'I know this will be a blow to you, Joan. I know you will miss me. After all, you do keep mentioning me in your election literature. But, sadly, what we had is over.

'This relationship ends here, this morning, as of now.'

At least one or two of the Labour entourage had the good grace to chuckle.

27

MY NAME IS NICK DE BOIS
AND I AM AN EX-MP

Iain Dale, the LBC primetime broadcaster and political blog-
ger, warned me in 2014 that there was nothing more useless
than a one-term MP. We were sitting in the elegant Radisson
Edwardian Hampshire Hotel on London's Leicester Square,
close to LBC's studio, when he dumped this unwelcome fact in
my lap.

'I am being serious,' he continued; albeit that he was not invited to continue, he did so quite bluntly. 'If you are thinking
of not standing at the next election, make sure you have some
other employment lined up because otherwise you will join a
long queue of under-employed former MPs, of which you will
be pretty close to the bottom of the pile.'

To think I was paying for this advice. Or rather, I had bought
him his drink, which was vastly overpriced in this particular hotel.

Like all good friends, though, he was showing me the respect
of being honest with his opinion. In his defence, I was at the
time in the throes of another severe bout of Marginal Agitation
and Despair syndrome, which temporarily but briefly led me
to consider not defending my seat at the next election. Iain put

the kibosh on that one pretty swiftly. As it turned out, I had the chance to test his thinking after the defeat at the 2015 election. Before doing that, however, I was overwhelmed by the compassion of the parliamentary authorities within days of the defeat.

> Dear Mr de Bois,
>
> We realise this will be a difficult time for you, but we wanted to take this opportunity to remind you of your responsibilities for winding up your parliamentary and constituency office in accordance with the obligation under IPSA [the Independent Parliamentary Standards Authority]...
>
> Yours,

How nice. One of the first things I get after the election is the bloody expenses police telling me to make sure I settle all my gas, rent, electricity payments and so on before they will release a single penny of money owed to me or my staff. The letter went straight in the bin.

It was then immediately, and wisely, retrieved by Helen, my senior caseworker. Again, she was doing the thinking, while I was still looking around for something to kick.

'We will', she continued, 'need that to make sure this office is shut down swiftly and efficiently so that we all get paid the redundancy and expenses owed. Don't worry, Leanne and I have it in hand.' Which speaks volumes about how well served I was during my time in Parliament, by all my constituency and Westminster teams.

Leanne, Helen, Tom, Carmen and James were the unfortunate casualties of my defeat who worked with me until the election. Through no fault of their own, all of them were made redundant overnight, with no guarantee of a job elsewhere. Their fate was inextricably linked to mine and, frankly, very few people outside Westminster understood that.

The IPSA redundancy process that they went through would be an embarrassment to any self-respecting private- or public-sector organisation and, I am in no doubt, would be heavily criticised by any employment tribunal if they were ever faced with one. There was no adequate process for trying to re-employ defeated Members' staff, no credible consultation period (an entitlement that all companies and employees have else-where), and absolutely no suitable advice process. Sweet sod all.

Which is why, after sending a note recommending all my team to my successful former colleagues and new Members of Parliament, I was so chuffed that Helen and Leanne were snapped up immediately by other MPs. Young James went on to work for an election strategy organisation, where I hear he was far more successful for his clients than he ever was for me. Tom, as I would expect, had his plans neatly mapped out and goes from strength to strength, as does my very feisty and com-petent event manager, Carmen, who is working in the law. Even our young apprentice Eve is enjoying a new career – thankfully for her, I expect, one divorced from politics. Maddie, Jack and Leslie had all very wisely left long before Election Day.

Which left me, the now ex-MP, the only one wondering what to do next.

'Take a few months off,' suggested my wife.

I was fooled for a while into thinking that this was a genuine measure of sympathy, until it became very clear that my services were not needed back at my old company, which she was now running. In fairness, how could I go back and seize the reins of leadership just because I had lost an election? Apart from the prospect of facing a huge constructive dismissal case from my wife, the company was doing far better under her leadership than it ever did under mine. That was not an option.

Some ridiculously over-optimistic researcher from the BBC

rang up and asked me if I would like to take part in a documentary on ex-MPs trying to find a job via the Job Centre, for which
I would – and here's the best bit – take whatever job was offered
to me. How the BBC would have loved that.

'Well, that's a fascinating thing to do, and I would love to take
part.'

'Great!' replied the startled but very happy BBC researcher.

'Just one thing: this would be a complete fabrication of my
circumstances.'

'Sorry, I don't understand. You did lose the election, right?
And you are now looking for a job?'

'Well, the first part of that is true, but I did run my own business, have income from that business, and am fortunate enough
not to have to take any job offered to me that I might not want,
which, I think, is the point of your documentary, right?'

'Yes, indeed. But it's also about following an ex-MP trying to
find work.'

'Well, it's up to you. Why not check it out with your bosses?
I am very happy to join in so long as we make it clear in the
programme that it's all a bit of a sham, eh?'

I never heard from them again, of course, and I never saw the
programme go out, if it did at all.

Meanwhile, back to reality.

I had another thought. Maybe LBC would want me as a guest
broadcaster? That way, I could maintain my interest in broadcasting and current affairs. After all, I had guest-presented on
their show.

Unfortunately for me, with LBC's huge success over the previous five years, there was little room for me when they had the
pick of the big names. That door shut fairly swiftly.

Recovery, it seemed, was not going too well. I cheerfully
kicked the proverbial cat on a few occasions, set about conjuring

up fiendishly wicked spells on the 20,172 people who had voted against me, and occasionally retreated into a self-indulgent sulk.

I was not helped by the fact that I couldn't shake an overwhelming sense that I was not done with politics. It would perhaps have been better had I happily said, 'OK, I get the hint, voters, you are done with me and it's probably best all round if I'm done with you. It's been a great ride, thanks very much!' and took myself off to the nearest beach for a few months.

But that isn't how I felt.

I believed I had more to offer and there was unfinished business for me to achieve which had been cut short by an unwelcome exit from Parliament. Overnight, I went from a position in which I could make a difference to one where anything I had to say would more often than not be met with indifference. I had at one time been able to influence outcomes and fulfil a desire for change. Frankly, I missed that. Inevitably, I clutched at any passing straw that appeared to offer a way back into an active political life, albeit not as an MP. And it was only a matter of days after the 2015 general election that the first passing straw came along in the shape of the Prime Minister.

'David Cameron here, Nick. I just wanted to call to offer my condolences on your defeat in the election.'

It was Saturday, two days after the 2015 general election, when I took a call from the Prime Minister. He had found time to call those few MPs, myself included, who had not quite made it over the line.

'Thank you, I really appreciate the call, and it is generous of you to make the time to do so,' I said – which frankly it was. Very decent of him.

'Not at all, and we will help you sort something out to keep you busy, we won't leave any colleagues behind. So do contact Jenny in the Public Appointments department at No. 10.'

It was good of him, and I told him I hoped to stay active in politics, either helping out at party HQ or following my special interests developed during the last parliament. If that could be done with the help of his office, then who was I to say no?

My thinking went like this: if knife crime, something I was deeply interested in, had continued to spiral upwards, and if the government wanted someone to spend time digging into root causes and trying to do something about them, then I would be more than happy to do this. If they wanted help in promoting UK exporting, I was ready and willing. If they wanted help within the party machinery, I was up for it and, judging by what the Prime Minister had just told me, this would not be a problem to achieve.

Looking back, I was ridiculously optimistic about the probability of that happening. Indeed, none of that did happen, and so that particular straw turned out to be one of a number of well-meaning but empty promises. What I struggled with was: why make the promises in the first place if there was no intention to deliver on them? Don't get me wrong, I liked the sound of them, but I didn't ask for them. Unfortunately, though, they kept coming.

'Nick, what are you up to these days?' I hear you on the radio every now and then, but what now?'

'Not a lot, Minister, I'm thinking of writing a book.'

'Wonderful, but what a waste to us.'

Crikey, I thought. He gets it. I wonder if he's going to make up for stopping me being a trade envoy? Yes, it was the same chap.

Turning to his special advisor, he instructed rather grandly, 'See what we can do to help this great fellow.'

I never heard from them, of course.

My recovery as an ex-MP was not going quite to plan. Worse,

Iain bloody Dale was, once again, correct. I wanted to be useful, but it seemed that few thought I would be of any use. His timely warning that there is nothing as useless as an ex-MP was proving irritatingly accurate.

Not all was doom and gloom by any means. While the parliamentary party hierarchy showed no real interest in helping out, friends within it did.

I was deeply gratified by the generosity of former colleagues, who always gave me a warm welcome and would offer a nudge of help if ever needed. Many close colleagues formed an unofficial support mechanism and understood that the most difficult thing I had to adjust to was suddenly being on the outside of the decision-making, outside the camaraderie, outside the influencers; if you like, very firmly outside the club.

Rob Wilson, then a minister in the Department for Culture, Media and Sport, actively supported my search to do something useful, doing whatever he could to champion my cause. It was ironic that he also found himself defeated in the 2017 election. Tracey Crouch, Minister for Tourism at the time, came to the rescue and offered me a part-time role as chairman of a joint ministerial and industry body in my old business sector. With no salary attached to the job, the process was much simpler and, helpfully, I even understood what the job needed. I am still enjoying that role today.

Zac Goldsmith was quick to invite me to help his London campaign and, in particular, work with the voluntary party across the city. This meant travelling to virtually every borough to campaign and meet with all sections of the voluntary party. I loved it and it made me feel useful again for six months.

Tracey, Rob and Zac, and others, illustrate what most people already know – that friends matter.

Ironically, these supportive gestures fuelled my belief that I could still be active in politics in a more permanent fashion, which in turn only lengthened the time I needed to realise the otherwise glaringly obvious: 'You lost, old chap, and the system needs you to go quietly, please.' But I was presently far from that conclusion. In fact, as the months rolled by, I grew even more determined to get a role that kept me active in politics and so my next move was to take up David Cameron's offer of getting a public appointment in an area where I could be useful.

He had promised that his Public Appointments team would help me find something and I was, frankly, looking forward to their help. Why not? After all, I had no problem with 'It's not just what you know, it's who you know'. So it was with some anticipation that I contacted them at their office in No. 10.

The help that materialised was somewhat underwhelming, but why was I surprised? My first contact was to be sent the published list of public appointments, which, unsurprisingly, anyone can get from the internet. Not an encouraging start.

To be fair, I did have a meeting where certain future positions were discussed as being suitable for my interest and political experience. Then I never heard from that team again, in part because David Cameron lost the Brexit referendum and his job, along with the head of his Public Appointments team, who was subsequently appointed to a seat in the House of Lords.

About that time, I started to think seriously about writing this book, from my new seat, our replacement sofa in the lounge.

However, this was not before I had submitted an application for one job that really interested me, and I met all the criteria to qualify for an interview. Better still, I thought, I had the full backing of No. 10 to go for it. The role was head of an independent organisation in the judicial system.

Maybe it was No. 10's backing that worked against me, however, since I did not even get invited for interview. I pressed for an explanation from the team responsible for public appointments, who had assured me an interview was a no-brainer.

'Hi Nick, I just wanted to let you know I've had some feedback on your application and why you didn't get an interview.'

'Great. Do enlighten me.'

'You had no experience of running a public-sector organisation.'

Silence.

'But that was not a key requirement.'

'No.'

'And isn't it government policy to try to engage more people from the private sector to step up and work in the public sector?'

'Yes, well, sort of.'

I had never come across a 'sort of' policy before.

'Sort of?'

'Well, it's to be encouraged.'

'So, let me get this straight. The Appointments Office in No. 10 supported my application, the Cabinet Office believed it was a very strong application, the Home Office had no objections whatsoever to me applying, and we as a government want to encourage people from outside the club to apply for posts like these... but, in fact, all that's pretty bloody meaningless.'

'I can see why you might think that.'

So much for clutching at that straw offered by the Prime Minister. The good news is that at least the public can be reassured that 'jobs for the boys' doesn't exist. In fact, even 'interviews for the boys' is non-existent.

Why the promise of help was made remains a mystery, because it was a promise that could not be fulfilled. For the vast majority of public appointments, the selection process is specifically designed to weed out political influence, and rightly – if, on this occasion, annoyingly – so.

But one area that is completely without any sense of controversy, and well within the party's gift, is the party's own voluntary sector. Surely they would happily take advantage of my offer to help?

With that in mind, my optimism recovered from the few minor setbacks in my recovery process. It didn't take long for that optimism to be dispelled once more.

'We don't hand out senior positions within the party to just anyone, you know.'

This was the chairman of the Conservative Party, Patrick McLoughlin, sharing his opinion with me in February 2017. Theresa May was Prime Minister, the new order was settled and the party was hugely popular, with a reported twenty-point lead in the opinion polls.

Patrick had invited me in for a chat, having bumped into me in the House of Commons. I had thought he might want me to do something to help out with our campaign strategy in London, given the upcoming local elections in 2018. The surprise general election was not yet on anyone's radar.

I was excited at the prospect of putting some time and experience to use to help the party, more so since no one really knew what to do with me, and I clearly was not going to go away. On the one hand, I was well versed in party, politics and elections, but on the other hand, I didn't fit neatly into any pre-defined role. As a defeated MP, if I needed a loan, CCHQ might be able to help. If I wanted to be a candidate again, they most certainly could help.

But anything else?

To date, that had seemed a big ask, and I hoped this meeting with Patrick might finally produce a way forward.

'Patrick,' I continued, 'I am basically sitting on my arse, fortunate enough not to have to work, and we as a party have a huge challenge in London. I can help if you wish?'

'Indeed,' he concluded wisely.

'Well, I'm happy to help out across London, using what we have learned from the 2015 general election and 2016 mayoral election to help rebuild a London campaign machine.'

Huge sigh from Patrick.

Hmmm. 'Is that what you might have wanted to talk about when you invited me to come and see you, Patrick?'

'Well, it's interesting, certainly.'

'Was there something else you wanted to talk about, perhaps?'

Clearly, this was heading nowhere and once again I was about to be left wondering why so many former colleagues go through the motions of pretending they value you and want to see 'what they can do to help'.

'Patrick, I didn't ask for this meeting, but I want to make clear I am available to help in any capacity you want if it is a worthwhile role.'

And that's when he told me that they didn't hand out senior positions within the party to just anyone.

Although this was a bit of a distraction, I confess to being quite stunned. The party dished out voluntary roles with various job titles almost on a monthly basis.

'Actually, Patrick, you do dish them out to all and sundry when it suits you. And when I say you I mean *you*, since you were Chief Whip and dished out loads of meaningless roles as vice-chair of this or that just to make sure MPs voted with the government!'

Silence.

'Well, it's different if you're an MP.'

Ah, of course. I had forgotten that since losing my seat I was outside the club. I was clearly being reminded of that in a rather charmless way.

'Patrick, I think you are missing the point. I want to help, but you seem to see only barriers, not opportunities. You can give me whatever job title you like, but if you do want help, let's make it a meaningful role.'

No response. I pressed on.

'Look, we lost in the general election in 2015 by around 300,000 votes across London to Labour. And in the mayoral election a year later, while we pretty much held our vote, we lost to a hugely increased Labour vote, beating us again by some 300,000 votes. We have no reason to think that things will get better unless we change things dramatically.'

More pause for thought by Patrick.

'Are you personally all right for money?'

What? Had he been listening to a word I'd said?

'Patrick, I'm not here for money.'

And that must have ticked a box of some sort, because within minutes the meeting was over.

Two months later, we embarked on the doomed surprise 2017 general election campaign, which saw a further wipeout of London Conservative MPs, including Kensington and Chelsea, Battersea, Enfield Southgate, Croydon Central and Twickenham, and saw other incumbent MPs clinging on for dear life in seats where they had previously held comfortable majorities. This time we lost to Labour by about 800,000 votes in total across London.

It also brought the conclusion to my personal recovery programme a lot closer. I may not have succeeded in developing some form of political role, but at last I realised it had been far from failure.

In fact, the past few months had been an outstanding success, bringing me back from the Westminster bubble and into reality. I had had a life before Westminster and there was most definitely life after Westminster.

I had thought, when I wanted to pursue a public appointment, that it was because I needed a platform to be active in key policy areas of interest to me. But that was not the case. In truth, it was my way of seeking validation because the electorate had cut short my time and that sucked and I wanted to compensate for that.

When David Cameron had promised that no one would be left behind, I believed him for the same reason.

I even thought, when I wanted to be a broadcaster with LBC, that it was to stay engaged in politics. It wasn't. It was to be a radio broadcaster first and political commentator second, something I have been lucky enough to fulfil occasionally these days with talkRADIO.

In truth, losing your seat is much like any redundancy, except that it is carried out in a very public arena. It takes time to come to terms with it.

How did I figure this out?

Because when I left Conservative campaign headquarters after that meeting with Patrick, I realised that I was quite relieved he had not put together an offer of some kind. He clearly wasn't interested, and the thought of being handed something as a compensation prize rather than out of genuine merit pretty much undermined everything I valued, and what I had always urged upon my constituents. We make our own opportunities, we cash in on our own luck and we tackle our own misfortunes. I had not seen my own advice staring me in the face.

Meanwhile, the British public's fascination with politics and MPs, be they loved, liked or loathed, continues.

Turnouts at elections have been growing in recent years, our country's future post-Brexit has stimulated huge political debate in the country, and young people are voting again. Those are all good things.

But we the politicians, former, current and future, must recognise that when most people vote, they do so with hope. Whatever they may think their MP does, should do, or more importantly can actually do matters far less than what the future holds for them, their families and their country. Because when it comes to MPs, many folk tolerate our shortcomings, are patient for success and, I suspect, may even think their local MP is all right on the whole. I hope so, but you have kindly read this book, so you decide.

When I started out in politics, I had no idea what the relationship between MP, constituents, ministers, press and the very institution of Parliament itself was really all about.

When I finished writing this book, I realised how much I missed it.

Mrs Jennings's meat pie and all.

ABOUT THE AUTHOR

Nick de Bois was born in 1959 into an RAF family. His father served on flying boats during the Second World War, then remained in service until his retirement in 1970. His mother worked as many hours as she could to help keep Nick and his brother Tony at boarding school, which they were both despatched to at the age of eight.

After leaving school and spectacularly flunking his A-levels, Nick attended Cambridgeshire College of Arts and Technology (now Anglia Ruskin University), where he left in 1981 armed with an HND in business studies and little idea what to do next.

Having taken jobs as a trainee betting shop manager, door-to-door salesman, fork-lift driver and bar assistant, he began working for the Advertising Standards Authority as a PR officer in 1982, where he at last held down a job for longer than six months. He joined Rapiergroup in 1984 and, thanks to the generous support of his then boss, he acquired the company in 1988. He became MP for Enfield North in 2010.

Nick has four children by his first marriage, Jessica, Laura, Madeleine and Alexander, and presently two grandchildren,

Henry and Isabell. He wants more grandchildren, but rightly has no say in the matter.

Nick was married again in 2009 to Helen, former financial director at Rapiergroup and now managing director. Helen has taken the business to new levels never achieved by her predecessor. Nick rather weakly insists he laid the foundations for success. Helen has two children by her first marriage, Bethany and Matthew.

He is currently chairman of the government's Events Industry Board and an advisory board member of the UK charity KidsCount.

Nick is available for radio and TV broadcasting, after-dinner speeches (preferably in a warm climate), 50+ birthday parties or pretty much anything that has a platform for him to be indiscreet, occasionally funny, and fed.

@nickdebois
https://www.facebook.com/NickdeBois2017/
www.nickdeboisbooks.com